The Author

Margaret Ricketts was an 85-year-old retired teacher when she wrote the main part of this book but it was completed over 2 years later. She has been a one- parent family for the past fifty years, bringing up four children and having a very successful teaching career. She has always been fascinated by what motivates people and the book reflects her interest in this.

Acknowledgements

I should like to record my grateful thanks to Sue Brewer my copyist, Caroline Mylon my editor and Karen Dowie my illustrator for their hard work and dedication to the success of my books.

OTHER MEMOIRS AND MAGINATIONS NOVELS

Autumn Leaves

Winter Frost

MEMOIRS AND MAGINATIONS NOVEL

Margaret Ricketts

Summer Sunshine

Michael Terence
Publishing

First published in paperback by
Michael Terence Publishing in 2021
www.mtp.agency

Copyright © 2021 Margaret Ricketts

Margaret Ricketts has asserted the right to be identified as
the author of this work in accordance with the
Copyright, Designs and Patents Act 1988

ISBN 9781800941670

No part of this publication may be reproduced, stored
in a retrieval system, or transmitted, in any form or
by any means, electronic, mechanical, photocopying,
recording or otherwise, without the prior
permission of the publisher

Cover image
by Karen Dowie

Cover design
Copyright © 2021 Michael Terence Publishing

I dedicate this book to my son Philip for his constant encouragement and his ability to navigate the wonders of technology on my behalf.

Chapter One

August 1985, Swanton, a market town in Oxfordshire

The front door clicked behind her as she turned and leaned back against the wall. The hall was in semi-darkness, lit only by the light from the porch. As she stood there, she heard the sound of a car's engine and then it drove off up the road. She waited until she could hear it no longer. The silence in her house seemed to wrap itself around her and she took a deep breath before switching on the hall light.

Leah looked around her, glad to be in familiar surroundings. She loved her home; it always made her feel happy and content. But tonight, she was particularly relieved to be there. Earlier that evening she had happily gone off to her friend's housewarming party. Leah had known Jen for many years and she and her husband Barry had recently moved into a new home. Barry had been promoted to assistant manager at his job in Oxford and the party was his way of getting to know the staff. Barry had invited his manager who was also new to the office. He had come from up north and Barry assumed that he would not know anyone in the area. This would be a good opportunity to introduce him to some new faces. Jen had asked him the manager's name and Barry had replied:

"His name is Adam Richards."

Jen had looked at Barry in astonishment.

"Do you know him?" Barry asked.

"I know someone with the same name," she replied and quickly left the room.

On the day of the party, Jen kept telling herself that it would be a fleeting dream, not a nightmare. Barry had answered the doorbell and as he brought the new guest to meet her, she knew her worst fears were becoming true.

"Hello, Adam," she said.

"Hello, Jen," said Adam and kissed her on both cheeks. Barry just stood there with his mouth open.

"Leah is here," said Jen. "Do you want to meet her?"

Adam looked at Jen and she saw the answer in his eyes.

"I'll take you over to her," she said.

And so it was that Leah met her estranged husband after no contact with him for eleven years.

Now, in the peace and quiet of her home, she felt that she could begin to relax. She had had quite a shock and she now realised that her heart had been beating too fast for comfort. She walked into the kitchen and put the kettle on. Then she sat at the table to collect her thoughts. She was normally in control of her emotions but this evening her thoughts were all mixed up in her head. After the initial surprise her basic good manners took over and she had managed to be civil but it had been a difficult conversation.

Leah stood up from the table and made herself a cup of coffee. I think I need to add some 'medicinal' she said to herself as she reached for the brandy bottle. She smiled as she was reminded of her friend Jen. They had often had a laugh about a drop of 'medicinal'. She decided it was time she went to bed and had a good night's sleep, to clear her head and hopefully feel better in the morning.

She picked up her cup of coffee and went up the stairs. After a quick wash in the bathroom, she was soon sitting in bed with her drink. Before long she switched off the bedside lamp and she was fast asleep.

The next morning, Leah was woken up by the phone ringing. The sun was streaming in through the window as she looked at her bedside clock and saw it was 9.55 a.m. Sitting up in bed, she reached for her phone, wondering who on earth would be calling her at that time on a Sunday morning. She didn't recognise the number it was displaying and hoped it wasn't one of those wretched scam calls.

"Hello?" she said rather briskly.

"I was getting a bit worried," said the voice at the other end and she realised who it was.

"Adam, I was asleep. You woke me up."

"Sorry about that," he replied, not sounding sorry at all. "I just wanted to make sure you were alright."

"I'm fine. I've had a good sleep and I have quite recovered my composure," she said with a hint of amusement in her voice. "How are you this morning?"

There was a slight pause in the conversation.

"I didn't sleep that well. I kept thinking about you and hoping that you weren't too upset at seeing me."

"I assure you that I was not upset at all. I was just so surprised. That was what hit me the most."

There was another brief pause.

"Leah, I really would like to keep in touch, but only if you want that too."

She thought for a moment. Despite all the emotions of the last evening, she had recognised that Adam was a very different person from the man who had left her eleven years before. She was interested to find out more about him.

"I would like to see you again," she said. "We have a lot of catching up to do."

Adam breathed a big sigh of relief.

"I'm so glad you said that," he said softly. "Can I take you out for a drink this evening?"

"I was counting on a relaxing day today. I'm not a fan of pubs so I would rather not go out. I'm looking forward to a day at home so if you would like to join me here this evening, I could offer you a cup of tea and a biscuit?"

His response was immediate. "I shall look forward to coming. I'll be there at about 7 pm if that is okay with you?"

"That's fine, I'll see you then," and she put the phone down.

Adam sat down on the nearest chair. His mind went over the conversation he had just had with Leah who was still legally his wife. He sensed that there was something different about her. When they married twenty years ago, they had truly loved each other and had worked together in bringing up the children. He had always been jealous of the confident way in which she had faced up to every problem or new experience. Now he was beginning to see that she still had that basic assurance in her life but she had other attributes. She was obviously a very good and successful teacher and she had an air of contentment about her. It would appear that she had managed the transition to single parenthood very well. He had never really stopped loving her but he realised that their relationship would never be the same. He would have to get to know her again and this would take time.

He needed to go shopping for groceries so he put on his coat and drove up to the supermarket, deciding that he should take something with him this evening. He kept looking as he shopped and at last, he found it, a beautiful bouquet of pink roses. He carried them carefully to his car and feeling very pleased with himself he drove to his house.

Leah quickly dressed and went downstairs. She made a cup of coffee and took it into the dining room. As she sat at the table, she looked out of the window. It was a beautiful day and she wished she had time to go out and deadhead the roses in her garden but she knew there were other more pressing things she needed to do. Her thoughts were interrupted by the sound of her phone. She picked it up and immediately recognised the number.

"Hello, Jen," she said. "How are you this bright morning?"

"Surrounded by the mess left from last night but more to the point, how are you?"

"I'm fine," said Leah. "Fully recovered my senses."

"I was really worried about you. Are you sure you are okay?"

Leah laughed.

"Of course, I'm sure," she said firmly. "I'm just going shopping and I'll call in on the way back and give you a hand with the clearing up."

"That's great," said Jen. "Don't be long. I'm dying to hear what happened after you left."

Leah took the car out of the garage and headed off to the shop. Forty minutes later she arrived at Jen's house. She walked through the back door into the kitchen. Jen was sitting on a stool with a glass of wine in her hand.

"I know, I know," she said. "But it seemed a pity to waste what was left," and she held up the empty bottle for Leah to see. Jen slid off the stool and put her arms around her friend. "I'm so sorry," she said quietly. "I should have warned you."

"I'm glad you didn't," said Leah. "I wouldn't have enjoyed any of the evening if I had known."

"Adam is Barry's boss," explained Jen. "He has recently been promoted to be the manager of the new branch which has opened in Oxford. Barry has been there for the past three months, ever since it was opened. They have had a temporary manager until Adam was appointed and came down from Leden office. Apparently, he is highly thought of by the directors and possibly destined for greater things."

Leah looked at Jen in surprise.

"But how does someone get from being a mediocre civil servant to become a top manager in a building society?"

"I can't answer that," replied Jen. "You'll have to ask him yourself."

The kettle had boiled and Leah made two cups of coffee. She made a space on the worktop and they sat there, each with their own thoughts.

Leah was the first to break the silence.

"When did you know that it actually was the Adam you knew coming to the party?"

Jen thought for a moment.

"Barry told me that he had invited his boss and his name was Adam. I asked what his surname was and Barry said Adam Richards. Little alarm bells began to ring but then I thought it was probably a coincidence, that there must be other men with the same name. But when I answered the door and saw him standing there, I knew my worst fears had come true. Hello Adam, I said. Hello, Jen, he answered and kissed me on both cheeks. Barry just stood there with his mouth open. Then my duties as a hostess kicked in. Come in, I said. I knew by then that I couldn't avoid it so I told him that you were here and would he like to meet you. Without a moment's hesitation, he said yes please and you know the rest. It was quite a surprise for him too but he was very anxious about the effect it had on you. So, what happened after you left?"

"Nothing really," answered Leah. "He held the door for me to get into his car, asked me if I was still living in the same house and drove me home. He helped me out of the car and went with me to the front door. He unlocked it for me and I thanked him for seeing me home. It was all very proper and stilted. I went into the house and he got into his car and drove off. I went to bed and slept like a log and didn't wake up until 10 a.m. when the phone rang."

"Well, that wasn't me. I was still in bed," said Jen.

"I know it wasn't you. I'd recognise your number anyway. Actually, it was Adam phoning to make sure I was okay. I told him I was fine and after a few more words I found myself inviting him over this evening. First of all, he asked me to go out for a drink with him but I said no thanks, I'm not a big drinker and I was looking forward to a relaxing day at home. So, we shall probably have a chat over a cup of tea and a biscuit."

"I suppose you will be chatting over old times?"

"Certainly not," said Leah decisively. "We can't change history. Might as well let go of it. There is no way we can pick up where we left off. That is assuming of course that we both want the same thing. After all, we are two different people from who we were eleven years ago. We have developed our own lives and characters and I think we have to make a fresh break in getting to really know each other and that is going to take time."

When Adam returned from his shopping trip, he carried the bags in and dumped them on the kitchen worktop. Then he returned to the car to collect the roses. They really were beautiful: he hoped Leah would like them too. He looked around for something to stand them in but he couldn't see anything suitable. He walked out into the hall. There were boxes of his stuff everywhere. At last, he noticed one box which was taller and thinner than the others. Holding the flowers in one hand he tipped out the contents of the box and then stood the roses in it. He found some newspaper and stuffed it around the stems. Then he lifted the box and put it near the front door where it was quite cool. He turned around and saw that the hall floor was now covered in books. He picked them up and stacked them in a corner.

He needed a drink and after rummaging in one of the shopping bags, found the cans of beer which he had bought earlier. He carried his drink into the living area which was at the back of the house. In the middle of the room was a sofa which was piled high with cushions, lamps, boxes and an assortment of bits and pieces. Adam cleared a space and sat down. He looked around him and felt slightly depressed. How on earth was he going to find the time to sort out this muddle?

Two days before, a removal van had arrived from Leden carrying all his worldly goods. He had taken time off work in order to be there when it had arrived but unfortunately, it had been delayed on the motorway and was two hours late. Adam was not in a good mood when it turned up and he had told the men to unload as quickly as possible and that the only thing he made sure of was that his bed was in place upstairs. The result was that there was furniture piled up and boxes all over the place. To make matters worse, he had no idea what was in each box. He had left the packing up to the removal company and they had not labelled any of the boxes.

He looked at his watch. It was nearly twelve-thirty and he suddenly realised how hungry he was, time for a good Sunday lunch. He was not really interested in cooking and in any case, he had no idea where any of his kitchen goods were. He knew where there was an excellent pub and restaurant about two miles away. He had visited it several times already and was getting to know the landlord.

Two hours later, he returned home after enjoying a good meal and convivial company. He certainly felt more relaxed as he sat on his sofa and soon fell asleep.

Adam woke with a start two hours later. It was beginning to get dark outside. His watch told him that it was six o'clock and his brain swiftly reminded him that he would be seeing Leah in an hour. He jumped up and went into the kitchen. All his groceries were still on the worktop and he put the milk and the beers into the fridge, deciding that the other things could wait until later. Then he went upstairs to the bathroom. It didn't take him long to freshen up and he was soon in the car. The roses in their box were secure on the back seat.

At seven o'clock he was ringing the front doorbell. He was feeling slightly nervous. Leah opened the door.

"Hello," she said. "Come in."

Adam stepped inside and held the roses out to Leah.

"These are for you. I want to say sorry for upsetting you last evening."

She took the flowers and looked at him.

"They are really beautiful," she said. "What a kind thought."

They were still standing in the hall. She turned and walked towards the kitchen.

"Adam," she called. "Will you come and hold them while I find a vase?"

He took the flowers from her and Leah went to find a suitable container. She came back with a large glass vase which she filled with water and then arranged the roses in it. She carried it into the lounge and placed it on a side table. Then she stood back to admire them again.

"They are really beautiful," she said. "And they have a gorgeous smell."

She sensed that Adam was standing behind her. She felt his hands lightly touch her shoulders as he turned her around to face him.

"They are not as beautiful as you," he said softly. "You are very special."

His eyes were drawing her to him like magnets. She could feel his arms tightening around her and her hands went up and caressed the back of his neck. She knew exactly what was going to happen next. Her body was pressed against his as if they were one. By the time his lips touched hers, they were both floating on air.

As they pulled apart, Leah said breathlessly:

"It is a very long time since I was kissed like that – over eleven years actually. I had quite forgotten the effect it can have."

They sat down side by side on the sofa.

"Believe me," said Adam. "There were eleven years of longing in that kiss. I've had a recurring dream when I imagine what it would be like to kiss you again and now my dream has come true."

"I hope you weren't disappointed," said Leah with a twinkle in her eye.

"It was the perfect fulfilment of my dream," he replied. Then he looked at Leah's face. "You were teasing me, weren't you? You never used to tease me."

She looked at him intently and in quite a serious tone, she said:

"I expect I do many different things now from years ago."

They were both silent, thinking their own thoughts. Finally, Adam spoke:

"It didn't take me long to realise that I had made a dreadful mistake but I was too ashamed to admit it. In less than six months I had decided to find my own accommodation. It was a very difficult period but that is a story for another time. I thought of you every day and I never stopped loving you. I just couldn't find the courage to contact you. I was too afraid of being rejected."

"You must have been very lonely," said Leah sympathetically.

"Yes, I was," he replied. "But eventually I made some good friends who helped me through the low times and I really put all my effort into getting a good degree from Leden University. That was the foundation of my new career and I'm very happy in my work."

Leah stood up.

"I'm going to make a cup of tea," she said.

Adam followed her out into the kitchen.

"What about you?" he asked. "How have you managed these last eleven years?"

Leah switched the kettle on and reached in the cupboard for two mugs.

"I don't even know if you take sugar and milk in your tea," she said.

"Not too much milk and one sugar, please," he replied.

"There is a tin of biscuits in that cupboard," she said. "Can you get them and take them into the lounge?"

She made the tea, put the mugs on a tray and followed Adam. They sat on the sofa together until finally, Adam said:

"Well. Are you going to tell me or not?"

Leah took a deep breath.

"Of course, I'll tell you," she said. "But there is not a lot to tell. After you left it took me two or three months to sort things out at home with the children. There were plenty of problems and teenage tantrums but we worked through it. They couldn't understand why you had abandoned us and I found it difficult to give them any satisfactory explanation. Since I was now the only wage earner, I knew it was important for me to have a regular teaching post and I moved schools a couple of times and I was lucky enough to get a job at a local private boarding school. It was a completely different experience from teaching in the state sector but I quite enjoyed it. Then I transferred to their junior department and I am still there on a part-time basis. For the past ten years, I have run a tutorial system at home and this has been an extra income for me."

"Did you ever consider moving to a smaller place?" asked Adam.

"You forget that the mortgage is in both our names. I couldn't have sold it if I had wanted to. In any case, it is the family home and the family comes first as far as I am concerned. It is my home too and I am very happy here."

Her voice was beginning to quiver with emotion. Adam reached out and took her hand. He really did not know what to say. They sat in silence for some time, each with their own thoughts. She was feeling upset because of the direct way that she had answered Adam. He had suddenly realised that he had no understanding of the difficulties she had faced over the past eleven years. A wave of shame rolled over him and suddenly he was re-living his life in Leden. The intense feeling of loneliness returned. He wanted to take Leah in his arms and comfort her but his courage failed him.

She stood up, lifted the tray off the table and took it into the kitchen. She took several deep breaths before she returned to the lounge. Adam was still on the sofa, his head resting on the back and his eyes were closed.

"Are you asleep?" she said softly.

Adam opened his eyes but he did not move.

"No, I'm resting my eyes and thinking."

Leah looked down at him. He did look rather weary. She sat beside him and took his hand.

"Tell me what you were thinking," she said gently.

He looked at her intently.

"There is no way that I can lie to you," he said with a sigh. "I have to be honest." He sat up in his seat so that he was directly looking at Leah. "In my dreams, I imagined that one day we would live together again as man and wife. I thought when we met, we would simply pick up that relationship where we left it and we would live as we used to. But I am beginning to realise that it is not going to happen like that. My dream is falling apart and I'm not sure about the future."

She felt sorry for him and she reached out and touched his arm.

"There have been a lot of changes since we were last together," she said. "We are two very different people. Circumstances made us both take a different route through life. The experiences we have had over the past eleven years have changed us. We have both come through the dark times and we are both in the better times. We have shared memories but they are history. We really do not know each other but there is one thing I know for sure. I still love you and always will. I am a 'one-man' girl and you are the man. Unfortunately, love alone is not a firm enough foundation for a relationship. It is only the beginning of a journey of discovery about each other. I don't know how long this journey will take or what the end result will be. But I am willing to try it."

He looked at her with tears in his eyes.

"You are amazing," he said. "You have just given me an explanation which I could never have worked out for myself. You have placed a quite different perspective on my way of thinking. Thank you for that – you have really helped me to begin to understand. I have a lot of thinking to do. But the most important thing to say right now is to tell you that I love you. I always have and I always will. I shall never run away from you again whatever the future may hold. I promise I will always look after you."

He reached over and kissed Leah on the cheek.

"I think a celebratory cup of tea is called for and maybe a biscuit," he said.

Adam drove home that evening with his mind in a complete whirl. He remembered what Leah had said about being different people and he knew instinctively that she was right. But it had shattered his own conception of what their future would be like. He wasn't even sure that they had a future together. He knew that whatever the outcome he would never stop loving her and he believed her absolutely when she said she loved him. He was beginning to realise what a relationship was all about. Love was an important part of it but it was not just physical attraction. It went much deeper than that. It embraced the meeting of two minds and included so many other emotions and attributes such as patience, consideration, companionship and friendship. Quite a formidable list, he thought. And this was only the beginning.

He took a beer out of the fridge and sat down on his sofa surrounded by all his muddles and mess. What a contrast to Leah's house, he thought and a reflection of how he felt right now. He stood up knowing that he had to pull himself together. He had a busy week ahead. Then he switched off the lights and went upstairs.

He showered and laid out his clothes ready for the morning. The double bed stood in the middle of the room and he shivered a little as he flopped into it. He pulled the duvet up around his shoulders and lay there, staring at the ceiling. It had certainly been an eventful evening although not quite what he had expected. He remembered the kiss and the passion he had felt with Leah's body pressed against his. He remembered his feeling of shame when she had talked about the house, her words of wisdom which had made such an impact on him but his vivid memory was at the end of the evening. When he stood up to go, he had put his arms around Leah and kissed her. Her response had lifted his spirits.

"The way ahead may have its difficulties," she had said to him. "But please remember that I do love you very much. I want us to be friends right now and not to be concerned about the future."

Adam turned over in bed. "I will always be there for you," he said aloud. "We shall grow old together, that is the only sure thing about the future. But before that, we have our lives to share in so many different ways." A feeling of contentment washed over him and he fell asleep.

Chapter Two

When Adam went to work on Monday morning, he knew that he had a busy week ahead of him. He went into his office and sat at his desk. It was all very neat and tidy, not a bit like his house and life, he thought. He decided to take a walk around the main public area. This would enable him to speak to some of his staff even if it was only to say good morning. He was basically a sociable person and he knew the importance of a good staff relationship.

He returned to his office having reassured himself that everything was running smoothly. He looked at his diary and saw that he had no specific appointments that morning so had time for coffee and called for his secretary to bring him one. As he waited for his drink, his mind turned to the events of the weekend.

There was a knock on the door.

"Come in," said Adam and expected to see Sally his secretary with his coffee. But it was Barry who came in carrying two cups.

"Sally said she was making your drink so I offered to bring it for her. Have you got a few minutes to spare?"

"Yes, of course" replied Adam. "Sit yourself down."

Barry sat down and looked at Adam across the desk. He hesitated for a moment.

"I feel I owe you an apology."

"An apology?" said Adam in surprise.

"Yes. I'm sorry that I landed you in such an awkward position. I had no idea that you and Leah were married. If I had known, I would have warned you that she would be there."

Adam looked at him and smiled.

"Apology accepted," he said firmly. "I wanted to meet Leah again but I didn't know how to make it happen. Actually, you solved the problem for me."

"But it was such a shock for both of you," continued Barry, relieved. "It was a big enough surprise for me."

"Well, it was not quite the meeting that I envisaged but it had the desired effect. At least we now have contact with each other."

"Leah has been a single parent ever since I've known her. Jen knows a lot more about Leah's history than I do. She has never discussed it with me and I certainly won't be quizzing her about it."

"I appreciate what you are saying," said Adam. "What I tell you now is in confidence. We are still legally married and we have never discussed divorce. Twelve years ago, I did a very foolish thing when I left Leah for someone else. It didn't take me long to realise my mistake but I was too proud to admit it and too afraid of rejection. I channelled my frustrations into building up my career but I never stopped loving Leah. When I was offered the job in Oxford, I knew there was a possibility that we would meet but by now I felt more confident about it. I knew that I had something that would make her proud of me and that is the success I have achieved in my career. We still enjoy each other's company but it is very early days. We have to get to know each other all over again."

"I think you have enough determination to win through," said Barry, as they both stood up and shook hands. "Thank you for taking me into your confidence, Adam. I give you my word that I shall not break your trust in me."

He turned to leave the room but Adam stopped him.

"There is one more thing," he said. "Please don't tell anyone that Leah is my wife. As far as other people are concerned, we are simply good friends."

"I won't say a word."

"And ask Jen to keep it secret too?"

The rest of the week passed quickly for both of them. Leah was busy at school and her evenings were taken up by her private commitments. Adam's diary was filling up with appointments and consultations. He was thankful that he had a competent secretary in Sally. He tried to bring some order to his house but only succeeded in piling the boxes in the second bedroom. He rearranged the furniture in his own bedroom so that he could move around more easily. The sitting room was still in a bit of a mess but at least there was a space on the sofa to sit down in the evening.

It was Wednesday evening before Adam spoke to Leah again. He missed hearing her voice and there was something he needed to ask her. He left it quite late before he phoned because he knew that she was usually busy in the evenings. Leah was relaxing in the lounge when the phone rang.

"Hello Leah," he said.

"Hello, Adam. How has your week been?"

Adam gave a little laugh.

"My week has been busy. A new job always brings a few problems but nothing serious."

"I know the feeling," she said. "It takes time to adapt to a fresh environment."

"I've missed you. Can we meet again this weekend?"

"I can't do Saturday," she replied. "Peter is coming down with his two children and I've promised to take them to the local garden centre where they have a children's playground. But I have nothing planned for Sunday."

"Sunday will suit me fine. I shall probably spend Saturday trying to sort out a few more of these wretched boxes. I'd like to take you out for lunch on Sunday. Will you allow me to do that?"

"Yes, I would like that," she replied immediately. "Thank you. I prefer to eat at lunchtime rather than late in the evening."

"Good. I'll book a table for 1 pm and pick you up at 12.30."

"Where are we going?"

"Somewhere nice," he said. "That's all you need to know. I'll see you on Sunday."

"Adam, before you go, can I ask you something?"

"Ask me anything you like," said Adam, wondering what was coming.

"Obviously, you have my number but I have no means of getting in contact with you. Can you tell me what your number is?"

"Of course, I can," he said, laughing, then dictated his number for

Leah to write down.

"Thanks. Now I can ignore you or pester you depending on how I feel. See you on Sunday."

He could hear the teasing in her voice.

"You are a witch," he said, firmly. "And I shall have to deal with you."

"How are you going to do that? I'm curious to know?"

"Never you mind," came the decisive reply. "You will know when it happens. Bye."

She put the phone down. She sensed that Adam was gradually relaxing and she was pleased about that. She suddenly felt a bit threatened by the speed at which it was happening. She realised that she would have to be very careful not to let events overtake them. It was not that she wanted to take control of the situation but she knew the importance of allowing a relationship to develop gradually and she had no intention of being carried along in a flood of emotion.

When Adam arrived at the office the next morning Sally was already there.

"There was a phone call for you from James Brown," she told him. "I said you would ring him back as soon as you came in."

"Who on earth is James Brown?" asked Adam.

"He is the area manager," replied Sally. "He did say that it was quite urgent."

He thanked her and she left the room. He sat at his desk wondering why the area manager wanted to speak to him and what was so urgent about it. Finally, he picked up the phone and dialled the number which Sally had left for him. He assumed that it was a secretary who answered the call and she immediately put him through to James Brown. After the initial introductions, James came straight to the point.

"I have been instructed to contact you by Head Office," he said. "A problem has arisen in one of our offices and they think that you could help sort it out."

"But I'm not a trouble-shooter," replied Adam.

"I think that is what you would be in this instance. Head Office is quite insistent that you are the man for the job. The office in question is in Leden."

Adam could hardly believe his ears.

"But when I left it a month ago, it was running quite smoothly," he stammered.

"Yes, you left everything shipshape. Unfortunately, the assistant manager was temporarily in control and frankly, he made a mess of it. A new manager has just been appointed but could do with some help to restore confidence and pacify the staff."

Adam sat in his chair feeling rather stunned. After a minute or two, he heard James say:

"What do you think. Will you do it?"

"What do you want me to do?"

"I want you to go up to Leden on Monday for three days. I know the staff have great respect for you and you will also meet the new manager. This is his first managerial position and he needs some support and encouragement. When you have written your report, send it straight to Head Office."

"I enjoyed my time at Leden, I'm sorry this has happened. I'll do my best."

"I know you will," said James. "Good luck." And with that, the phone went dead.

Adam sat there considering what he had just heard. He had always had a niggling doubt about his assistant manager and he wondered what he could have done to upset people so much. He would find out soon enough, he decided. Meanwhile, he had a few immediate problems of his own. He stood up and went into the main office. It was Thursday morning and everyone was busy. He walked through to Barry's office and knocked on the door.

"Come in!" Barry shouted. He was surprised to see Adam and noticed that he looked rather worried.

"I need to speak to you," said Adam. "Come to my office at 11.30 and bring two cups of coffee with you."

Barry arrived with the coffee at 11.30 exactly.

"I've told Sally that I don't want to be disturbed and she will deal with any calls that come through," said Adam.

He paused for a moment and looked at Barry who was beginning to feel a bit uncomfortable. Adam sensed that Barry was getting anxious and he hastened to reassure him.

"Don't worry," he said quickly. "You've done nothing wrong, In fact, I am looking for your support."

Barry breathed a sigh of relief as Adam began to explain about the phone call.

"But you've only been here a few weeks," he said in surprise. "Why would you want to go back to Leden even if it was just for a few days?"

"The powers that be have spoken," sighed Adam. "And it would reflect badly on me if I refused to go. In any case, I suppose I am more familiar with the office and the staff. I'll do what I can to help them out."

Barry nodded his head.

"When are you going?" he asked.

"Monday morning and back on Wednesday evening. And that is why I needed to talk to you. There is no time to bring someone in to take my place and in any case, I don't think that would be necessary. I feel quite confident in leaving you in charge and it is very easy to keep in touch while I am away. How do you feel about it?"

"I had some experience of running this office before you came so I'm sure I could do it again. Thank you for your confidence in me. There is just one question I would like to ask you," said Barry, nervously.

"Ask away."

"How do you feel about going back so soon?"

"I'm certainly not looking forward to it. I know I shall enjoy living in this part of the country and I'm already looking forward to the future here. There is such a contrast between living in a crowded town like Leden and being able to breathe fresh air in the countryside. My life is here now and I was hoping that I had escaped from the stresses and tensions of the past twelve years."

Barry stood up to leave.

"Well, you needn't worry about this place," he said. "All we hope is that you will be able to help and we shall look forward to your return." And he picked up the two empty cups and left the room.

Adam didn't move from his desk. He had just had a disturbing thought. How was he going to tell Leah and how would she react to the news that he was going back to Leden? He couldn't explain it over the phone so it would be Sunday before he could talk to her.

He was kept busy for the rest of the week making sure that everything in the office was in good order. He had complete faith in Barry's ability to look after things whilst he was away. He summoned his secretary into his office and explained that he would be away for three days and told her to refer any problems to Barry.

As he went home on Friday evening, his thoughts turned to Leah and how he was going to tell her that he was going up to Leden. He had not yet had an opportunity to talk to her about what had happened to him whilst he was there. He knew he would see her on Sunday but he didn't want to spoil the day by talking about his experiences.

Saturday was spent trying to put his house in order. It was a much smaller place than his previous flat and he knew that there was too much furniture in it. He had rented the house for six months while he decided where he wanted to buy his next property. He did not want to get rid of any furniture so he piled it up as tidily as possible in the living room. He only needed to have the sofa and coffee table for his day to day use; he didn't want pictures on the walls, nor china on the mantlepiece. It is called minimal living he said to himself and it suits me very well.

He opened some of the boxes but did not unpack them. They would only have to be packed again in a few months, so best to leave them as they were. He carried most of the boxes up to the second bedroom which had been turned into a storeroom. He could now close the door on them and forget them for a while.

He had managed to find his crockery and kitchen equipment and now he unpacked it and stacked it in the kitchen cupboard. He cleared away the shopping which was still on the worktop from last weekend and put the rubbish in the outside bin. Then he looked around and was pleased with what he saw. The whole house was now reasonably tidy and a much more inviting place to live. He washed his hands and was soon on his way to his favourite pub. He was very hungry and looking forward to a good lunch and a cold beer. He had a chat with Bob the landlord and asked him if he could recommend a restaurant nearby which served a good Sunday lunch. Bob suggested an old coaching inn near the river which had an excellent reputation, and he gave him the telephone number.

"Shan't see you on Sunday then?" asked Bob.

"Just a blip, just a blip," laughed Adam. "Don't worry, I'll see you again soon."

He went back to his car. He sat in the driver's seat and dialled the number Bob had given him and two minutes later, he had booked a table for 1 pm on Sunday.

Leah's week had been straightforward. There had been no major hiccups at school and her evenings were very busy. The exams for the private sector were fast approaching and this always increased the pressure on the students and Leah. She had been pleased to hear Adam's voice on the phone and she was really looking forward to their Sunday lunch.

By the end of the week, she felt tired and a little bit grumpy. Peter had arranged to bring her two young grandchildren to see her and she had planned to take them to a local park. Then at the last minute, he had phoned to say that one of them had been sick so they wouldn't be coming. Leah was disappointed. She made herself a cup of tea and went outside to sit in the garden. It was really peaceful and she could hear the birds singing. As she sat there, a squirrel appeared on the lawn looking for any crumbs left over by the birds. Leah watched as it scampered into the bushes then she lay back and closed her eyes.

She did not go to sleep because she suddenly had an unwelcome thought. She had told Adam a little bit about herself but she had said nothing about any of their four children. She suddenly realised that he had not mentioned them either. He didn't even know he was a grandfather! She pondered this problem for a while and finally decided that Sunday would not be the right time to broach the subject.

Adam drove over to Leah's house the next day feeling rather apprehensive. He had not slept well and he still did not know how he was going to tell Leah about his trip up north. He parked his car on the drive and rang the bell. When Leah answered he said:

"I hope you don't mind me parking in front of the garage? We won't need the car so I thought it would be safer off the road."

"I don't mind at all," said Leah. She had no idea where they were going for lunch but obviously, it was within walking distance. "Where are we going?"

"I've booked a table at the Old Coaching Inn. Do you know where I mean?"

"Yes," she said. "It's down by the river. The food is very good there so I have heard."

She collected her handbag and locked the door. As she turned back to look at Adam, she couldn't help noticing the pensive look on his face and knew something wasn't quite right. They walked down the road hand in hand but there was little conversation between them. The lunch was tasty and enjoyable but the atmosphere remained heavy. Leah was beginning to get worried. She had no idea what was troubling Adam.

It was a bright, sunny afternoon and Leah suggested that they should go for a stroll along by the river. She hoped that the fresh air might improve Adam's mood. They walked along the riverbank past the tennis courts and the crazy golf until they found a bench to sit on. It was comparatively quiet with just a few families who were going up to look at the weir. It was Leah who spoke first.

"Adam, I don't want to pry into your life but I know there is something wrong. Is there anything I can do to help?"

He looked at her with tears in his eyes. He knew that her offer was totally genuine but he was still worried.

"Adam, please tell me why you are so upset. You are beginning to make me feel uncomfortable."

He swallowed hard and began to tell her what had happened.

"There has been a lot of unrest in the Leden Branch and Head Office seem to think that I am the person to sort it out. I suppose I know the place and the staff very well and everything was running very smoothly when I left. A request from the directors in Head Office can't be ignored so I said I would go."

"If you know them that well it shouldn't be difficult for you to sort out the problem. Why are you so worried about it?"

"I'm not worried about sorting out their problems." He replied tersely. "I am more worried about you."

"How is it going to affect me?" she asked incredulously. "I've never even been to Leden."

"I haven't yet had a chance to tell you about my life up there." He spoke quickly and Leah could clearly hear the emotion in his voice. "I don't know how you have imagined it but, in my head, I thought that you might wonder about my friends and who I might be meeting up with."

"I don't know why you had to make it so complicated. What you are saying is that I might be jealous of you having the opportunity to renew old acquaintances. I'm not the jealous sort, Adam. I would have thought that you might well bump into people you know." Leah's tone was quite indignant.

Adam looked at her in surprise.

"You think I've been making mountains out of molehills?"

"I think you have stressed yourself out unnecessarily. Why not concentrate on the positive side? If the directors think you can do a job, it is up to you to prove them right. When will you be going?"

"Tomorrow morning and back Wednesday evening. I'll phone you on my way back."

"Come on," said Leah. "Let's go home."

They stood up and Adam put his arm around Leah.

"You are amazing," he said. "You seem to have a deep understanding of every problem and the ability to put it into perspective. I feel better already."

The sun was getting low in the sky and the air was feeling chilly. They walked home briskly and were glad to get into a warm house. Leah put the kettle on and made two cups of tea which she took into the lounge. Adam was sitting on the settee, deep in thought. Leah sat down beside him and sipped her tea. She waited for Adam to speak and eventually he said:

"I really want to tell you about the last eleven years but I'm not sure if you want to hear it. I don't know how to begin." He sounded so sad that Leah wanted to take him in her arms and comfort him. Instead, she reached out and held his hand.

"Adam," she said. "If it will help you, I am quite prepared to listen. You don't have to tell me anything if you don't want to. All I ask is that you are honest with me."

He did not answer immediately but his eyes were searching her face as if he was looking into her very soul.

"I will be honest with you," he said. "You are the only person I would trust with my innermost thoughts. For the past eleven years, I have dealt with the shame and guilt of what I did to you and my family. The time has come for me to admit it to you and myself. I will tell you about my life and I am ready to accept the consequences. It is in your hands to judge me as you will."

"I do not judge people on their past actions," she answered. "I do not like to judge people at all. The past is gone, it is the present that matters. So long as people learn from their mistakes and make the necessary changes, I accept them as they are."

"This is quite a long story," Adam said anxiously. "Are you sure you want to hear it?"

Leah was just about to tell him to get on with it and Adam saw then the steely look in her eyes and thought it was no wonder she never had any discipline problems at school. He knew now that he was committed to telling her and took a deep breath and began.

"I suppose I was like everyone else in thinking that the grass is greener on the other side, but it wasn't long before I realised that I had made a dreadful mistake. It was difficult to find a job similar to the one I had left and before long my money began to run out. I was desperate enough to take a job in the local supermarket stacking shelves. The family I was living with was noisy and quarrelsome and after six months, I decided to move out. I had managed to save enough money to pay the rent for a bed-sitter and I was still working at Asda.

"Then one day the store manager called me into his office. My first thought was that I would be sacked but instead, he offered me an assistant manager's post which I gladly accepted. I stayed there for about two years and learned a lot about retail and customer services. I got on well with the staff and the manager. Then one day he said that I had the potential to be a good manager but it would help me to have a paper qualification in business studies. He suggested that I enrolled at the local college for a one-year diploma in finance and business. I took his advice and at the end of the course I came out with the top place for the year in finance. The college advised me to take a further qualification and so I applied to Leden University and was accepted for a two-year degree in finance and business studies.

"I worked very hard for those two years and I got my reward when I finished with a top degree. I had managed to save some money from my retail job and I was able to move into a two-bedroom flat. It was only then that I started to feel some pride in my achievements. Until that time I had lost all confidence in myself and there were many occasions when I was lonely and depressed. I used to spend a lot of time in the local pub and it was from there that I made some good friends who really helped me through my low times."

Adam paused in his story remembering some of his darker moments. Leah had been listening intently. Now she looked at him and quietly said:

"Go on, you haven't finished the story, have you?"

Adam was beginning to feel weary. It was not easy for him to drag up all those unhappy memories and he still didn't know how Leah was going to react.

"Yes, there is more to tell," he sighed. "But it does get a bit more cheerful. My degree made me realise that I could consider a new career. I'd had enough of vegetables and groceries and so I applied for an assistant manager's job in the local building society. It was the first application that I had made and I wasn't very hopeful. But to my surprise, I was offered the post. It was much better paid and I was able to buy a flat at a very reasonable price. I enjoyed working with the staff and had good relations with the customers. Then after I had been there for a couple of years, the manager announced his retirement and it was he who suggested that I applied for his job. There were other applicants as well but I was lucky enough to be successful.

"It was a very happy place to work in and I was there for three years until one day the area manager came to see me. He congratulated me on the smooth way the office was functioning. He then said that Head Office was looking for a manager to take charge of a new office which was down south and they would be putting my name down as a very strong contender. I then asked him where this new office was and he replied that it was in Oxford. I was speechless and I remember him looking at me curiously. Don't you like the idea of working in Oxford?

He asked me. You don't look too keen.

"I managed to find my voice and told him that I knew the area very well and would be quite happy working there. So, after three interviews I was appointed and you know the rest."

Adam stood up and went to the kitchen for a glass of water. He was glad to have finally told Leah and he felt as if a weight had been lifted off his shoulders. But he was still anxious about her reaction.

Leah was still sitting on the settee and her face gave him no clue as to what she might say. He sat down beside her and waited.

After a while, she turned to face him and said:

"Have you told me the whole story? The person you went up there with, what happened to that relationship?"

"It was not a proper relationship. I suppose you might call it a fling," he said. "When we first arrived in Leden, we stayed with her parents but it soon became obvious that they were not my kind of people. The house was crowded and when my money began to run out, they made it perfectly clear that I was an outsider and they had no intention of helping me out. That was when I decided to move out and since I left that house, I have had no contact with any of them. It was the hardest time of my life. I was alone with no real friends and very little money. Looking back, I don't know how I managed to keep going but somehow, I found the strength. I was at rock bottom and it was then that I decided the only way was up."

He was still waiting for Leah's reaction to his story. Then, at last, she spoke.

"I know you found it very difficult to tell me your story and I appreciate your honesty. But I don't understand why you were so stressed about telling me. I heard nothing that you should be ashamed of, on the contrary. When you were in the deepest hole you pulled yourself out of it and should be pleased with that. You have steered your life into a good place and you have every right to be proud of where you are now. It is obvious that you are a very competent manager and this has been recognised by the hierarchy of the company. You deserve your success and I feel sure there is more to come in the future."

She stood up and went into the kitchen to make a cup of tea. She waited for the kettle to boil then carried the two cups into the lounge.

Adam was still sitting on the settee but the tears were streaming down his face. Leah was alarmed.

"I'm so sorry," she cried. "I didn't mean to upset you."

She put her arms around him. He rested his head on her shoulder and she waited for his sobs to subside. She gently wiped the tears from his face. When he finally calmed down, she looked at him anxiously and said:

"Whatever I said to make you feel so bad I'm truly sorry for."

Adam looked straight into Leah's eyes and quietly said:

"Those were not tears of unhappiness, they were tears of relief."

"Relief?" she asked. Relief from what?"

"I am relieved that I have at last been able to tell you my story. I was worried that you would think so badly of me that I might lose you again. I was just overwhelmed by your response. You have a very special way of expressing your feelings in words and it was as if a heavy weight had been lifted off my head. I have never met anyone who is as calm and sensible as you are when there is a problem. I am not expecting you to forgive me but I hope I will be able to make it up to you in the future."

"I have had plenty of practice when it comes to solving problems," Leah said shortly. "Don't expect too much of me" she added. "Only you can do that."

Adam stood up and put his jacket on.

"I think I'd best be going," he said. "I have to leave early in the morning." He turned and took Leah in his arms. "Thank you," he whispered, "for helping me to come to terms with the past."

"Don't think so much about the past," she said. "You can't change anything. The present is more important and it is best to let the future take care of itself."

He kissed her goodnight and she went to the door with him.

"Drive carefully," she said. "I'll see you when you return."

"I will phone you on my way back on Wednesday evening," he said.

She closed the front door and went to collect the dirty cups from the lounge. She sat down in her favourite chair to think about the events of the evening. She had no idea that Adam had been so stressed out. She began to appreciate the depth of his shame and the guilt which had been ever-present for the past eleven years. She had never known him to lose control of his emotions as he had that evening and she hoped that he would have a good night's rest and that his trip would be successful. Besides she had a thought which would no doubt cheer him up on Wednesday evening. It will be a case of déjà vu, she said to herself with a smile.

Chapter Three

On Monday morning, Adam was up early and by 8 o'clock he was on his way to Leden. The journey was uneventful and he arrived at 11.30 a.m. He booked in at an hotel which was just around the corner. He left his car in the hotel car park and walked down the road to the office. Everything was very familiar and he even met one or two people who greeted him warmly. He walked through the front door and was instantly recognised by the receptionist.

"Why Mr Richards," she cried. "What a lovely surprise."

He went over to speak to her and after a few pleasantries, he said:

"I'd like to see the manager, please. What is his name?"

"He has only been here for ten days," said Rose. "His name is Robert Preston. I'll see if he is free." She picked up the phone and contacted the secretary. "Susie," she said in an excited voice. "You'll never guess who is here. It's Mr Richards. He wants to see Mr Preston."

"The manager is busy until 12.30," Susie answered. "I'll come out at once to fetch Adam," and she put the phone down.

Two minutes later, the inner door opened and Susie came rushing out.

"Adam," she gushed. "How nice to see you. Come with me. You can wait in my office."

Adam followed her in. Susie had been an efficient secretary but he had always been a little wary of her. She was an attractive woman and he made sure to keep her at arm's length. Now she looked at him curiously.

"What are you doing here?" she asked in her no-nonsense manner. "I didn't know you were coming. Does Mr Preston know you are coming?"

"I'm not sure," said Adam. "Possibly the area manager has mentioned it."

"I suppose you know we've had some trouble here in the past month? Sam took over as manager on a temporary basis and he made a right pig's ear of everything. He tried to make changes which were quite out of order and he bullied the younger cashiers into resigning their posts. We were glad to see the back of him. This new manager seems to be a good chap although he is still a bit wet behind the ears."

Adam remembered how forthright Susie could be with her opinions when the manager's office door opened and two men came out. They said goodbye and the other man went to go back into the office. But Susie jumped up and said:

"There is someone to see you, Mr Preston. This is Mr Adam Richards who was the previous manager here."

Robert Preston looked at Adam and held out his hand.

"Good to meet you, Mr Richards, please come in," and he ushered Adam into his office. It was not very different from when he had left it a month before.

"This must be familiar to you," said Robert. He picked up a photo which was standing on the desk. "This is the only thing that I have added. It is a picture of my wife and one-year-old son."

Adam smiled.

"You've only been here one week," he said. "Plenty of time to expand your stacks of paper and files."

"I'm quite forgetting my manners," said Robert. "Would you like a cup of coffee? I'll get Susie to bring it in. How do you like it? Milk? Sugar?"

"I guess Susie will remember how I like it," he laughed. "After all the coffee kept me going for four years."

Five minutes later, Susie came in with two cups of coffee, one of which she put in front of Adam.

"Milk and one sugar," she said.

Adam smiled and thanked her.

"Because this is my first post as manager," said Robert, after Susie left. "And there are a few problems to iron out, the area manager promised that he would get me some help. Are you that help?"

"Yes, I suppose I am," said Adam. "But I'm not here to criticise or interfere. I know the staff and I am hoping that by chatting to them I can help to improve staff relations which have been under a strain. You need to get to grips with the responsibilities of your new position and I am here to give you support and encouragement. I assure you not to intrude on your authority."

Robert looked closely at Adam. He felt that he would be quite comfortable with him.

"I'll tell Susie to cancel my appointments for tomorrow. Then we can talk all day if necessary. Feel free to talk to any of the staff. Ask them anything you want to know," said Robert and he stood up to shake Adam's hand. "By the way," he added. "Please call me Robert although most of my friends call me Rob."

"And I'm Adam and it is impossible to shorten that," Adam said easily. "I'll see you tomorrow, about ten o'clock if that is convenient for you?"

"That's fine," he answered.

Adam left the office feeling confident that he would get on well with Robert. Susie had been very busy spreading the news about his arrival and as he went through the main office, he spoke with many of the staff and heard a lot of complaints. He believed that most of the problems would disappear now that they had a new manager and he realised the importance of his meeting tomorrow. It was 3.30 p.m. before he managed to escape.

He walked down the main street until he reached his solicitor's office. He had sold his flat and he knew that it only required his signature to seal the deal. It was approaching closing time but he hoped that Mr Turner, his solicitor, might still be there. He asked at the reception desk if it might be possible to see his old friend. The receptionist recognised him and rang through to the inner office. A minute later the solicitor came out. He was smiling.

"Adam, my friend," he said. "This is a surprise. Come into my office."

Adam went in and they sat opposite each other at the big oak desk.

"It's only about a month since you left us," said the solicitor. "What brings you back so soon?"

Adam explained the problems in the building society and how Head Office felt he was the best person to sort it out.

"I would have preferred not to come back," said Adam. "But I didn't think it a good idea when the instruction came from up high."

Mr Turner looked at Adam and said very firmly:

"Never look a gift horse in the mouth, Adam. You must make full use of your abilities."

"You are right. I sometimes doubt myself but I am getting better at being more confident. I wonder if you have the final document for me to sign for the sale of my flat? I can't start seriously looking for a place in Oxford until I have that money in the bank."

Mr Turner put his glasses on and smiled.

"By a strange coincidence," he said. "I received the final form today and I was going to post it to you tomorrow." He burrowed through the mass of paper on his desk until he found a particular brown envelope. "Here it is," he said. "It needs your signature and mine plus a witness. I'll just see if my secretary is still in the building." He pressed the intercom and a woman's voice answered. "Come into my office," he instructed. "I need you to witness." He placed the form in front of Adam and showed him where to sign. Then the solicitor added his name, the secretary witnessed it and the deed was done.

Adam breathed a sigh of relief as he came out of the solicitor's office. Now he would have a significant amount of money in his bank account and he would be able to start looking for the next property in Oxford which would be a real home. He decided to go back to his room in the hotel and start to write his report. Later that evening, after a good dinner, he sat in the lounge area with his coffee. He picked up a paper to catch up with the day's news but he couldn't concentrate on it. He suddenly felt rather tired; it had been a long and busy day and he decided he needed an early night and went upstairs to bed.

He slept soundly and woke the next morning feeling better. He lay in the bed considering what the day ahead might bring. He was not particularly looking forward to it. He knew that he had to be diplomatic when speaking to Robert and any suggestions he made had to be carefully worded. He found himself wondering how Leah would manage this tricky situation. He got dressed and went downstairs for breakfast.

An hour later, he went to his office to meet Robert. Adam had decided on his plan of action. Together they would make a thorough tour of the building, including the upper floor which was being used as a storeroom and the paved area at the back. This would give them something concrete to talk about before they got on to more personal matters. Adam intended to take Robert out for lunch so that they had an opportunity to get away from prying eyes and wagging tongues. He sensed that the staff were curious as to why he was there but he had decided to wait until the next morning before he spoke to them.

"I'd like to take an in-depth look at the whole of this building. Is that alright with you?" Adam asked.

"That's fine," replied Robert. "I'm in your hands."

They walked through the main office. Many of the staff said good morning to them but they did not get involved in any conversations. Adam led the way out of the front entrance and across the street. On the opposite side of the road was a small café.

"This way," said Adam and took Robert into it.

A woman was busily tidying up and clearing tables.

"Hello Morag," said Adam with a smile.

The lady spun around.

"Mr Richards," she said and shook his hand. "Whatever are you doing here?"

"Just visiting," replied Adam. "I'd like you to meet Mr Preston. He is the new manager and I'm sure he will be as regular a customer as I was."

Morag shook hands with Robert.

"I'm pleased to meet you," she said warmly. "You will always be welcome here."

"Now could we have two cups of your excellent coffee?" said Adam. "We have some business to discuss."

They sat at the table by the window. Morag brought their coffee over and Adam turned to Robert who was looking a bit bemused by what was happening.

"When you look across the street," he said. "What do you see?"

"I see my place of work."

"Yes," said Adam. "And let me assure you that you are quite secure in that. Now I want you to imagine that you are an estate agent looking at a property. How would you describe it?"

Robert began to look nervous.

"Are you suggesting that they are considering selling the building in which case I should lose my job?"

"Of course not," said Adam quickly. "I asked you to use your imagination."

He began to see how very insecure Robert was and he realised that he would have to be careful not to upset him.

"Let me explain what I mean," said Adam. "For four years I felt the same, that is, it was just my place of work. Then I moved to Oxford and found myself in the middle of a busy city, surrounded by modern architecture and great glass-fronted windows. I did not anticipate how big a culture shock it would be. Modern offices are always flooded in light, usually of the artificial kind. Looking across the street now I see a building opposite in a very different way. It has a character of its own. It is one of the oldest places in this street but it is in need of some attention to return it to its former glory."

"What have you in mind?" asked Robert.

"The stonework on the façade needs to have years of dirt and smoke removed. The windows need a good clean so it is just cosmetic work which would be dealt with by Head Office," replied Adam.

Robert was still gazing out of the window.

"I see what you mean," he said. "It is a question of looking at something in a different way."

Adam felt relieved at Robert's reaction.

"Good," he said. "Shall we get back inside now?"

They said goodbye to Morag and walked back into the office. It was very busy so they went straight through to the back. The rooms there were small and cramped.

"It may be a good idea to remove some walls to give more space for decent sized offices, to cater for the different services we offer," said Adam.

"We also need to clean the windows," said Robert, smiling.

Adam felt pleased that Robert was starting to think more positively. They unlocked the back door and went out into the yard which ran the whole width of the building. The sun was shining and it was pleasantly warm.

"What a waste of space!" said Adam. "How do you think it could be put to better use?"

"Well, it is quite nice in the sun," he replied eventually. "If all the rubbish was removed, maybe we could install some benches and tables which could be used at coffee breaks?"

"Good idea," said Adam enthusiastically. "To be able to stretch your legs and take in some fresh air is very invigorating. I'm sure the staff would appreciate that."

They went back inside, locking the door behind them.

"Let's have a look upstairs?" said Adam. "It is a long time since I was up there."

They went up the stairs which creaked at every step.

"It's a bit eerie, isn't it?" said Robert nervously.

Adam felt inclined to agree with him but didn't say anything. They reached the landing and saw four doors ahead.

"Which one first?" asked Adam.

He opened the first door and they found themselves in a big empty room at the front of the building. They had a quick look around and Adam could sense that Robert was getting rather agitated.

"You stay on the landing," he said. "And I'll just have a very quick peep into the other rooms."

When he came back to Robert he said:

"The rooms are all big and empty. This would make an excellent flat."

They went downstairs and into Robert's office. He was looking very pale and Adam felt really sorry for him.

"That was quite a morning," he stammered. "Not what I was expecting at all."

Adam looked at him.

"It was not my intention to take you so far out of your comfort zone," he said apologetically. "But the experience may have done you more good than you realise right now."

"I know I'm not the most confident person in the world but I am trying to improve."

"Experience takes effort," said Adam. "I feel sure you will achieve it. Now I'm going to take you out for a stiff drink followed by lunch."

They went back through the main office followed by curious glances of the staff. Adam was well known in the area and he soon found a table in a quiet corner of his favourite restaurant. As they ate their meal, they talked together. Robert was feeling more comfortable in Adam's company and listened carefully to his advice. He told Adam about his family and how proud he was of his son, even though he was only one year old. Suddenly Adam thought of Leah. She had brought up their children by herself and he had never even mentioned them to her. He realised that Robert was looking at him rather oddly and he pulled himself together.

"I'm sorry," said Adam. "I was reminded of my own family which is not as happy as you obviously are."

They finished their meal and by the time they went back to Robert's office, it was mid-afternoon.

"This has been a funny old day," said Robert. "I think I shall go home early today."

They said their goodbyes and Adam walked out of the office. He went around the corner to the hotel and straight up to his bedroom. He sat down and closed his eyes. He knew he should continue writing his report but he was exhausted by the intensity of the day. His realisation about his children was the last straw. How could he be so wrapped up in his own so-called problems and not even spare one thought for his children, he thought. Once again, the old foreboding hit him and he wondered how Leah felt. He took off his shoes and lay on the bed. He was soon asleep. Two hours later, he woke up and looked at his watch. It was time for dinner. He wasn't very hungry but he could do with a drink. He went down to the bar and had a chat with the barman, then he chose a light meal from the menu. As he sat there, he started to think about the day. It had certainly been a busy one, not so much physical as emotional. He had a good idea of what he would write on his report but he felt that the really tricky part might be the next morning when he was going to speak to as many staff as possible.

Adam thought of Robert. Once Robert had got rid of his suspicions regarding Adam, they got on very well. They had discussed the role of manager and Robert had reacted positively to Adam's advice. Adam had made some suggestions to improve the fabric of the building and to provide a better standard of furniture and fittings. But most of all he hoped that he had given the courage to enable Robert to make any changes with an air of authority.

After his meal, he went upstairs and sat at the desk in his room. He opened his briefcase and took out the report which he had started the previous evening. He knew exactly what he was going to write and it didn't take him long to complete it. He put it back in his briefcase and got ready for bed. As he lay there, his mind drifted away from the events of the day and his thoughts turned to tomorrow. He was really looking forward to going back to Oxford. He had found the whole situation in Leden quite depressing. It dawned on him how much had happened since he moved away and it reinforced his hopes of a brighter future. He couldn't wait to see Leah again even though he knew there were still difficulties to be faced. I must be patient, he told himself. It was almost like the beginning of their courtship when they first met. A tremor of excitement fluttered through him and he vowed not to make the same mistake again, but to cherish their love and he pulled the duvet around him and went to sleep, feeling relaxed and content.

The next morning, he checked out of the hotel and went straight to the office. He went to say good morning to Robert to explain to him what he intended to do that morning.

"I would like to speak to the staff today. I won't disturb the business of the office but I need to find out what happened here in the weeks before you were appointed."

"I understand," said Robert. "Please, go ahead. I will make one of the offices available to you."

"Thank you. Do you mind if I start with Susie? I'm sure she will be a mine of information."

"I'm sure she will be," replied Robert with a smile. "I have several appointments this morning and I can manage without her."

Adam returned to the main office and spent a few minutes looking at the décor and general state of repair. He made a note to recommend a refurbishment of the interior. Some of the staff had been appointed after Adam had moved away. He had a quick word with them and heard no complaints. He felt a tap on his shoulder and a familiar voice:

"Mr Preston says that you want to talk to me. He has told me which office we can use."

Susie was not her usual ebullient self. She thinks I am going to be cross with her, he thought.

"What did you think I wanted to talk to you about?" he asked when they were seated in the office.

"I don't know. But it must be something I've done or said."

Adam looked at her; she seemed to be worried and anxious. He decided to put her out of her misery.

"Actually," he said. "It's neither of those two but if you have something on your conscience, now is the time to tell me."

"I don't think I have done anything wrong," she said thoughtfully "I have tried to do a good job in some difficult circumstances but I know I sometimes speak my mind when I really should keep my mouth shut."

"You are a very competent secretary and I'm sure that you will do as good a job for Mr Preston, as you did for me. Now you have my permission to speak your mind fully and tell me exactly what happened after I left."

Susie looked so relieved that Adam wanted to smile but he managed to keep a straight face. Once Susie started talking, she was hard to keep up with. She described how Sam the assistant manager had been asked to take over until a new manager was appointed.

"By the end of the first week," she said. "Half of the staff had given in their notice and left. The remaining staff had carried on as best they could but Sam was like a slave driver until the bullying got so bad, that the whole staff walked out. It was then that the area manager became involved. Sam was immediately dismissed and the office was closed for three days. The area manager himself took over and he consulted the staff. The problems were slowly resolved but the whole administration side of the business was affected. Some new staff members were appointed but they were mainly part-time. The few remaining staff worked very hard to get everything in order but by the time Mr Preston arrived, there were still some outstanding issues." Susie stopped to catch her breath then suddenly burst into tears. "I wish you had not left," she said. "It was a happy place while you were in charge."

Adam was taken aback at her outburst.

Yes, he thought. It was a happy place but she had no idea of the pain it had cost him to get there. By now her sobs had subsided.

"We all experience dark periods in our lives, Susie," he said. "But there is a strange satisfaction in finding our way out of them. It makes us appreciate the good times and not get obsessed with the bad. Life is constantly challenging us and the only way forward is to face up to those challenges. Things will improve I can promise you that. This is Mr Preston's first managerial job and he has to overcome his fears and anxiety in order to succeed. Can you imagine how big that challenge is? You were always very supportive to me and I really hope you will do the same for him."

"You are a very kind person, Mr Richards," she said. "I'd better wash my face and powder my nose before I go back on duty. Thank you."

When Susie had gone, Adam sat there deep in thought. He had all the information he needed but he was stunned by her emotional outburst. He had never seen her like that before. It must have affected all the staff who had remained quite deeply. He decided that he was not going to discuss it with them anymore because of the unhappy memories which would resurface. He would chat to them about the positive improvements which he knew would happen as a result of his report.

He stood up and collected his briefcase from the table. He desperately needed some fresh air and walked briskly out of the main entrance. Outside, he paused and took some deep breaths. He crossed the road and went into Morag's café. Morag greeted him warmly.

"Can you find me a quiet corner, please? I've had a difficult morning," he said.

Morag took him over to a table that was partially hidden from the rest of the café then went away and soon came back with a steaming hot coffee and a bun.

"On the house," she said as Adam thanked her.

He took out a notebook and began to jot things down. He remembered what Susie had told him but he needed to remember it exactly and made notes of what he had heard. As he wrote it down, he thought of the people involved and how hurt and bewildered they must have felt. He admired them for their loyalty to the company and he sincerely hoped that his visit and subsequent report would help to make their working lives better. He thought about Robert Preston and the challenges which lay ahead of him. He was a lucky man in that he had a loyal staff but Adam knew that Robert had a lot to learn about personal relationships. He made a note to speak to the area manager about this. Maybe a more mature assistant manager would be helpful.

Although Susie had provided him with all the information he needed, he went back into the main office and made a point of speaking to the other staff members who had worked with him. They all told him the same story and he did his best to reassure them that things would get better. Finally, he went to say goodbye to Robert. The two men shook hands and Robert said:

"Thank you for coming. I have enjoyed your company and you have given me the confidence to be more positive about the future. I should very much like to keep in contact with you if you don't mind?"

"I should be pleased to hear from you at any time," replied Adam, warmly. "I am sure you will be successful."

Robert accompanied him to the main entrance. They shook hands again.

"Have a safe journey home," said Robert.

Adam walked around the corner to where his car was parked in the hotel car park. He unlocked it and slid into the driver's seat.

"Home!" he said aloud. "Yes, I am going home."

He set off down the road and was soon speeding southwards on the motorway. As he travelled, he could feel his spirits lifting. The last three days had not been enjoyable but he had not realised how stressed he had been. He reckoned that he was about halfway to Oxford so he decided to stop at the next service station. He needed to stretch his legs and to phone Leah. He pulled into the car park and got out of the car. The night air was fresh as he walked in to buy a cup of coffee and a sandwich. He carried it to one of the outside tables and sat down. There was a continuous stream of cars and lorries coming and going around him but for a few minutes, he was lost in his thoughts. He took out his phone and pressed Leah's number.

Leah was saying goodbye to her last student when her phone rang. She hurriedly closed the front door and went to answer it.

"Hello?" she said breathlessly.

"You are out of breath," he said. "What have you been doing?"

"I'm out of breath because I rushed to answer the phone before it stopped ringing," she said firmly.

"I would have phoned again."

"Never mind that," she said. "Where are you?"

"Halfway to Oxford, about 1½ hours away."

"Have you had a good trip?"

"Yes, very good but I shall be glad to be home."

"I've been thinking," she said rather too quickly. "You won't have any food in the house or even milk for a cup of tea."

"That's true," said Adam wondering what was coming next.

"Would you like to come here for the night? The bed is made up in the spare room and I could get you something to eat?"

Adam was speechless. He wasn't sure what to say.

"Are you there?" came Leah's anxious voice.

"Yes, I'm still here," he said, finally. "I'd like that if you are sure it is not putting you to too much trouble?"

"It is no trouble at all," said Leah lightly. "I'll expect you in 1½ hours. Bye."

Adam sat staring at his phone for several minutes, then he pressed the call ended button and made his way back to the car.

It was a kind thought but he couldn't help feeling there would be more to it, knowing what a tease she could be. As he drove off, he sensed an interesting evening ahead and found that he was quite looking forward to it.

The rest of the journey to Oxford was quite straightforward. As he approached Leah's house, he realised how much he had missed her. He parked the car, collected his overnight bag and briefcase and rang the doorbell. Leah answered the door and as he stepped inside, he kissed her on both cheeks.

"I've missed you," he said.

"I've missed you too. Come on in."

Adam followed her into the kitchen.

"I'll make you a nice cup of tea," she said. "Or would you prefer coffee?"

"I have drunk enough coffee in the last three days. A cup of tea will be fine."

He sat down at the kitchen table and sighed. She made the tea and gave it to him then studied his face.

"You look very tired. Have you had a difficult time?"

"It wasn't easy but I think I achieved what I set out to do. I'll finish my report tomorrow; then it is up to Head Office to take what action they feel is necessary."

"Have you eaten today?" she asked.

"I had a bun this morning and a sandwich this evening," he replied. "I suppose I am rather hungry."

"Go and relax in the lounge. I'll get you something to eat."

He stood up and went into the lounge. He flopped down on the settee and closed his eyes. The activity of the last three days had drained his energy. It had left him with very mixed feelings. In addition to that, he now found himself in a situation which he did not understand and which was out of his control. It was a new experience to have someone actually looking after him and caring about him. He was so used to being independent and looking after himself. He didn't understand but he was determined to enjoy it.

"Your dinner is ready," she called.

He went back to the kitchen and there was a plate of sausages, mash and beans.

"That looks good," he said, sitting down.

"You know me. I'm no gourmet cook but I can just about manage the basics."

Adam laughed, remembering the cooking disasters which had taken place when they were first married.

"That's not changed then?"

As he finished his meal, he looked at up at her.

"Thank you," he said. "That was good. I had not realised how hungry I was."

He stood up and stretched and yawned.

"You need a good night's sleep. Come on I'll show you to your room."

He followed her up the stairs. He knew that Leah slept in the front bedroom. He pretended to go into it but Leah took him firmly by the arm and showed him into the spare bedroom.

"None of that," she said sternly as she switched on the light. "This is your room."

Adam looked around. He remembered it well because it had been their room when they had first moved into the house. Even the big bed felt familiar.

"Sleep well," she said and kissed him goodnight. "I'll bring you a cup of tea in the morning," she added but he did not notice the twinkle in her eye.

Adam had a quick wash and was soon in bed. It felt strange to be here and he couldn't quite shake the feeling that she was up to something. But the bed was very comfortable and he was so tired that he was soon fast asleep.

When Leah left Adam in the bedroom, she went downstairs, cleared up the kitchen and laid the table ready for breakfast. Then she took two mugs out of the cupboard and put them on a tray. She knew exactly what she was going to do the next morning.

She slept well and woke quite early. She took a few minutes to reflect on the fact that her husband was asleep in the next bedroom, then she got out of bed and put on her dressing-gown which was hanging on the back of the door. She went downstairs and made two mugs of tea which she carefully carried back up the stairs. She knocked gently on Adam's door and went into the room. He was still fast asleep so she kissed him softly on his forehead.

"I've brought you a cup of tea."

Adam was having a lovely dream where Leah was in bed with him and he was holding her in his arms. He was just about to kiss her when he felt something warm touch his leg. He awoke with a start and saw Leah lying in the bed beside him. He was too surprised to speak but eventually, he mumbled:

"What are you doing?"

"I told you I've brought you a cup of tea. I was just waiting for it to cool enough to drink and I was getting cold standing by the bed and the bed looked so warm and inviting that…" she suddenly stopped speaking and looked at Adam. He was laughing so much that tears were running down his cheeks.

"You are impossible!" he chuckled, holding her in his arms and pulling her closer to him. They lay there in peaceful contentment until Leah suddenly said:

"Déjà vu."

Adam was puzzled and asked what she meant.

"Do you remember?" she said. "Before we were married and you were a lodger at our house, I used to bring you a cup of tea in bed at the weekends and I got in bed with you and we had a cuddle. It was all very innocent just like this."

"I assure you this is not innocent!" said Adam in a stern voice. "You are a witch and you know it. One day you will tempt me too much and then I shall have to deal with you."

Leah laughed.

"Drink your tea," she said. "It will cool you down. It is time to get dressed anyway. We both have work to do."

She slid out from under the duvet and went into her bedroom, thinking she had quite enjoyed teasing Adam but she must take care not to tempt him too fast. She heard him go into the bathroom as she went downstairs. He soon followed her and they sat together at the kitchen table.

"Did you sleep well?" she asked.

"Yes, I did, thank you, better than I thought I would."

"What do you mean by that?" she asked, surprised.

"I thought I would feel disturbed knowing you were in a different bed next door but I was so tired I could have slept on a clothesline."

"What will you do today?"

"I must phone Barry first and let him know that I shall be coming into the office later this morning. The most urgent thing is to finish writing my report and send it to the directors. Once that is done, I can relax and get on with my proper job." He stood up and looked at her. Thanks for looking after me. I'll phone you later in the week," he said and kissed her.

"No problem," she said, smiling at him. "It was a pleasure. We must do it again sometime."

"Make that sometime soon," he whispered in her ear and with that he was gone.

Leah listened to the car driving away. It had been an interesting time but now she thought maybe she should remind him about being just good friends.

Adam drove back to his house, mulling over the time he had just spent with Leah. He knew there had been a hidden agenda but had to admit it was quite a surprise to wake up and find her in bed with him. He believed he had still been in a dream but she soon showed him he wasn't. Déjà vu she had said and he knew exactly what she meant.

Chapter Four

Adam was relieved to get back home. He picked up his post as he went through the front door. Most of it was junk mail and it went straight into the bin. He had remembered to stop at the supermarket to buy milk and bread and he carried it into the house, together with his overnight bag and briefcase. He then phoned Barry and told him that he would be coming in later that morning. Barry reassured him that there were no problems and Adam was pleased to hear him say that. He carried his bag upstairs and sorted out the contents, putting some clothes to be washed. He went into the bathroom and decided to have a shower to wash away some of his long-term memories and look forward to the future.

Half an hour later, he felt fresh and clean and ready to face the day. He collected his briefcase and drove into work. As he walked through the main door, he was struck by the contrast between that entrance and the one he had been using for the past three days. He had certainly moved on and greeted the staff all hard at work. The receptionist had seen him come in and she immediately phoned through to Sally his secretary. Sally had been talking to Barry and they both came out to welcome him back.

"Everything seems to be working smoothly without me," said Adam, drily, then saw Sally and Barry look at each other a little uncertainly. "But I know it is because you have both been working hard. Well done both of you."

"You had us a bit worried there," said Barry. "No doubt we shall get used to your sense of humour."

"I'm sorry," said Adam "There has been no opportunity for humour in the past three days. It has all been deadly serious."

"Was it really that bad?" asked Barry, sympathetically.

"Let's just say I'm glad it's over," he replied. "I have to finish writing my report and once that has been sent to Head Office, I hope it will be closure."

"There are some messages for you," said Sally. "Shall I bring them in to you?"

"I need to talk to Barry first," said Adam. "I'll call you when I'm free but could you please make us two cups of coffee?"

"Yes, of course," said Sally.

"Let's go into my office, Barry," said Adam. "And you can fill me in about what's been happening here."

They made their way to Adam's office which was exactly how he had left it. Sally came in with the coffee and they sat facing each other across the table.

"Tell me everything," said Adam.

"There is not much to tell," replied Barry. "The staff are all very professional. They work hard in their different departments and I haven't heard any complaints. The place runs like a well-oiled engine."

"I'm glad to hear it," said Adam. "What a contrast to the last three days."

"I don't want to break any confidences but was it really as bad as that?" Barry looked genuinely shocked.

"It was actually a very depressing place, both as a building and general atmosphere inside it. Within a week of my leaving, the assistant manager had bullied the staff so badly that half of them resigned and left. The few remaining loyal staff members tried to carry on but the bullying continued and the staff walked out. That was when the area manager reasonably took over and sacked the bully. But the damage was done and it will take a big effort to rescue the branch. I've written all this in my report. So, the Head Office will make any necessary changes."

"But I understood that they have appointed a new manager," said Barry. "Surely that will make a difference?"

"Yes, there is a new manager but he is young and inexperienced. He is lacking in confidence and I'm not sure he has the steel in him to make these changes. He is a nice enough chap but totally out of his depth."

"Are you glad you moved away from Leden?"

"I am glad for any number of reasons," said Adam. "Most of which are to do with work but some are a lot more personal."

"By the way," said Barry. "How is Leah?"

"She was very well when I saw her last night and she looked fine this morning too," replied Adam and he sat back on his chair and pretended to be looking through some papers but all the time he was watching Barry out of the corner of his eye.

"You spent the night with her?" spluttered Barry.

"Leah and I are friends," said Adam primly. "Friends often spend time together."

"But you said you spent the night with her?"

"Ok. Perhaps I should have said night time. Does that persuade you that we are just friends?" said Adam and burst out laughing.

"You do wind me up," said Barry a little grumpily. "I'd better go before you tell me any more stories."

Adam returned to the serious business of being a manager.

"Ask Sally to come in as you go out?"

Before long, Sally came in carrying a handful of papers and some files. She placed the files on one of the shelves and said:

"I've checked them out and removed any outdated material to put in the archives. I will do the same with the other files and sort out the rubbish."

Adam watched her. He knew she would be a most efficient secretary.

"How did you get on with Barry, as your boss?" he asked.

"We got on fine," she replied. "He works hard and has good relations with the staff. He is learning a lot from you. He says that he enjoys working with you."

Adam was pleasantly surprised at what he heard. He had already decided that Barry would be a very good manager and when the right time arrived, he would have no hesitation in recommending him.

Sally opened one of the folders and took out some paper.

"There are three applications for you to deal with. I thought best to keep them for you to see."

"Thank you," said Adam. "Is there anything else?"

"Yes, one other thing. I had a phone call from James Brown, the area manager, yesterday. He wanted to know when you would be back and he wanted you to phone him today. He was very insistent. He wants to come and meet you."

"The last time I spoke to him I ended up doing something which I really didn't want to do," said Adam, thoughtfully. "I might have to grow a thicker skin where he is concerned."

Sally left the office and Adam picked up the phone and got through to James's secretary.

"I'll put you straight through," she said.

"Hello Adam," he said. "When did you get back?"

"I came back last night."

"How was the trip?" James asked.

A man of few words thought Adam.

"I think I achieved what I set out to do," replied Adam, tersely.

"I shall look forward to seeing a copy of your report."

"It will be with you tomorrow."

"Good," said James. "I would like to come and meet you. When would be a convenient time?"

"I do not have my diary with me. I will ask my secretary to arrange an appointment," said Adam. He was getting rather fed up with this conversation. "I will put you through to her right now."

He pressed the intercom to Sally's office and explained what he wanted her to do. Then he went back to James who by this time was getting impatient.

"My secretary has my diary now and she will sort out a possible date for you to come to Oxford. I look forward to seeing you."

He finished the call. He knew he would have to complete his report that afternoon so that it was ready for Sally to send it to Head Office and now the area manager as well. He just had the last page to write up and he would make that his priority after lunch. He went to Marks and Spencer and bought a sandwich and a drink and returned to his office. He told Sally what he intended to do and asked her to deal with any calls which came in. By 3.30 pm he had finished writing. He sent for Sally and asked her to read through the report to check for any mistakes. When he was sure that it was okay, he put it in his briefcase.

"That is your first job in the morning," he told Sally. "And I shan't be sorry to see the back of it."

Adam went home in the evening feeling pleased with what he had achieved that day. He was most relieved that the report had been completed but decided to check it over one more time, just to make absolutely sure he hadn't forgotten anything. He had bought a readymade meal, which he now put in the microwave. When it was ready, he took it into the lounge to eat. He sat back on his settee and closed his eyes. He was comfortable in the quietness of his surroundings after the frantic activity of the last few days. As he began to relax, he thought about his visit to Leden. He hoped that he could help improve things for the people there. His three years in that office had opened his eyes to the complexities of relationships. He now realised that it had been the start of his own journey of acceptance. He had been in a position where he was responsible for the well-being of the staff and that had prevented his mind from dwelling on his own misfortunes. His move to Oxford had continued this process and he was beginning to feel that, despite the past, he could make a worthwhile contribution both in his work and in his private life.

He went to the kitchen to get a beer out of the fridge and returned to his seat on the settee. He had been in Oxford for less than a month but so much had happened. He was confident that he could make a success of his appointment to such a well-established office. He felt fortunate that he had a competent second-in-command in Barry. The staff and the general public he had met had been most welcoming. He felt he could go on making a long list of his blessings and was suddenly hit by a sense of wonder. It seemed so unfamiliar and he realised he had never considered he had blessings in his life.

For a long time, he sat there contemplating this mind-blowing discovery. It was like a watershed moment when he saw his whole life from a different perspective. He knew he would never be totally free of guilt over how he'd let down Leah and the children but for the rest of his life, he wanted to be there for them. He would try to make amends for what he did and hoped that one day they would forgive him enough to allow him to do that. He laid his head back and closed his eyes. All sorts of thoughts were racing through his mind and he knew his heart was beating too fast. He didn't move until his whole body had relaxed then he got up and walked a little unsteadily into the kitchen. He stood by the sink gazing out of the window. It was dark outside and he closed the blinds. He opened the fridge door and reached for a can of beer. It was the last one and he knew he needed to go shopping. The next day was Friday and he decided to call at the supermarket on his way home from work.

He returned to his settee and sat down again. He felt much calmer now after the tumult of the past hour. He was beginning to feel quite at home in his little house but he knew that he really wanted to buy his own place. The problem was: where did he want to settle down? He actually knew the area very well but that was twelve years ago and many more large housing estates had been built since then. The choice was endless and he would need some help in order to make the right decision.

He decided to visit some estate agents on Saturday. He wouldn't tell them who he was and thought it would be very interesting to find out about the property market. He switched off the lights and went to bed wondering what Leah would do.

Chapter Five

The next morning, he arrived early at the office. Sally was already there checking that the computer and printer were both in good order. Adam took the report out of his briefcase and passed it over to her.

"One copy to Head Office, one copy to the area manager and one copy for my personal file," he said. "When they are printed, I will sign each one before you send it."

"I'll do it right away," said Sally and disappeared into her office.

Half an hour later, she was back in Adam's office.

"They are ready for you to sign," she said, handing him the folder.

He signed each one and gave two of them back to Sally.

"You can send them off now," he said wearily.

He put the third copy in his private file which he kept locked away in the filing cabinet. Then he sat back with a huge sigh of relief. Then he called Barry to come to see him. When he came in Barry found Adam sitting in his chair deep in thought.

"Is something wrong?" asked Barry. anxiously.

"No. everything is very right," replied Adam. "But I was just thinking that we need a decent coffee-making machine in the establishment. See about one please?"

Before Barry could reply, Adam's phone started ringing.

"Head office is on the phone," said Sally. "I'll put them through."

Barry stood up as if to leave the room but Adam gestured to him to sit down.

"Hello, Adam Richards speaking."

"This is the chairman of the directors here," said a disembodied voice down the phone. "Just ringing to thank you for your report received this morning. Good work! Job well done. Be in touch when we have studied its contents." The phone went dead.

Adam sat there quite speechless. Eventually, he said:

"You'll never guess who that was."

"Someone quite high up judging by the tone of his voice," said Barry.

"I don't know his name," said Adam. "He said he was the chairman of the directors."

"Wow, you can't get any higher up than that."

"It makes a big difference when someone says thank you. It makes you feel that all your effort has been appreciated. That is a lesson to remember," said Adam.

"You've hit the jackpot there. Who knows what it might lead to?"

"I don't want it to lead to anything," Adam said with a hint of anger in his voice. "I want to be allowed to get on quietly with my job here."

"I hope you have your wish," said Barry soothingly. "But I think you might not."

Barry left the office and Adam sat there thinking about the phone call. He would never have expected to speak to the chairman or any directors. What did he mean when he said 'be in touch?' He had a funny feeling that there was something going on which he knew nothing about. I hope I'm not getting neurotic, he thought. He needed some fresh air and he went out into the street.

There was a slight smell of diesel in the air but the breeze was gradually dispersing it. He bought a coffee and strolled up the street taking in all the sights and sounds of the city. He passed several estate agents and picked up a Property Paper from a stand outside one of them. It was dinner time when he arrived back at the office and he sent Sally out to buy him a sandwich.

When she returned, Adam told her about the phone call.

"This is all confidential," he reminded her. "I don't want any rumours floating about the place. I really have no idea what he means."

"We've never had a phone call from the directors. Any information has usually come through the area manager," said Sally, thoughtfully.

"Ah yes, the area manager. That's another mystery: why does he want to come? By the way, did you manage to arrange a date?"

"Yes, he wanted to come on Monday but I told him that you had prearranged appointments for the first three days of next week so he is coming on Thursday at eleven o'clock."

Adam looked at his diary then looked at Sally.

"I don't appear to have that many arrangements here," he said.

Sally looked a bit sheepish.

"I hope I haven't done the wrong thing but I thought you might like a couple of quiet days after all the stress of this week?"

Adam did not answer immediately and finally said:

"That was very thoughtful of you but next time please let me in on your little secret?" He smiled gently at her.

As Sally left the room, she was not sure if she had done the right thing or not. She enjoyed working for Adam. She found him a very interesting person and found herself wondering if he was married or not.

Adam finished his sandwich and went out into the main office. It was nearly closing time and there were only a few customers. He was glad to be able to chat to the staff who were busily finishing the business of the day. This was one aspect of his job which he thoroughly enjoyed and he was very aware of the importance of personal relationships.

He returned to his office feeling satisfied that everything was running smoothly. He told Barry that he was leaving and would see him on Monday. He drove home calling at the supermarket on the way to pick up some groceries. The first thing he did was to switch on the kettle. A nice cup of tea, he thought and that's exactly what Leah would say. He reminded himself to call her this evening.

He went into the lounge and sat down. A feeling of weariness suddenly came over him. What a week, he thought, feeling like a wet rag. All the conflicting emotions of the week crowded into his mind. He closed his eyes and stretched out his legs, thinking he needed time to unwind and he knew just the person to help him. He picked up his phone and pressed Leah's number. It only rang a couple of times before she answered it.

"Hello," she said. "Are you okay?"

"Not really," he answered sorrowfully. "I'm in need of some t.l.c. Do you know anyone who could help?"

"I need to think about that" Leah replied. "But in the meantime, can

I be of any assistance?"

"What do you suggest?" he asked a little too eagerly.

"Well, I would need you to come here for a consultation before prescribing any treatment," she said firmly. "I can see you at four o'clock tomorrow afternoon. Is that convenient for you?"

"Yes, that will be fine," he replied. "Shall I bring an overnight bag with me?"

"You can bring one," she said. "But I can't guarantee that you will need it."

"I'll see you tomorrow," he said. He felt better already now that he could look forward to seeing her again.

Almost immediately, his phone rang again.

"Hello?" he said.

"Is that Adam?" asked a woman's voice.

"Yes."

"This is Jen," she said.

He was pleased to hear from her. She was Leah's best friend and he had known her for many years.

"Hello Jen," he said. "Lovely to hear from you."

"How are you doing?" she asked. "Barry tells me that you had quite a week of upheaval."

"It certainly wasn't an easy week but it is behind me now and I hope I shall be able to move on."

Jen hesitated for a moment then said:

"How are you getting on with Leah?"

"Actually, we are getting on very well," he said. "We both accept that it is not possible to just return to our old relationship and that we almost have to start all over again. We are good friends."

"I'm really glad to hear that. The way in which Leah has dealt with the last twelve years is really remarkable. She is a very strong-minded person which is just as well considering all the problems she has had with her children."

Adam couldn't speak for a minute or two. He was too shocked by what he had heard.

"Are you still there?" asked Jen, anxiously.

"Yes, I am still here. I'm feeling very bad about what you have just told me. We haven't really talked about the children and Leah has said very little about the problems she faced."

"That is typical Leah. She gets on with life and always puts others first. She is well known and highly respected. Anyway," said Jen. "I was ringing to see if you would like to come to supper one evening next week. How about Wednesday? Barry plays darts that evening so we can have a nice long natter. Would seven o'clock suit you?"

"That's fine," said Adam. "I shall look forward to it."

Phew, he thought. Things seemed to happen more decisively down here that they did up north. The whole pace of life moved more quickly and he needed to get used to it. His hope for a quiet life was rapidly disappearing. The odds were he would get busier and he would have to learn to go with the flow.

The next day, he didn't rush to get up. A nice lie-in was a real treat. Eventually, he dressed, had some breakfast and put some washing in the machine. It was a lovely sunny morning so he put on his coat and walked up to the local shops. There were two estate agents in the area and he had a good look in their windows. The prices were much higher than up north and there was a great variation for different parts of Oxford. He would have to do his sums very carefully. But still, as a Building Society manager, he should be capable of getting a good deal for himself. He called in at the local pub and had a pub lunch but made a mental note to avoid it in future because he did not find the food appetising.

He arrived back home early afternoon and removed his washing from the machine. He draped it over the radiators and hung his shirts to drip dry above the bath. He packed his overnight bag and put it in the car. Soon he was on his way to Swanton. He parked the car in front of the garage and went in through the back door.

"Hello Leah," he said. "The patient has arrived."

She kissed him on the cheek.

"My therapy includes practical elements," she said seriously. "And the first task for you is to put the kettle on."

"I'm very good at that," he said. "Do I also have to make the tea?"

"Yes please, that is the second element. I've nearly finished doing these potatoes so we will have the tea in the lounge."

"What are you cooking?" he asked, innocently.

"It is a surprise. You must eat it whatever it is, that is the third element."

"Kill or cure," he muttered; fortunately, Leah didn't hear him.

They went into the lounge with their tea.

"Am I allowed a biscuit?" he asked.

"Yes, if you fetch it yourself."

"Would you like one?"

"Why don't you bring the whole tin in? That would be the fourth element; using your initiative."

Adam smiled as he went to the kitchen. He could see why Leah was such a good teacher. She could add light-heartedness to any situation. The kids must love her.

"Well, you have passed the first test," she said. "The second one begins after dinner."

They sat in silence for a while until Adam said:

"How has your week been?"

"Quite busy but no major excitements."

There was another silence. This time Leah spoke first:

"How about you? What has your week been like?"

"I'm just glad it is over," he replied.

"Has it been that bad?"

"Yes," he said shortly and Leah knew that now was not the time to ask any more questions.

"I'll go and start the dinner," she said getting up from her seat. "You stay here and have a rest."

Adam was not sorry to have some time alone. He appreciated the quiet order of Leah's house. The atmosphere seemed to calm him and stop his mind from racing. He took off his shoes and made himself comfortable lying full length on the settee. With a start, he remembered that he always used to relax in the same way many years ago. Other memories came flooding back to him as he lay there and some of his doubts returned, wondering sadly if it would ever be the same; he didn't want to lose her again. He remembered what Jen had said to him on the phone about the problems Leah had dealt with. How could he have been so selfish? He began to feel very despondent and not sure that even Leah could help the way he felt now. He sighed deeply.

Leah came into the room and heard the sigh. Oh dear, she thought. This may turn out to be harder than expected.

"Dinner's ready," she announced. "Come and get it."

Adam reluctantly rose from the settee and followed her into the kitchen. He didn't feel very hungry but he appreciated that Leah had made an effort and actually it looked really appetising.

"This looks good," he said as he sat down at the table.

"Mostly the work of Tescos," she said. "But I did have to cook it."

He smiled at her.

"Well done," he said. "You've cooked it very well," and he tucked into the meal.

"That was good. I did enjoy it," he said eventually and Leah was pleased with his reaction.

"Now for the second test," she said. "You clear the table while I go and sit down. It's called job sharing."

Adam smiled at her.

"I think I can manage that. Off you go and leave me to it."

Leah left the kitchen and went upstairs to freshen up. When she came down Adam was already in the lounge.

"That was quick!"

"We workers don't hang about," said Adam, sternly. "Now what is the next test?"

"I have to demonstrate this one," she said and sat down next to him on the settee.

She put her hands around his face and kissed him fully on the lips. Adam responded immediately and put his arms around her. They held each other close and Adam whispered in her ear:

"Why are you so kind to me? I don't deserve it. I've treated you so badly. I'll never be able to make it up to you," and his voice cracked with emotion.

They sat there, side by side. Adam still had his arm around her.

"I think that our biggest problem is wondering what sort of relationship we might end up with," she said eventually. "Maybe we have different opinions on that but I do not think we should worry about it right now. I think it will develop naturally whatever the final result. To my mind, a personal relationship is like a slow-burning fuse of friendship. You light the end of the fuse and it slowly burns through different stages of friendship. You start by becoming a friend or maybe an acquaintance then the next stage is being a good friend when you might do more things together like going out for a meal for example. After that, you become a very good friend when your feelings start to change and you spend much more time with each other and you want to do things to surprise them, in a pleasant way of course. Then by the time you become very, very good friends you know a lot more about your relationship. Here endeth lesson number four."

Adam had been listening intently to Leah's lecture. It all made sense to him and he couldn't help wondering how Leah had developed such a wise understanding of human nature. She had a clear and honest way of expressing it. He knew he could learn a lot from her.

"How far do you think our fuse has burnt?" he asked quietly.

It was several minutes before Leah answered. Adam waited while she considered her answer. This was too important to rush to a conclusion.

"We are certainly friends," she said, eventually. "And I think we may be as far as good friends. We haven't fallen out and we enjoy each other's company. That is how I feel but what about you?"

"I think you are right in what you say," he replied. "But I know there are bigger challenges ahead. I am starting to understand what you meant when you said that we were two different people from how we were many years ago. Maybe we were almost childlike in our dependence on each other. Now we have grown up and our experiences have changed the way in which we view ourselves and the world around us."

Leah nodded her head in agreement. "It is almost as if we are meeting each other for the first time and yet we are not strangers. It is like starting from the beginning again but going about it in a different way. I feel we have made a good start but the next stage will be harder."

"You mean that arriving at the very good friends' position is going to take a lot more effort on my part?" smiled Adam.

"I don't think that the problems of the past should colour our perspective of the future but I honestly feel that the ball is in your court."

Adam stood up.

"I'll go and do my duty and put the kettle on," he said.

But Leah stopped him by saying:

"I'll go."

He sat down again trying to make sense of the conversation which had just taken place. He wasn't quite sure what Leah had meant by her last remark. He was still trying to figure it out when she came back carrying a bottle of wine and two glasses.

"I thought we deserved something a little stronger than tea after all the soul searching," she smiled as she put it down on the coffee table.

"Let me open it," he said, picking up the bottle and reading the label. "Pinot Noir? My favourite." He turned to Leah and said in amazement: "You remembered didn't you."

She said nothing and held out her glass. He filled both glasses and clinked them together.

"A toast to us," he said. "May we become very, very good friends."

As they drank their wine Adam suddenly said:

"I must be careful not to drink too much, I don't want to be caught over the limit."

"I don't think that is very likely tonight. I assume it is your overnight bag in the hall?" she said in an innocent voice.

Adam heard what Leah said and he burst out laughing.

"Don't pretend to be so innocent," he spluttered. "You are a witch and you know it. You had the whole evening planned."

"Of course, I did," said Leah primly. "It is part of the treatment I promised you."

"Well," he said still chuckling to himself. "I know one thing for sure, I shan't be recommending this particular treatment to anyone else. It is worth more than gold to me and I feel much better already."

"You are not yet fully recovered," she said firmly and Adam couldn't help wondering what was coming next.

They spent the rest of the evening chatting until the wine bottle was empty. By then Adam was feeling quite relaxed and Leah was getting sleepy.

"Time for bed," she said. "You go up first and I'll put the lights out down here."

She heard him go to the bathroom and back across the landing to the bedroom, then she went up the stairs. She had a wash and got ready for bed, then she noticed that Adam's light was still on. She knocked gently on the door and went into the room. He was already in bed.

"Are you okay?" she asked him.

"I'm fine," he replied. "Come and join me."

"I can't refuse an invitation like that," she said without hesitation and slid under the duvet beside him. "Just a quick cuddle."

Adam held her in his arms and whispered:

"Just a quick cuddle between very good friends."

"Yes," she said sleepily and relaxed into his arms.

A minute or two later she was fast asleep. Adam lay there for a while thinking about what had happened that evening. Being with Leah had felt so comfortable and relaxing but there was also a sort of mystery about her which he could not understand. She seemed to have the ability to look into his very soul and he knew that he would have to work hard to regain her trust. He kissed the top of her head and vowed to do whatever was necessary for them to spend the rest of their lives together.

The next morning when Leah woke up, she knew that she was not in her own bed. The sun was streaming through the window and it never shone into her bedroom in the morning. There was something heavy laying across her body and as she went to move, she came to her senses. She looked down and suddenly realised where she was. She pulled back the duvet and stood up. She felt a bit wobbly but couldn't decide if that was the result of a hangover or shock. She crept out of the bedroom and into her own room. Sitting on the bed she tried to remember what had happened last night. She recalled having an invitation which she accepted and ended up sleeping with her husband. She hoped he hadn't forgotten his manners. She dressed quickly and went downstairs, deciding not to disturb him this morning. They had the whole day in front of them. She made herself a cup of tea and went to sit in the garden.

I really must deadhead those roses and pull up a few weeds she thought. And the grass needs cutting back and front. She found some gardening gloves and the secateurs and set about trimming the rose bush. She had nearly finished when she was startled by a voice behind her:

"I wondered where you were. What are you doing here?"

"The garden needs TLC too," she said. "I'm tidying it up and then I shall cut the grass."

"I could cut the grass for you?" he said. "If you tell me where to find the mower."

"That would be really helpful. The mower is in the shed and the extension lead is in the garage," she said gratefully.

He was pleased to be able to do something practical to help Leah and they worked together for the next hour.

"I've done enough for today," she said, finally. "I think it is coffee time."

She went into the kitchen and made two cups of coffee which she took to the outside table.

"Do you have any help to work in the garden?" he asked.

"Gardeners cost money," she replied. "I can manage. Thank you for cutting the grass. That has made it look much tidier."

"What would you like to do this afternoon?" he asked.

"I haven't any plans," she said. "Have you anything in mind?"

"When I was up North," he said "I completed the sale of my flat so now I can seriously start looking for a place of my own down here. But there are so many choices and I am not sure what I want or where it should be. I need some help and I wondered if we could just go for a ride around this area and see what is available? There must be some nice country pubs around where we can get something to eat. The only thing I am sure about is that I don't want to live in Oxford or the surrounding area."

"Yes of course I'll come with you. It's a lovely part of the country for a Sunday afternoon drive. I'll just go and put something decent on," she said and dashed upstairs.

Adam washed his hands and tidied himself up and before long they were getting into his car.

"You look very nice," he said.

Leah smiled at him.

"Have a Brownie point," she said. "You don't scrub up too badly yourself."

"Cheeky monkey. By the way, did you sleep well last night?"

"I had a peaceful night with no disturbances thank you," she said firmly.

"Are you sure of that?" said Adam with a fake measure of concern in his voice.

"I'm sure of it unless it is proved otherwise. Why are you so bothered about it?"

"I believe you implicitly," he said. "It was just a casual conversation."

Adam smiled, knowing he had managed to rattle her. He was determined to be just as much a tease as her and he gave a little laugh.

"Keep your eyes and mind on the road," she said grumpily and he laughed again.

They drove through the Oxfordshire countryside until they reached a pub high up on the downs. They chose a simple pub lunch and took it outside to eat. The sun was still shining and the scenery beautiful.

"I don't think I would want to live in a village," said Adam suddenly. "I like to have people around me".

She looked at him curiously.

"When we were first married, we lived in some very isolated places," she said. "You never complained about that."

"It was all part of my job. I suppose it goes to show what a different person I am now."

They sat in silence while memories came flooding back.

"If you don't want to live in a village, where would you like to live?"

He took some time to consider his answer.

"I would really like to live in Swanton but I don't know how you would feel about that?"

She looked at him in surprise.

"I am very happy living in my house. It is the family home and the children all regard it in that way. If you want to buy a house in Swanton, I don't mind. After all, it will be your home."

He was taken aback by her answer. He had hoped that one day they would live together in the same house. Was she saying that this could not happen?

"Time to move on, I think," he said, standing up rather abruptly.

They drove back in uneasy silence. Leah knew she had really upset him and wondered what he was thinking. When they arrived home, he said:

"I'll go and collect my bag then. I must be going."

He went upstairs and Leah stood in the hallway uncertain what to do. She walked into the lounge and sat on the settee. She could feel the tears welling up in her eyes and they began to roll down her cheeks. She did not know that Adam had come into the room until she felt his arms around her.

"Leah?" he said in a voice full of concern. "Leah, what is it?"

She was still sobbing her heart out as he tried to wipe away her tears. "Leah, please tell me what has upset you so much?"

Her sobs were quietening down until at last, she felt able to speak.

"I'm sorry," she said. "I'm really sorry."

"What are you sorry for?" he asked gently.

"I'm sorry I upset you by what I said. I didn't mean to hurt you."

Adam was thinking back to what was said outside the pub. Leah's words had certainly upset him but he thought he had succeeded in hiding it from her. He realised that underneath that confident exterior there was a sensitive and vulnerable person. He knew that he had to be honest with her.

"Your words did upset me. They shattered my dream of us living together at some time in the future. I'm not sure what the alternative is. I have a lot of thinking to do."

"Can we still be good friends?"

"Of course, we can," he replied instantly. "Nothing can change that." He kissed her on the forehead. "I'm going to make us both a nice cup of tea. You stay there and blow your nose."

Leah gave him a little smile.

"I've been rather sniffy," she said. "I'm sorry."

When Adam returned with the tea, Leah was feeling much calmer. It was quite unlike her to collapse like that and she realised she really did care about him.

"I think we have many things to talk about," he said. "But not tonight. I really must go. I have another busy week ahead of me but I will find time to ring you every day to make sure you are alright."

"I shall be fine. I shall be busy too but I always look forward to hearing your voice."

They stood up and Adam put his arms around Leah.

"I do love you. Nothing will ever change that," he said and kissed her.

"I love you too," she said as she saw him to the door.

She stood there until he had driven up the road then she went back into the lounge. It felt strangely empty now that Adam had gone. She had become so used to spending time in her own company and always been very comfortable doing that. She wondered if she would really want Adam here all the time? This was a new thought which would need careful consideration she decided. It had been a day of contrasting feelings and Leah was ready for bed. She went upstairs, had a quick shower and before long she was fast asleep.

Adam drove back once again with a mind full of mixed emotions. His idea that they could slip back into their old relationship had completely disappeared. He was beginning to understand that they certainly were two different people but with a common bond of love which bound them together. He understood what Leah meant when she said that love was the foundation but a relationship needed to be carefully built on it. His thoughts began to turn to the week ahead. He had the feeling that it was going to be very interesting.

Chapter Six

The next day he went to work quite cheerfully. He was fortunate that he was able to put his personal problems to the back of his mind whilst he was at work. Each morning he spent time in the main office getting to know people who worked there. He was basically a sociable person and his staff were all impressed by his attitude towards them.

He called Sally into the office and they discussed his appointments for the day. There were not too many of them but it was useful to have the input of Sally's local knowledge. In between business meetings, Adam had time to think about something that had really bothered him the previous weekend. He knew that Leah had continued to pay the mortgage on the house after he had left. It must have taken a substantial part of her salary each month. I must have been out of my mind, he thought. How could I have been so selfish?

He decided that he must find out the details. He switched on his computer and scrolled down until he found what he was looking for. The mortgage was still in both their names. That was one thing he definitely had to change. He noticed that the payments had been very regular and Leah had never been in arrears. He would need to do some sums and proceeded to work out exactly how much she had paid in the past twelve years. He was shocked at the total amount and switched off the computer.

By the afternoon, he had worked out his plan, but he knew that it would be unethical to implement it himself. He decided to discuss it with Barry the next morning, as he prepared to go home. He said goodbye to Sally and went out into the street. It was already getting dark and he noticed that the leaves were beginning to fall from the trees. Typical Autumn weather he thought, we are nearly in October and then soon it will be Christmas. He remembered last Christmas when he had spent the day alone in his flat. He had been to several Christmas parties but he couldn't forget the feeling of loneliness which had engulfed him. What will this Christmas be like, he wondered and hoped it would be a happier time. Also, he had a birthday to come before that. He suddenly stopped walking as another thought entered his head. Leah's birthday was before his, in October. He was determined to get her a present, a real present to show how much he loved her.

It didn't take him long to drive home and the first thing he did was to phone Leah as he had promised.

"I know you are probably busy," he said. "But I needed to know that you were alright."

"I'm okay," she said. "I've been busy but I've nearly finished for the evening. I think I will have an early night."

"Sleep well. I am still your very good friend," he said and put the phone down.

That evening, Adam went up to the back bedroom and found the box which contained the television. He plugged it into the socket and for the first time in a month, he switched it on and listened to the news.

The office was already busy when he arrived the next morning. He went to find Barry who was helping one of the staff to sort a computer problem. Adam had a quiet word with him and asked him to come to his office when he had finished what he was doing. He then checked his appointments for the day with Sally and asked her to handle any calls whilst he was talking to Barry. He went into his office and closed the door. He needed to check that he had worked out the figures exactly before he explained to Barry what he wanted him to do. Barry came in carrying two cups of coffee. He put one down on the desk in front of Adam.

"That smells good," said Adam. "Just like real coffee."

"It is real coffee," replied Barry. "Out of our new coffee machine."

Adam looked at him and burst out laughing.

"You didn't waste any time, did you?" he chuckled. "When did it arrive?"

"It was installed in the staff room yesterday," said Barry. "And it certainly earned you some brownie points. The staff are well pleased."

"They work hard. They deserve the best we can offer them."

He looked straight at Barry and said:

"There is something I want you to do for me. It is a personal matter and absolutely confidential. Do you understand that?"

"Yes. I give you my word."

"It is to do with Leah."

Barry's eyes widened and he opened his mouth to speak but Adam raised his hand.

"Don't say anything, just listen. The mortgage on Leah's house is in both our names but for the past twelve years, Leah has made all the payments herself. I have been so selfish that it never occurred to me that this was happening. Now I have to put things right and this is what I want you to do. Luckily the mortgage is with us so you will have no trouble getting access to the information. I do not want anyone else to be involved in this, do you understand?"

"Yes," said Barry. "What do you want me to do?"

"I want you to transfer ownership of the house to Leah's name only. Then cancel her standing order for each month but take the mortgage payment from my account. Work out the total of the payments she has made over the past twelve years and I will pay that amount off the mortgage. When you have completed this, let me know exactly how much is still owed on the mortgage itself."

Barry was feeling a bit shocked by all these instructions and by the information which Adam had given him.

"That is quite a lot to remember," he said faintly. "I need to break it down into more manageable pieces. Can I check with you after each part? I don't want to make a mistake."

"Yes, keep me in touch with your progress, Barry. No doubt there will be papers to sign along the way."

"Adam, does Leah know about this?"

"No, she doesn't," he replied quickly. "I'm not telling her anything about it until the deed is done. I've made up my mind and see no point in giving her the opportunity to disagree."

"I'd like to be a fly on the wall when you do tell her," said Barry with some trepidation.

"I can deal with Leah," he said confidently. "By the way Barry, I have worked out my own set of figures but I'm keeping them under wraps until you have done the same, then we will compare them."

"How soon do you want the result?"

"It is Leah's birthday early in October. I would like it to be part of her birthday present."

"I'll do my best," said Barry as he left the room.

Adam wondered if this fell into the very good friend category. But it was only part of her birthday present.

Adam stood up. He had suddenly remembered something else very important which he needed to tell Barry. He called his office to see if he was back.

"There is something I forgot to tell you," he said, as soon as Barry answered. "I'm having supper with your wife tomorrow evening."

"That's nice," said Barry. "Sorry I can't join you but we have a very important darts match I can't possibly miss. You'll be able to have a good chat with her or should I say a good listen to her," he said, chuckling.

That evening when he phoned Leah, she was not her usual chatty self.

"I don't feel 100 per cent," she said. "I think I may be going down with a cold."

"Have you been to school?" he asked.

"Yes, I managed but thank goodness I only had two lessons."

"Would you like me to come over? I could mop your fevered brow."

"My brow is not fevered," answered Leah. "It just needs a Lemsip and a couple of Paracetamol which I can manage myself."

"I hope you feel better tomorrow. By the way, I must just mention that I might not be able to phone you tomorrow. I shall be going for supper with a friend." He waited for her reaction.

"That's nice," she said weakly. "Is it anyone I know?"

There is a touch of jealously there, thought Adam.

"I think you know her. She only has three letters in her name."

"Oh, you mean Jen!" said Leah feeling relieved. "She is a great talker. I don't envy you the state of your ears by the end of the evening," and she put the phone down.

Adam was actually feeling rather apprehensive about the evening with Jen. He knew that he was probably going to hear a lot more uncomfortable facts about Leah's life but he was determined to listen, or he might never manage to get closer to Leah. This was one of those challenges which they had talked about the other night. He would have to grit his teeth and behave like a man.

The next day, Wednesday, he was at the office contemplating the visit of the area manager. He called Sally in.

"How do you like the new coffee machine?" he asked.

"It makes a great cup of coffee. The staff all love it," she said. "I think it should impress Mr James Brown tomorrow."

"No doubt he will want the guided tour. Have we any cups and saucers?"

"No," said Sally. "We all use mugs or paper cups."

"It would not make a very good impression to offer Mr James Brown coffee in a paper cup. I want you to go out shopping now and buy six coffee cups, basin, jug and coffee pot and we could possibly do with some proper spoons, not these plastic ones. The coffee set will only be used for important visitors. Now why do you think we might be having some of those?" he said dreamily. "Make sure you choose a china set but not too many girlie patterns on it."

Sally laughed.

"I'll remember that," she said and stood up to go. Adam was still thinking.

"Get half a dozen new mugs and a couple of nice plates to put the biscuits on. That should show them that we know how to entertain our guests in Oxford."

"May I take one of the junior clerks with me?" she asked. "She can help with the carrying."

"Yes, of course," said Adam. "Take the money out of the staff fund."

Sally went off to do her shopping and Adam stayed in his office. He had several appointments that morning. He was beginning to meet some of the business owners who were coming to him for advice. It was dinner time before Sally returned loaded with parcels. Her junior helper was also weighed down too. They put them down on Adam's desk. Sally took a small packet out of her bag and gave it to him.

"First things first," she said. "Sandwiches for dinner."

"Thank you," said Adam. "Most welcome."

Sally was looking very pleased with herself as she started to unpack the parcels. Julie, her helper, was putting all the paper in the bin and it was not long before the results of her shop were laid out on the desk.

"Thank you, Julie," said Sally. "Thanks for your help. You may go now."

Julie left the room taking the overflowing wastepaper basket with her.

Adam liked the china. It had a contemporary design printed on it but the shape was quite conventional. He noticed that one bag had not been opened.

"There's one more bag," he said to Sally. "What's inside it?"

Sally looked a little nervous as she opened the bag. She pulled out a beautiful oak tray and a tin of biscuits.

"I got it all from M&S," she said. "So, I can easily take anything back if you don't like it."

Adam looked carefully at the tray. It was big enough to hold 4 cups and saucers and could easily be carried through the door. It was a lovely piece of English oak and Adam ran his fingers over it.

Sally hesitated then said:

"I thought it would set off the coffee cups quite beautifully and really add a touch of class."

"And what about the biscuits?" Adam asked.

"We couldn't offer a digestive and a custard cream," Sally said nervously. "Do you want me to take them back?"

"No, of course not," said Adam. "It was very thoughtful of you. It is the smallest touches that make the biggest impressions. Now we are ready for a visit from Mr James Brown and anyone else who might turn up. I would feel even more confident to entertain the managing director and his bevvy of Boarders."

Sally laughed out loud.

"Stranger things have happened," she said. "I'll take this china into the kitchen and give it a good wash. Then I will put it in one of the cupboards with a notice on the door." She gathered it all up and cleared the surface of Adam's desk.

He sat there and thought about Sally's comment: stranger things have happened. He could not understand why he was getting a knot in his stomach. It was beginning to worry him a bit. He locked his desk and told Sally he was leaving the office. He knocked on Barry's door but he was not in his usual place. He decided Sally would let him know he'd gone and went out into the cold air. He drove straight home and had a shower before he got ready to meet Jen. Then at 6.45 pm, he was on his way to her house.

Jen was a good cook and she had prepared a homemade cottage pie with cauliflower cheese.

"It smells really good," said Adam as he came through the door.

"Well, I do enjoy cooking," Jen laughed. "Unlike someone else I know."

"Leah does try," he said. "But it has never been her favourite occupation."

"It is all ready," said Jen. "Let's see if it tastes as good as it smells."

They sat down at the supper table to eat.

"Full marks," said Adam when they had cleared their plates. "I did enjoy that."

Jen picked up the half-empty wine bottle and two glasses.

"Let's go and sit somewhere more comfortable," she said and led the way into the lounge.

A log fire was burning in the grate and there were two easy chairs either side of it. A coffee table was in place between the two chairs. Jen poured them each a glass of wine and they sat facing each other.

"Barry told me that you didn't want anyone to know that Leah is your wife," she said. "And of course, I shan't say anything. But you can't keep it a secret forever can you?"

Adam thought for a moment before he replied.

"Don't misunderstand me. I am not ashamed to admit it but at present, we are just good friends and that is how we both see our meeting again."

"I know you are spending time together. Leah has told me that but she hasn't talked about it much and I don't ask her too many questions. But it's my guess that she hasn't told you how she managed over the past twelve years."

"She has said very little about herself and we have not even mentioned our children. I'm not sure how to get her to open up to me," he said, sadly.

"Leah is a very private person. She may not want to tell you everything that has happened or how much it has affected her life. She will give you clues as time goes on and you will have to learn how to interpret them."

"I love her very much and always will but she is a much more complex and yet complete person than the woman I married."

"Of course, she is," said Jen emphatically. "You can't go through what she has endured without it affecting you quite strongly. It was a 'kill or cure' situation and Leah soon showed that it wasn't going to kill her."

"It's funny," said Adam. "But she has no photographs on show in her house. You have family photos here in your lounge and pictures of your children."

"Leah keeps all her memories inside her. She has always kept her own counsel, even in the most difficult situations."

"What do you mean difficult situations? What sort of problems has she had?"

"Mainly problems involving the children."

There was silence for a few minutes while Adam tried to come to terms with what Jen had said. He looked at her in amazement. It suddenly hit him what a dreadful father he had been. For the past twelve years, his thoughts had been locked into his longing for Leah and he had almost forgotten about the rest of his family.

"Jen, I feel utterly devastated. I have four children and I know nothing about their lives," he said, his voice cracking with emotion.

"You also have four grandchildren," said Jen in a matter-of-fact voice.

Adam was speechless. He stared at Jen and the tears started to run down his cheeks. She stood up and put a box of tissues on the table. She felt really sorry for him but she knew that she had done the right thing. If he really wanted to renew his relationship with Leah there were some facts which he needed to be told. She waited until he had regained his composure.

"I'm sorry, Adam, but I had to tell you. The sooner you know the better for you. In the long run, it will help you to understand Leah and to understand yourself. You are not going to rebuild your lives together overnight. It will take a lot of patience and effort on your part for you to get the result you most desire."

Adam paused and looked intently at her.

"It can't have been easy for you when you told me but I'm glad you did and I thank you for it. Now I understand what Leah meant when she said the ball is in my court. I shall go slowly and carefully and find ways of showing her how much I love her. But I don't know how to start building bridges with my children."

"Some problems offer their own solutions," Jen said wisely. "I would just wait and see and not make any hasty decisions if I were you. Even when they are grown up, children can be very unpredictable."

"I'll take your advice on that," he said, gratefully. "I can see a rocky road ahead."

"You won't be on your own. I'll be here to lend a hand if necessary and I'm sure Barry will support you as a friend."

"Thank you, Jen. I've coped on my own for so long that I have forgotten how important good friends are. Now I think I must be going. It is going to be a difficult day in the office tomorrow and I must be ready for it."

Jen accompanied him to the door and he kissed her goodnight.

"Thanks again," he said. "I have a lot of thinking to do."

She watched as he drove off into the night.

When Barry came home later, he kissed his wife and said:

"Had a good evening?"

"Yes, very interesting," she replied. "By the way, what is happening in the office tomorrow that is so important?"

"We are having a visit from the area manager. Why do you ask?"

"It is just that Adam mentioned it," she said as she went to tidy up the kitchen.

Barry was surprised. It was quite unlike Adam to comment on anything to do with the business outside his office. He made a mental note to check on him first thing in the morning.

Adam was glad to get home. He was stunned by what Jen had told him. However much he tried, he could not make sense of anything. He felt completely overwhelmed with remorse for what he had done. He knew that what Jen had said was only the tip of the iceberg and at some later time he would learn a lot more things which would upset him. It was a situation which he had never before experienced and he did not know what to do. He sat on his settee until his mind stopped racing and reasoning began to take its place.

He told himself not to anticipate the future but concentrate on the present. He knew tomorrow would be a difficult day and he needed all his wits about him. He went upstairs and had a nice hot shower before getting into his bed. He lay there trying to relax his body until he fell into a troubled sleep.

He woke early the next morning and immediately memories of the previous evening came back to him. He knew he could do nothing about that today and forced himself to put it out of his mind.

Chapter Seven

It was early when he arrived at work and the main office was quiet. Various members of staff were starting to arrive. There was an air of expectancy about the place. They had been briefed by Barry on the special visit which was due to take place and they all wanted to do their best to make the day run smoothly.

Adam went straight into his office. Soon there was a knock at the door and Barry came in. He looked anxiously at Adam who was sitting behind his desk staring vacantly into space.

"Are you alright?" Barry said with a voice full of concern.

"Too much on my mind."

"Jen told me about the evening. I suppose it was bad timing on her part?"

"Don't blame Jen," he said immediately. "It wasn't her fault. She didn't know about this meeting today. It is just that there are so many things happening all at once that I find it difficult to work out the priorities."

"Perhaps you should take each day as it comes? Then the priorities will take care of themselves."

"That's a very philosophical outlook," said Adam. "Where did you learn that?"

"I have a very good teacher sitting opposite me," replied Barry, quietly. "I am learning a lot."

Adam thought for a while.

"You are right of course. Now you have pointed me in the correct direction and I shall be fine. So, let's get down to work but first things first."

He rang to ask Sally to bring in two mugs of coffee. They discussed the arrangements for the visit and Barry then went off to check that the staff were happy. Adam called Sally back into his office.

"Are the coffee cups at the ready?" he asked her.

"Yes, it is all under control," she replied.

Sally noticed that Adam had a worried look and wondered what was bothering him.

"You look worried," she said, finally. "Can I help?"

He found it easy to talk to her.

"I am a bit concerned. I feel there is more to this visit that meets the eye. Have you ever met James Brown?"

"No, I haven't," she said. "He sounds a rather pompous and impatient person on the phone."

"I felt the same way. I get the feeling that I may not like him and that is unusual for me. I can get on well with most people. I must keep an open mind but I want you to keep an eye on him, Sally, if he starts to prowl around."

At 11.30 exactly James Brown arrived. The receptionist saw him come and she rang through to Sally.

"Visitor has arrived," she announced.

Sally went out to meet him. He was quite an elderly man, not long till retirement thought Sally, and he stooped a little as he walked. She introduced herself and James Brown eyed her up and down.

"I will take you to Mr Richard's office," she said.

She noticed that he had piercing blue eyes which seemed to dart all over the building.

"Lead on," he said with a toothy smile and he followed her down the corridor.

"Nice legs," she heard him say behind her as they reached Adam's door.

"Come in," said Adam and Sally introduced James to Adam. As she did so she gave James an indignant stare which he ignored but it was noticed by Adam.

"Have you travelled far?" Adam asked politely.

"My area is the West Midlands but I am based in Birmingham."

"Would you like a cup of coffee?"

"Yes, I would," said James, tersely. "It has been a long journey."

"I will ask my secretary to make it," said Adam rather stiffly.

He rang through to Sally and soon she brought in the coffee cups on the tray. She made the coffee in the coffee pot and when she had poured it out, she moved the sugar and milk in front of James. Adam couldn't help but noticing that she kept her distance from James Brown at all times.

"Thank you, Sally," said Adam. "I'll call you when I need you."

As she left the room, James Brown's eyes followed her.

"Buxom wench," he remarked. "You certainly know how to pick them."

Adam could feel the tension rising in the office. He was in no mood for games so he decided to ask the question which had been bothering him for the past ten days.

"Is there a particular reason for your visit Mr Brown or do you pay regular visits to different offices?"

"That is a loaded question and somewhat surprising," he said pompously. "I must say it is unusual for a general manager to request information in such a direct way."

He's trying to pull rank, thought Adam feeling as though he might actually enjoy this. He sat in his chair and waited for Mr Brown to formulate his reply.

"There were two or three matters which I needed to discuss with you," said James, eventually. "I had heard so much about you from Head Office and from your previous area manager that I wanted to make your acquaintance. I have read your report on the work you did in Leden last week. It is very comprehensive but it did not contain many useful solutions. Thirdly, I shall be retiring next year and your name has been mentioned as a possible candidate for my job. I wanted to see for myself if you were up to the mark for it."

Adam could feel himself getting very angry.

"It is good to meet someone face to face so that they are not simply a voice on the phone. It is impossible to get to know them unless you meet them personally," he replied. "With regards to my report, I was asked to gather information on what had happened there and to offer support and advice to the new manager. It is up to other people to decide on any action which needed to be taken. I do not understand the implication of your third point. As far as I am aware, appointments and promotions are made by Head Office, not by the outgoing incumbent of the post."

Adam could see that Mr Brown was angry at being spoken to in this way and he quickly said:

"This is a new building with all the modern facilities. Would you like to take a closer look at it?"

"Yes," James Brown answered shortly. "Your secretary can show me around."

"I'm very sorry but I need Sally in the office," said Adam, trying to sound apologetic. "I will get my assistant manager to give you a guided tour." He called Barry on the intercom. "Barry, could you please come into my office? Mr Brown would like a tour of the building and I am sure you would be delighted to be his guide."

Five minutes later Barry arrived. He took a good look at the two men. Adam was cool and composed but Mr Brown was seething with anger.

"It should take about forty-five minutes," Adam said sweetly. "Do make sure you show Mr Brown everything and come back to my office when you have finished."

"I shall be delighted to show him around," smiled Barry and off they went.

As they passed Sally's office, she looked up from her desk. James Brown scowled at her and walked swiftly by. Barry noticed the scowl and he moved quickly on. He whizzed James around the building not giving him any opportunity to stop and speak with the staff. When he returned James to Adam's office, he noticed that Sally was not there. Adam had left some files piled up on his desk and he was leafing through some papers. He was giving a very good impression of being a busy man. He looked at James.

"I hope Barry was a good enough guide?" he said.

"He showed me everything," said James shortly and looked at his watch. "I must be off. I'm having dinner with the Lord Mayor this evening."

He said goodbye to Barry and Adam accompanied him to the main entrance. The two men briefly shook hands and Mr James Brown walked away towards the station.

Adam watched him go, thinking that no doubt he had a first-class rail ticket, not wishing to mix with the hoi polloi. Then he turned and went back to his office.

"Where's Sally?" asked Barry. "It's not like her to go missing."

"I sent her out on an errand," said Adam. "I thought it would be safer that way."

Barry looked at Adam in horror.

"You don't mean that James Brown assaulted her in any way?"

"No, thank goodness it didn't get that far but he would certainly have laid his hands on her given the chance," said Adam.

"You mean he is a predator, a sexual predator?" asked Barry in astonishment.

"I'm not saying that he is but he certainly gives that impression."

"How did you get on with him?" Barry asked.

"I thought he was a pompous git who did his best to patronise me. Please don't repeat that comment to anyone. He could be a dangerous enemy, but I think his time has passed and he knows it. He is just clinging on by his fingernails."

Just at that moment, a message came through on the office phone.

"I'm back," said Sally. "Has he gone?"

"Yes, he's gone," replied Adam. "Come into my office and please bring three cups of strong coffee with you."

Five minutes later, Sally arrived with the coffee and some biscuits.

"I realised that I haven't had anything for dinner. Thank goodness for chocolate biscuits."

Adam thought for a moment then he turned to Sally.

"What did you think of Mr James Brown?"

Sally came straight out with her reply:

"He is a most horrid man who preys on women. He is not fit to be in a position of power."

"That won't be for much longer. He retires next year so he told me. But I can't help wondering how many have suffered his advances over the years. Do you want me to make an official complaint to Head Office?" asked Adam.

"The whole episode did not last long but I did get the feeling that he knew it had been noticed and your subsequent handling of it confirmed that. I think he has had quite a fright today. Maybe we should make the relevant authorities aware of it without making a direct accusation?" she said.

"You may well be right," said Adam. "I think we should keep a record of it. It could be used as evidence at some time in the future. What do you think Barry?"

Barry's reply was instant:

"I think he is a horrible character and certainly not fit to be working where there are girls. I noticed him leering at some of them as we went around. It was really embarrassing."

"Tomorrow, you must write down what happened and how you feel about it," said Adam. "And I will put it in a safe place in case it is ever needed."

Barry went back to his office but on the way, he called in at the staff room. Several of the girls were having their coffee break. They stopped their conversation as Barry went in.

"Is something bothering you?" Barry asked.

The girls looked at each other uncertainly.

"We were talking about the visitor we had this morning," said one.

"What about him?" asked Barry.

"I don't know exactly. He just made us feel uncomfortable. But perhaps we were just imagining it?" she added hurriedly.

"No, you weren't imagining it," said Barry. "We were all affected by his visit. But don't worry, it has been noted and it won't happen again."

The girls were very relieved.

"Can we tell the others what you have just said?" asked the same woman.

"Yes, of course, you can," he replied.

He left them in the staff room looking much happier and went straight back to Adam's office. He told him what had happened and Adam looked concerned.

"I have a suspicion that we haven't heard the last of this. I think you and Sally had better write your brief reports this afternoon and I will do the same."

By the end of the day, all three reports were safely locked away in the filing cabinet.

Adam was glad to get home that evening. It had been a strange day. He realised he had been so concerned with the problems at work, he hadn't had time to think about himself or his life. He thought maybe he should take a step back and let life look after itself. He suddenly felt extremely hungry, having missed lunch on account of Mr James Brown and deciding he deserved a good dinner, went off to his favourite pub.

Later that evening, when he had returned home, he phoned Leah. She answered immediately.

"This is a late call," she said. "I'm in bed."

Adam looked at his watch. He hadn't realised that it was after ten o'clock.

"I'm sorry," he said. "Did I wake you up? How are you feeling today?"

"Getting better thank you. I am not infectious any longer but it has left me with no energy."

"Have you been into school?" he asked anxiously.

"No, I cancelled all my lessons for the rest of the week."

"I'll come over on Saturday and feed you up. You will soon get your strength back," said Adam, decisively.

"I haven't been shopping and there isn't much food in the house. I've not felt hungry."

"Don't worry, I'll soon sort you out. I'll be there at about twelve o'clock. Now have a good sleep. I love you," and he put the phone down.

That's what I need, he thought, a good sleep, ready to face another day. He wondered what tomorrow would bring and couldn't dispel a feeling of uneasiness.

The next day was Friday and Adam wasn't sorry that it was nearly the end of the week. He went into work feeling more cheerful than he had the previous day. He did his usual tour of the main office and spoke to some of the staff. They all seemed happy and Adam hoped that the day would go smoothly. He went into his office and almost immediately his phone started ringing.

"I've got Head Office on the phone," Sally said breathlessly. "I'll put them through straight away."

Adam felt his good mood begin to disappear.

"Good morning. Adam Richards speaking."

"I'll put you straight through to the managing director," said a woman.

"Good morning, Adam. This is Dominic West, managing director."

Adam was speechless but he managed to say:

"Good morning, Mr West."

"I'll come straight to the point," continued Mr West in a business-like tone. "I understand that you had a visit from James Brown the area manager?"

"Yes," said Adam. "He was here yesterday."

"I have received a very curious e-mail from him this morning. He was not complimentary about you or your staff. I want to hear your view on this," said Mr West.

Adam thought quickly. He was not going to compromise himself or his staff by not being honest.

"I found him a difficult person to communicate with and he certainly intimidated my staff. He made the girls in the office feel very uncomfortable by his attitude and the way in which he kept looking at them."

"Thank you," said Mr West. "That is all I need to know at this stage.

I'll be in touch." He ended the call.

Adam tried to concentrate on the paperwork on his desk but before long the phone rang again.

"Head Office want to speak to you again," said Sally and Dominic West's voice came down the line.

"There have been developments," he said. "I'm coming down to see you today. I will be with you at two o'clock." The phone went dead.

Adam sat in his chair feeling as if a brick had hit him. He looked at his watch. It was nearly twelve o'clock already. He couldn't imagine what had happened to create such urgency. He roused himself and began to tidy his desk. Then he told Sally and Barry to come to his office at once. When the three of them were together and the door was firmly shut, he told them about the morning's events.

"I am telling you this in absolute secrecy," he said, very firmly. "I have no idea what is meant by developments but I want you both on stand-by whilst he is here." He turned to Sally and smiled. "It looks as if the coffee cups will be used again sooner than we expected. Make sure everything is prepared and tell the receptionist that we are expecting an important visitor but don't say who it is. I don't want any gossip or speculation among the staff."

"I'll see to it immediately," said Sally and hurried off.

"I did try to warn you," said Barry.

"What do you mean?" asked Adam. "Warn me of what?"

"Not to expect a quiet life."

Adam looked very closely at Barry.

"Do you know something that I don't know?" he asked suspiciously.

"No, I don't actually," replied Barry. "But I have heard rumours."

"From where?" demanded Adam. "Where have these rumours come from?"

Barry could sense that Adam was getting more and more uptight.

"Don't look so worried," he said. "The rumours only contained good news." Adam visibly relaxed as Barry went on. "I have a friend who works in the office up north. We met at University and have always kept in touch. His area manager is the same one that you had and Bill says that he was always quoting you as a good example and then one day he told Bill that he believed you were destined for higher office."

"He was a good man that area manager," said Adam. "I always respected his views but I think he might be wrong in this case."

"I'll go and check that everything is okay and then I'll wait in my office," Barry said as he left the room.

Adam looked at his watch. It was ten minutes to two. He wasn't worried about the meeting with Mr West, just very curious as to the reason for the visit. It all seemed so cloak and dagger.

At two o'clock exactly, a chauffeur-driven car pulled up outside the office. A smartly dressed man carrying a briefcase came in through the main entrance. The office was very busy but Sally had been nervously watching the door. Now she stepped forward.

"Mr West?" she asked politely.

"Yes, that's me."

"I'm Sally, Mr Richard's secretary. I will take you to his office."

"Thank you, Sally," he said and shook hands with her.

What nice manners, she thought. So different from yesterday.

He followed her along the corridor until they came to Adam's office. She knocked on the door and Adam opened it himself.

"Thank you, Sally," he said and she went away.

The two men shook hands and introduced themselves. They seemed to have an easy rapport and the difference in the status was soon forgotten.

"Would you like a coffee before we begin?" Adam asked.

"That would be most acceptable, yes, please."

Adam called Sally and asked her to bring in the coffee. Five minutes later it was on the desk. Sally poured it into the cups and gave one to each of the men.

"Thank you, Sally," said Adam said as she left the room.

Mr West looked at the china cups approvingly.

"You have an excellent secretary." He said.

"Yes," said Adam. "I also have an excellent assistant manager. We work together as a team."

"I must say I was impressed by the friendly atmosphere as I walked through. Everyone was busy and they gave the impression that they were all very competent."

"A happy staff is essential for a successful business," said Adam with a smile.

"Now we must get down to business. No doubt you are wondering why I am here. I will fill you in on the reason for my visit," said Mr West and took a folder out of his briefcase. It was quite thick with papers. "This is a folder with Mr James Brown's name on it. It contains a number of complaints which we have had about the way in which he carries out his duties. When I received his e-mail this morning, it was so critical of you and this office that I became concerned about what happened during his visit yesterday. It was so damning that I knew it couldn't be true. I needed to hear your side of the story and that is why I phoned you this morning. You gave me straight and honest answers and so I decided that the time had come to take action but first I needed your permission to do this because it is quite possible that you will be called to give evidence. We want to deal with this as an internal matter and there will be a disciplinary hearing. We do not want it to leak into the public domain as it would reflect very badly on our ethical values."

Mr West paused to drink his coffee.

"Do you mind if I have a refill?" he asked.

But Adam did not hear him; he was deep in thought, so Mr West helped himself.

"My secretary, assistant manager and I all felt that there was something unpleasant about him," said Adam, eventually. "But I had no idea how serious it actually is. As a matter of fact, we all agreed to write a report detailing how we felt. I have them here," and he opened the filing cabinet, took out the three reports and handed them to Mr West.

He read them all carefully.

"This is very useful evidence. May I keep them?"

Adam hesitated.

"You may certainly have mine," he said. "But I think the other two people need to give their permission in case of any future legal problems."

"You are right," agreed Mr West. "That is important."

"It will mean that Sally and Barry will need to be given more detail about the case but I trust them both to keep it confidential. Will you tell them, or shall I?" asked Adam.

"I think it best if I tell them. I am sure you will discuss it with them once I have left."

"I'll call them both in," said Adam and he summoned Sally and Barry into his office. "I think you already know Sally but may I introduce Barry who is my very competent second-in-command."

Mr West smiled and nodded at Sally and the two men shook hands. He then gave them a brief outline of the reason for his visit and finished by asking if they would allow him to take their reports. They looked at Adam. He seemed quite relaxed about it.

"What is written there is a true and honest account of the way we felt," said Barry. "And the effect it had on us personally and the office as a whole. I would verify it in any court of law."

"How do you feel about it, Sally?" asked Mr West.

"I totally agree with what Barry said," she replied. "If it saves other women from the threat of unwanted attention, then I am happy to make the contribution."

"That's settled then," said Adam to Mr West. "You can have all three reports but first I would like Sally to photocopy them so that we have our own record."

Mr West handed the papers to Sally and she went back to her office. A few moments later she returned and gave Mr West the original copies. She gave the photocopies to Adam and he returned them to the filing cabinet. Mr West sat and watched. He was most impressed by the efficiency of the office.

"I'd better go and check that everything is running smoothly," said Barry.

"It's been a pleasure to meet you, Barry."

"Thank you, Mr West," he said and left the room.

Sally was still standing by the desk and Mr West shook her by the hand.

"Thank you for your help. You have done a very brave thing by speaking up. Adam is very lucky to have such an efficient secretary."

Sally felt a blush on her cheeks and didn't know what to say.

"I think I can hear your phone ringing," said Adam. "You had better go and answer it."

"Thank you," she stammered and quickly made her exit.

"I didn't mean to embarrass her," said Mr West with a smile. "But I must say you handled the situation in a most sensitive way."

Adam hesitated before answering.

"I do try to keep a level head at all times but it can be difficult sometimes."

He sounded quite sad as he spoke and Mr West looked at him closely as if he could tell that Adam had been through some trauma in his life. He decided to look into it further. He pushed back his chair and stood up.

"You have been most helpful, Adam, and it has been a pleasure to meet you. We must have another chat at some future date. In the meantime, I will keep you informed of the progress in this case and I will be in touch."

"It's been a pleasure to meet you too. Now I can attach a face to the voice I hear on the phone," said Adam with a smile.

He accompanied his visitor to the main entrance where a car was waiting to whisk him away. They shook hands.

"I will be in touch," he said and left Adam standing at the door in total surprise at his parting words.

Adam found his way back to his office in a complete daze. He sat in his chair, staring at the blank wall in front of him. That's how I feel he thought, completely blank. He didn't hear Sally come in; he didn't notice her clearing the coffee cups; he didn't see her frantically contacting Barry. It was only when someone gently shook him that he emerged from his stupor. Barry was standing in front of him holding a glass of water.

"Have a drink," he said firmly and Adam did as he was told. The cold water began to revive him and he stood up.

"You gave us a fright," said Barry. "What happened?"

"I don't know," Adam said. "I've had so many shocks this week that they all seemed to attack me at once. My mind just went blank."

Barry felt sorry for Adam.

"It has been a dreadful week one way or another. I think you should leave the office now. Go home and have a good sleep and I'm sure you will feel better in the morning. I expect you will be seeing Leah this weekend?"

Sally was still standing by the desk and wondered who Leah was. Adam was not sorry to go home early. He felt as if his brain could not hold one iota more of information. He had to concentrate fully as he drove home and once inside his front door, he just flopped onto the settee. He kicked his shoes off and lay flat out. All his energy had drained away and he felt as helpless as a baby. He closed his eyes and immediately fell asleep.

Chapter Eight

When he woke up, it was dark outside. He sat up and looked at his watch; nearly eight o'clock. He had been asleep for four hours. The events of the day began to creep back into his mind. He felt relatively calm as the memories returned and he was able to think about them without the feeling of panic which had engulfed him earlier. He went to the kitchen and made a strong cup of tea which he carried back to the lounge. He was rapidly regaining his composure and thinking about what he needed to do.

His thoughts were interrupted by the ringing tone of his phone. He recognised the number.

"Hello, Jen," he said but the voice that answered was Barry's.

"How are you feeling?" he asked anxiously.

"I've been asleep for four hours and I've just woken up. I'm feeling much better and beginning to think about what I have to do this weekend."

"Sally and I were very worried about you," said Barry. "We know you have had a pretty torrid week but we felt that something must have been said to give you such a shock."

"I'll tell you about it on Monday," Adam replied. "Now I have to start thinking about tomorrow. I've promised Leah I will cook her dinner and I must think about the shopping."

"You don't have to worry about that. Jen has been around to see Leah and everything is under control. She will do Leah's shopping in the morning and she will leave your dinner ready for you to eat. You'll just have to heat them in the microwave."

"That is very kind of Jen. Please thank her from me."

"That's what friends are for. You need a relaxing weekend in order to be ready for Monday. Who knows what next week will bring?"

"Don't tempt fate," replied Adam. "But it can't be any worse than the past week."

Barry laughed.

"Enjoy your weekend," he said. "I'll see you on Monday."

Perhaps things are getting back to normal, thought Adam and he began to look forward to some quiet time with Leah. He picked up his phone and dialled her number.

"Adam, are you alright?" she said straight away. "Jen told me that you weren't very well."

"I'm feeling better now. I'll tell you about it tomorrow. How are you today?"

"I'm on the mend," she replied. "I should be okay by Monday but I could do with a couple more quiet days."

"I feel the same. Let's enjoy two days of peace and quiet. We might even watch the rugby on television. I'll bring a couple of bottles with me to help us relax."

"Sounds good," said Leah with a smile. "See you tomorrow then. Bye."

Adam made a mental note to call at the shop on his way in the morning and also not to forget his overnight bag either. He had a good night's sleep and felt much better in the morning. He had decided not to tell Leah the whole story of his week but he would try to find out a bit more about the children. He did all the necessary household chores and by mid-morning, he was on his way to Swanton. He had remembered to buy the wine and some flowers from the shop. This time they were bronze chrysanthemums which were the same colour as the autumn leaves. It reminded him that it would soon be Leah's birthday. He intended to ask what she would like as a present but actually, he had already decided what he was going to give her. There was something important he needed to do while he was at Leah's house but it had to be done in secret.

He parked the car in front of the garage and rang the front doorbell. Leah answered it with: "I really must give you a key."

He kissed her and gave her the flowers.

"What a gorgeous colour!" she said. "Just like autumn leaves."

Adam dropped his overnight bag in the hall and followed her into the kitchen.

"I had to throw out the rest of the roses. They were dropping petals all over the place," she said. "I do enjoy having fresh flowers in the house. Thank you, Adam," and she kissed him on the cheek.

The kitchen table was covered with bags of groceries and on the worktop was a large cottage pie.

"I see that Jen has been around," he said. "I feel a bit of a fraud. I promised to feed you up and now someone else is doing it for me."

"Jen was only too pleased to help. I've switched on the oven and I'll put the pie in to keep warm then we can have it whenever we want. I was just about to make some coffee. Would you like one?"

"Yes, please. I think I'd like a biscuit too."

"Take the tin into the lounge," she said. "I'll bring the coffee."

Five minutes later they were sitting on the settee drinking their coffee and talking about the week that had just passed.

"I haven't felt as rotten as I did this week for ages," she said. "I've been a teacher for so long that I'm usually immune to the coughs and colds. But I think this was a particularly nasty virus which was going around."

"I'm glad you had the sense to take some time off. It's never a good idea to push yourself too hard when you are not well. "What have you been doing with yourself all day?"

"Mostly sleeping," she replied. "But I also spent some time looking at the local paper, property pages."

Adam looked surprised.

"Were you looking for anything in particular?" he asked.

"Yes, I suppose I was. After you said you would like to live in Swanton, I was looking to see what was available to buy."

"And did you find anything that I might like?"

"There are quite a lot of nice houses available but I don't know what your price range is or even how many bedrooms you would like," she said. "Perhaps it would be a good idea to look at them together?"

"Maybe later on," he replied, shortly. He didn't want to bother with making any kind of decisions.

He was holding Leah's hand and stroking her fingers.

"You are known by your married name but you never wear your wedding ring. What do you say when people ask about your husband?"

"I say he has moved away because of business commitments. As a matter of fact, I couldn't wear my ring because it became too small for my finger. My engagement ring was the same. One day I had to pay for a major repair to my car and I have to confess that I sold the rings to help pay for it. I fully intended to buy a replacement for each of them but I could never afford it. Fortunately, I have a wedding ring which belonged to my stepmother so I use that when I need to. I'm sorry Adam. I hope I haven't upset you?" She looked at him sadly.

"You did what you had to do," he said. "I'm not upset. I'm very sorry you found yourself in such a situation."

They sat in silence. Adam was full of remorse but it only confirmed in his mind what he intended to give Leah as a birthday present.

"I'll go and lay the dinner," he said, standing up. "I'll call you when it is ready."

He decided this was his best chance. He put his bag on the bed in the spare room and then crept into Leah's room. Silently he opened the box which contained her jewellery. He quickly found what he was looking for and he took it out. He had brought in a notebook and a pen and he took the wedding ring out of the box. He placed it on the next page of his notebook and carefully drew around it. Then he quickly returned the ring to its box and went back into his bedroom. He put the notebook back into his bag and zipped it up.

"Dinner's ready," Leah shouted upstairs.

"Coming!" he replied and went down to the kitchen.

The pie was delicious and soon it was all gone.

"I'm full up," said Adam.

"So am I! I think we shall sleep well this afternoon."

Adam lay full length on the settee and Leah sat in her favourite chair with her feet on a stool. They slept for two hours.

She woke with a start. There was a strange scratching noise at the front door and then some insistent knocks. She went to investigate and when she opened the door, she was nearly flattened by two small people rushing at her.

"Granny Leah! Granny Leah!" they shouted and she threw her arms around them.

"Benjie, Lucy," she cried. "What a lovely surprise."

The children hugged her and then went running off into the lounge.

Leah waited at the door. Peter, her son, was coming up the path. He was looking at Adam's BMW parked in front of the garage.

"Nice motor," he said. "When did you get rid of your trusty Polo?"

"Don't be silly," said Leah. "It's not my car. It belongs to a friend."

Peter raised his eyebrows and followed Leah into the kitchen.

"I know you haven't been well," he said. "We've just come to see how you are."

"I'm feeling much better," she said. "I'll put the kettle on." She stopped for a minute then she said: "It's very quiet. I wonder what the children are up to?"

She walked towards the lounge and Peter went with her. They stood in the doorway and didn't say a word. Adam was still asleep on the settee and the two children were looking at him intently. They were prodding him with their fingers. Adam stirred and opened his eyes to find two small faces gazing at him.

"Who are you?" asked Benjie in a forthright way. "What's your name? Why are you asleep on Granny Leah's settee?"

Peter took a step forward as if to stop Benjie's questioning but Leah held him back.

Adam was rather bemused but he said:

"My name is Adam and I am a friend of Granny Leah." He looked closely at the children. "Now you tell me your names."

Benjie puffed out his cheeks and said:

"I am Benjamin, Adam Richards but I am called Benjie and I am five years old and this is my sister, Lucy, Ann Richards but she is only three."

Benjie jumped back and shouted at his sister

"Let's go into the garden!"

They ran through the hall to the back door. Peter and Leah followed. The full meaning of what he had heard began to dawn on him. He looked at Leah in astonishment. He didn't know what to say. Leah said it for him.

"Yes, that is your father. He is now working in Oxford and we have been in contact for the past month. We are just good friends, nothing more."

"But how can you be good friends with someone who abandoned you twelve years ago?"

"A lot of things have changed and we are only just beginning to know each other" replied, Leah. "Neither of us has made any commitments. We are honestly just friends."

"I suppose I will have to go and speak to him?" said Peter in a hesitant voice. "Although I don't know what to say."

"I'll keep an eye on Benjie and Lucy," she said. "But please be civil to him. You don't know the whole story yet."

She went out into the garden. She was feeling very uneasy about what was happening and she hoped that Peter would not be too unreasonable when he spoke to Adam.

Peter slowly walked towards the lounge. He was very nervous but he knew he had to do it. He went through the door and stood in front of his father. Adam had put his shoes on and was standing up. The two men looked at each other uncertainly.

"Hello, Dad."

"Hello, Peter."

He held out his hand and Peter hesitated for a second before he shook hands with his father.

"This is an unexpected turn of events," said Peter. "In fact, it's quite a shock. Mum seems quite relaxed about your return but I'm not sure what the long-term effects might be."

Adam thought for a minute or two before he replied.

"I am truly sorry for what I did and I shall never forgive myself for as long as l live. It has been a very difficult time for your mother and me. We have been living very different lives and we are both different people from who we were twelve years ago. We are just getting to know each other again. We enjoy each other's company and we are good friends. I know how much I have hurt Leah and my family but I am hoping that I can make amends for that."

"My mother has suffered in many different ways. She has been the rock in our family and always puts others' needs before her own. She has kept this family together while at the same time building a very successful career as a teacher. She is respected and admired by everyone who knows her. She has sacrificed a great deal for us and we love her. We shan't allow her to be hurt again," he said, his voice rising as he spoke and Adam sensed that he was near to tears.

"I too love your mother very much. I respect her for the way in which she has been a single parent to all of you. I give you my word that I will never hurt her again and I will do my best for all of you if you will allow me to."

"That's good enough for me," said Peter. "All I want is my mother's happiness and if you can make that happen then we shall all be pleased."

Adam did not have time to reply as the children came running in. They went straight into the conservatory at the back of the house because they knew that was where their toys were kept. Benjie took the box of Lego out of the cupboard and then lifted out a box of bricks for his sister.

Leah had followed the children in from the garden and she looked nervously at the two men. Peter went up and put his arm around her.

"It's alright, Mum," he said. "We haven't come to blows."

Leah heaved a sigh of relief.

"I'll make a cup of tea," she said.

Adam and Peter sat down. They were deep in conversation when Leah returned. The children were playing happily in the conservatory and the three of them sat amicably together in the lounge. Suddenly Adam felt a small hand tugging at his sleeve.

"Come to the 'servatory," said Lucy. "I've built a house."

"It's time for us to go," said Peter, standing up. "Mummy will be wondering where we are."

"Next time, I promise," said Adam, smiling at Lucy.

"Where is Janet?" asked Leah.

"She went to see her mother who hasn't been well," replied Peter.

"That's my Granny Tessa," Lucy informed Adam. "I've got a Grandad as well."

"That's nice," he said, smiling and thinking now she has two grandads.

They said their goodbyes. Adam turned to Peter.

"We must have a longer chat," he said. "Possibly over a pint?"

Peter nodded his head and got into the car. The children were waving through the window as they drove away.

Adam shut the door and went to find Leah. She was on her knees in the conservatory cleaning up the toys.

"I usually make them clear their muddles," she laughed. "But today they were too excited."

"Let me help you?" he said and knelt down beside her.

"So much for our quiet afternoon," she said with a smile. "Those two go through the place like a hurricane. I don't know where they get the energy from."

"They are young and healthy," Adam said wisely. "And perfectly charming!"

"Children have no inhibitions," she said, thoughtfully. "It is amazing how quickly they can ease the tension."

They both stood up and went back into the lounge. Leah cleared the mugs from the coffee table and took them into the kitchen. It was getting dark and she shut the blinds. When she returned to the lounge, she pulled the curtains closed and sat on the settee with Adam.

"Tell me how you got on with Peter?" she asked anxiously.

"We got on well. We had an honest conversation about the situation and we fully respected each other's views. I hope I will have the opportunity to talk to him again and get to know him and his family. He is very protective of you, that I did find out."

"There have been times when we have needed each other," said Leah. "Particularly when Thomas decided to emigrate to New Zealand."

Adam looked at Leah in amazement.

"Emigrate" he gasped. "To New Zealand. But why did he do that?"

"He completed his apprenticeship and wanted a different kind of life I suppose," she said, thoughtfully. "He had a friend who was already there and he told Thomas of the opportunities and lifestyle. I also think that he didn't relish the thought of being the senior man in the family."

"Do you keep in touch with him?"

"Oh yes. He writes letters home and sometimes phones. I tell him what's happening in the rest of the family. Births, deaths and marriages, that sort of thing."

Adam was feeling rather stunned. He had wanted to find out about his children but it was turning into a series of unpleasant surprises. He wondered how many more there would be.

"What about the girls?" he asked apprehensively.

"Last year Harriet decided to resign from her job and to go travelling. She teamed up with another girl and they went right across Europe, then to India, Thailand and China. She even visited the Great Wall of China. She then went to Australia and on to New Zealand where she is now. She has a good job and is buying her own house."

"So, has she settled there too?"

"I think she will eventually come back home but not for a few years. I think Thomas now considers New Zealand to be his home."

Adam sat on the settee feeling quite bewildered. Two of their children were now living twelve thousand miles away and Leah had seen them off all by herself. He couldn't imagine how she felt when they left. No wonder Peter was so concerned for her. Leah appeared to be quite matter-of-fact as she talked and Adam marvelled at her composure. There was one more daughter who was a stranger to him.

"What about Alice? How is she?"

"Ah yes. Alice," said Leah. "At least she still lives in this country which is a good thing."

"What do you mean by that?"

Leah paused and looked at him. Adam started to get worried, he wondered what was coming.

"Alice is the one I worry about most," she began. "She married a friend of Thomas but it only lasted eighteen months before they were divorced. She then started seeing a boy who she had been very friendly with during her last year of school. She was an attractive and sociable girl with lots of friends. I must admit that I never liked the boy and I was very worried when he came back into her life after the divorce." She paused and took a deep breath.

"What was the boy's name?"

"His name was William but he was always called Wills. Many of Alice's friends were worried too and tried to warn her not to get involved with him but he was like a spider catching a fly in its web. Once he had his hands on her he wouldn't let go and she was seduced by the lifestyle he promised her. Eventually, they married and now have two children, a boy and a girl. The sad thing is that he is a control freak and has been emotionally abusing her so much that she suffered a breakdown and had to spend time in a clinic as a result. They live in a large, five-bedroom house and now he is seeing another woman, his secretary, I think. So, it looks like another divorce is on the way."

Leah stopped talking and sighed deeply. Adam looked at her with eyes full of pity.

"Oh Leah, you must have been through hell and done it all alone. I don't know what to say. I feel so guilty for allowing this to happen. I don't know how to start to put things right but I am going to do my best to make it easier for you in the future."

"I haven't been alone," she said. "I have some very good friends who have always stood by me. I know how important good friends are!"

Adam looked at her face. She was so severe and almost peaceful.

"Leah," he said gently. "Do you think we are at the very good friends mark?"

Leah thought for a moment.

"Close, very close."

"How close?" asked Adam.

"I think a cup of tea would bridge the gap," she smiled.

Adam kissed her forehead.

"I'll do it," he said. "I need some practice at mending bridges."

He left the lounge and Leah remained on the settee. It's funny, she thought, how life sometimes presents itself in unexpected ways. If Peter and the children hadn't come to-day, she would have found it much more difficult to tell Adam about the other three. She was glad that she had managed it because she hadn't realised how it had been bothering her. Now it was over they could talk about their children openly.

Adam came back with the tea and they sat in comfortable silence. After a time, Leah said:

"What are you thinking about?"

"I was thinking of something Barry said the other day. Each day is a new experience. We should make the most of it and not waste our energy on what tomorrow might bring," he replied. "I've certainly thought of those words many times during the past week."

Leah looked at him curiously.

"I know I've been poorly," she said. "But surely that didn't colour your whole week?"

"It was part of it but so many other things happened at the same time."

"Was it really that bad?" asked Leah in a concerned voice.

"Yes, it was that bad. But I don't want to talk about work this evening. Maybe I'll tell you tomorrow. There is something far more important I want to ask you now."

Leah looked at him in complete surprise.

"I hope you're not going to ask me to marry you!"

"That is not necessary," he said, laughing. "We've already been there, got the t-shirt as they say."

Leah pretended to be relieved.

"Thank goodness that is not the question because I would have to say No Thank you."

"That's okay," he said. "Because I would have kept asking until you changed your mind."

"Stop teasing me and tell me what this important question is?"

"Well, it is your birthday soon and I wondered what you would like as a present?"

"That's an easy one to answer. I've no idea."

"That is not very helpful," he said, sternly. "So, a box of chocolates and a bunch of flowers will do."

"That is what I usually get and I always say thank you for them."

"But you wouldn't mind something a bit different this year, would you? Like a bunch of chocolates and a box of flowers?" and they both burst out laughing.

"In any case, it doesn't matter that you have no idea because I already know what you are going to have," he said with a smile.

"Aren't you going to give me a clue?"

"No, you will just have to wait. The subject is now closed," he replied, even more sternly.

"Typical man!" said Leah, under her breath but Adam heard it.

"What do you mean?" he asked, pretending to be cross.

"Always wants the last word," said Leah sweetly and she stood up and left the room quite smartly.

When she came back, she was carrying a bottle of wine and two glasses.

"I'm only going to have one glass this evening, she said decisively. "In case I end up in bed with my husband again."

"I'm going to have at least two glasses," said Adam. "So, I can be sure to end up in bed with my wife again."

They looked at each other with big smiles on their faces.

"I wonder who will be right?" said Leah dreamily.

Adam put his arm around her and pulled her closer to him.

"I'm a typical man," he whispered. "I'm always right."

They sat together in silence for a moment.

"I've been thinking again about your wanting to live in Swanton," she said. "According to the local paper's property section, there is plenty of choice but I have no idea what your preference is."

"If you were me where would you choose?" he asked.

"Well, I wouldn't choose a really big house with five bedrooms and I wouldn't choose a really small place with two and a half bedrooms. I wouldn't want to live in a block of flats or on one of the many housing estates which have sprung up."

"There can't be many left to choose from," he said. "Perhaps I should save time and move straight into an old people's home? Can you now give me a positive opinion?"

"I would want a modern apartment with all mod cons and a nice view out of the window," she replied, ignoring his sarcasm.

"You sound as if you have somewhere in mind," he said, suspiciously.

"Well, there was one place which rather jumped out at me. It was a luxury two-bedroom, ground-floor apartment in the Marina. It had a patio at the back where you could sit and watch the boats go by on the river. Imagine doing that on a beautiful sunny day."

"If it is that close to the river, imagine baling the water out of your house after a flood," he grumbled.

"Don't be such a spoilsport! All the houses in that development have been properly built so that there is no risk of water coming in."

"I don't even know where it is," he said. "I don't remember anywhere called the Marina."

"It is a fairly new development and rather exclusive. I'll show you where it is tomorrow."

She looked at her wine glass on the coffee table; it was full.

"That's funny," she said. "I'm sure it was empty just now."

She looked at Adam who had a most innocent expression on his face.

"You can't put it down the drain, can you? You'll have to drink it."

"Are you trying to get me drunk?"

"Now, why would I do that?" he said. "I can manage you very well when you are sober," and he kissed her.

"It's been a long day," she said, yawning. "I'm ready for my bed."

"You go up first," he said. "And I'll put the lights out tonight."

Leah was about to object but Adam had already picked up the empty bottle and the two glasses. She decided not to argue and went upstairs and got ready for bed. She heard Adam come up and go into the bathroom. She got into her bed but left the door slightly open.

"Good night," said Adam as he came back across the landing and went into his room.

He lay down on the bed and waited. He hadn't switched his light off and it wasn't long before Leah came in.

"Adam," she said. "Did you lock the back door?"

He pretended to be asleep so she went over and touched his shoulder.

"Adam, did you lock the back door?" she repeated making sure that he heard her this time by leaning over his face. Immediately his arms went around her and she was pulled under the duvet beside him.

"Of course, I locked the back door!" he said with a chuckle. "Any more questions?"

"Yes," she said. "What do you think you are doing?"

"I'm keeping you safe in case a strange man comes in through the window which I left open."

"You knew this would happen, didn't you? You were determined to get me into your bed," she said, accusingly.

"You didn't need much persuasion and now you are nice and warm, it would be a shame to go back to your cold bed."

Leah was too tired to argue.

"Alright, you win," she said and snuggled up against him.

Soon she was fast asleep but Adam lay there thinking how wonderful it was they had become very good friends. He wondered how much longer it would take for them to move up to very, very good friends and he leant over and kissed her on the forehead, vowing to be patient but hoping it wouldn't take too long.

Chapter Nine

The next morning, they had a leisurely breakfast and sat outside to have their tea.

"What would you like to do today?" asked Adam.

"I'd like to show you that apartment we talked about last night."

He wasn't that keen but he reluctantly agreed. They drove to the south of the town and along the road by the river. When the road came to a dead-end, Adam parked the car and they walked to where there were some very attractive houses.

"It is a mixture of houses and apartments," said Leah. "And most of them have their own mooring on the river."

They found the apartment with the 'for sale' notice in the garden and walked up the path to look through the window. At that moment, the front door opened and a girl came out carrying a folder.

"Oh, I'm very sorry," said Leah. "I thought the apartment was empty. We didn't mean to trespass."

"It's okay," said the girl. "I don't live here. I'm from the estate agency and I've just been showing a couple around."

"I know we haven't made an appointment," Leah. "But would it be possible for us to look at it while you are here?"

"I'll have a chat with the office," she said. "Excuse me for a minute, I'll use the phone in the house; it's still connected and I'm sure the sellers won't mind, considering you're interested in the property."

She went back into the house and they could hear her speaking to her manager.

"I have half an hour before my next appointment," she said, reappearing in the doorway. "The manager says I can show it to you but I must be sure to get your details."

"Thank you so much," said Leah. "Can we do the tour first and the details afterwards?"

"Try and show a bit of enthusiasm," she whispered to Adam. "She is being very helpful."

"Follow me, please," said the girl and led the way into the apartment.

Everything looked fresh and clean and it was finished beautifully. They went into the thoroughly modern kitchen which was filled with all the latest equipment. It was large enough to include a small dining area. The two bedrooms were at the front of the house and they both had en suites.

"That is unusual," said Adam.

"I think it will make more sense when we go into the lounge," said the girl.

"Oh, what a beautiful room!" said Leah.

The whole of the end wall was one big picture window which provided a magnificent view of the river and the fields beyond. The girl pulled back the double doors in the middle and they stepped out onto a patio which was the whole width of the house. It was sheltered at one end by a bamboo hedge and at the end was a wall of the garage. There were shrubs in pots and outdoor furniture dotted about the patio and in the corner was a gas barbecue.

"This is really lovely," said Leah as they went back in.

"It is finished to an exceptionally high standard," said the girl. "That is because it was the show apartment for the complex. It is to be sold exactly as you see it and includes all the furniture and fittings. Now if you would come back into the kitchen, I can make a note of your particulars?"

Leah left Adam to give his details while she had another look around. She noted that there were fitted wardrobes in both bedrooms but there were no radiators. It was obviously underfloor heating. The bed linen was all of the highest quality. There was a carport at the side which was quite big enough for Adam's car. All in all, it was a place you could comfortably live in from day one. Adam came out of the kitchen clutching an armful of brochures. He shook hands with the girl and went to find Leah, who was out the front chatting to a neighbour. Adam went straight to his car and Leah followed.

"Well?" said Leah, on the way home. "What did you think?"

"It's very nice; I could see myself living there if that is to be my home," he replied, briefly.

They drove straight back to Leah's house and sat in the garden with their coffee. Adam was very quiet; he hardly said a word. She could sense he was sulking but wondered what was bothering him so much. The brochures which the girl had given him were on the table and Leah noticed that Adam kept looking at them.

Suddenly it dawned on her what his problem was. He had not said much when looking around the apartment and Leah remembered his comment when they got back to the car. 'If that is to be my home' he had said with emphasis on the word 'my'. She knew that he had hoped that they would live together as man and wife. Now the realisation hit her that it would not work. They had been apart long enough to develop a different lifestyle. They enjoyed their time together but they also needed their own space.

Leah looked at him. She knew then what she wanted for the future but had no idea how she could explain it to him. He stood up and went into the house, returning with the tin of biscuits and the second bottle of wine. He put them on the table together with the glasses. He poured out the wine and handed her a glass.

"I think I'll get drunk and drown my sorrows," he said.

He looked so sorry for himself that Leah burst out laughing.

"Don't be silly," she said. "Getting drunk only makes matters worse. Tell me what is bothering you?"

Adam just looked at the brochures lying on the table and then he looked at Leah.

"Are you cross with me for telling you about that apartment?" she asked.

"I'm not cross," he replied. "It was a very nice place. I am disappointed that's all." And he lapsed into silence again.

Leah sat in her chair and considered her response

"Adam," she said eventually. "I know you were hoping to carry on as we were twelve years ago but that is not possible. We have already recognised that we are not the same as we were then. We have led very individual lives and we are used to having our own space. The fact that you have your home will make no difference to our relationship, we can still share our lives between the two houses. After all, they are only bricks and mortar. It's what happens inside them that matters."

"You've done it again haven't you?" he said, looking hard at Leah. "Explained the problem in a logical way."

She looked shocked.

"I'm sorry if I've done the wrong thing by telling you how I feel. I wouldn't want to influence your decisions," she said firmly.

"You'll never do that. I'm perfectly capable of making my own decisions."

"I'll go and see what I can rustle up for dinner," she said shortly and went into the house.

Adam sat back feeling shattered. They had just had their first disagreement and he didn't like it. He knew that Leah was right in what she said but he couldn't admit it to himself. His dream had now completely disappeared and he was unsure what would take its place; the one thing he knew for certain was that he would have to make things right with Leah before he left her that day. He collected the brochures from the table and took them into the house. He left them on the hall table and went into the kitchen.

"I haven't very much to offer you," she said. "I'm afraid it is going to be baked beans on toast."

"That's okay. I'm not very hungry."

He went upstairs and tidied his bedroom. He picked up his overnight bag and carried it down to the hall. He took the brochures from the table and put them in the bag. Then they sat at the kitchen table in an awkward silence until Adam could bear it no longer.

"Let's go and sit in the lounge?" he said.

Leah followed him and he sat on the settee. She went and sat on her armchair. Adam watched her in dismay. It was obvious that she was unhappy.

"Leah? Leah please?" he said and tapped the space on the settee.

Leah stood up and reluctantly sat down beside him. He put his arm around her shoulders but she didn't respond. He was starting to feel worried. He wasn't sure what to do. He could feel the stiffness in her body and a slight shiver of fear ran up his spine.

"Leah," he said again. "We need to talk."

"I don't need to talk," she said, bluntly. "It seems that I've done too much of that already."

Adam felt as if someone had punched him in the stomach. He had never before heard such resignation in Leah's voice. She was always so positive in her attitude. He suddenly realised that there was a very deep hurt inside her and he was the reason for it.

"Leah," he said. "If I talk, will you listen?"

"Yes, alright but don't expect any comments from me."

"I don't know how to start," he muttered.

"Begin at the beginning, that's the best place to start," she replied, crisply.

"If I do that, we shall be here all night. I'm going to begin with today. Until this morning, I was still holding onto my dream of us living together but when we looked around that apartment you were so enthusiastic about it that I resented the fact that you could already see me living there. I could no longer deny the reality of that but I felt that it had not been my decision. I suppose I felt that I was being drawn into a situation which was not of my making."

Leah had been listening carefully.

"I would not dream of pushing you into anything. You are your own man and that is a good example of how we are both individuals as well as being a married couple. I have become so adept at advising other people about their problems that I have lost sight of my own. That is why I sometimes need space to allow me to sort myself out."

"I'm sorry I snapped at you. I'm sorry I upset you."

"I'm sorry too," said Leah. "I shouldn't have frog-marched you into that apartment this morning. But it was a very nice apartment," she added, wistfully.

"I think you see yourself in it as much as you see me," he said, smiling.

"Perhaps I do," she said but quickly added: "but it is your decision of course."

"Can we be very good friends again?" he asked, kissing her.

"Of course, we can," she answered quickly and kissed him back.

They sat there each thinking their own thoughts until Leah said:

"When Barry told me that you were unwell, I was quite worried. He said that you went home early and that is unlike you."

"I had a very busy week and the problems seemed to hit me all at the same time and my mind just went blank."

"Couldn't you delegate some of them to other people? I'm sure Barry would have helped you out."

"Barry is always a great help to me but some things were too personal to share with him," he answered. "There are several ongoing situations which have yet to be resolved."

Leah knew better than to ask him for details so she said:

"I hope you get the answers you need but don't forget how very good friends can sometimes help."

He looked at her gratefully. He did not feel it was necessary to trouble her with all the details but it was good to know that she would be there to support him.

"I'll make a cup of tea," she said and went off to the kitchen.

He dwelt on what had been a busy weekend. He'd met his son and grandchildren, heard about his other children; he'd seen the apartment he hoped to buy and had his first disagreement with Leah. But at least they were still very good friends and that was all that mattered to him right now. Leah came back with the tea and they sat side by side on the settee. It was getting dark outside.

"I think I'd better be going soon," he said. "I've got a busy week ahead of me. I'll ring you in a couple of days but don't forget, you have my number in case you need anything?"

"I won't forget," she said. "I hope you have a better week."

"Who knows? Everything seems to happen twice as fast as it did up north. I shall just have to get used to it." He kissed her goodbye and whispered in her ear: "I love you."

"Nothing has changed," she said, smiling. "In spite of being told off by you."

"Cheeky monkey," he said and kissed her again.

She heard the car drive off as she closed the door then went back into the lounge and sat in her favourite armchair. It was the one place where she could truly relax. She thought about the events of the weekend and came to an interesting conclusion; she had been the student, not the teacher and felt truly put in her place. She would have to learn not to interfere too much in Adam's life. He had his way of dealing with things just like her. But it had convinced her of one thing: they could not live together in the same house but they could live happily together in two houses.

She took the dirty mugs into the kitchen and washed them up. Then she turned off the lights and went to bed.

Adam arrived home and unpacked his bag. He found his notebook and looked at the picture he had drawn in it, determined to make time this week to deal with it. Then he noticed the brochure which the girl had given him and realised he would have to find time to deal with that, too. It was going to be a busy week and that would be before he could think about work.

Chapter Ten

Adam went into work the next day in a cheerful mood. The weekend had been interesting and he felt re-invigorated. He said good morning to the staff as he walked through the main office and when he reached his own office, he called for Sally to bring in details of his appointments for the coming week. When she entered, she placed the files on the desk and looked at Adam.

"Are you feeling better?" she asked, anxiously. "You gave us such a fright."

"I'm sorry about that," he said. "But I'm fine. I had a relaxing weekend and I'm back to normal. Now tell me about my programme for the week?"

"Well, it starts off quite quietly but it gets busier later on. This morning has been peaceful so far as we have had no calls from Head Office," she said solemnly.

"Don't tempt fate!" he said abruptly. "You had better not be away from your desk for too long in case the phone rings."

She was not sure if Adam was joking or being serious. She looked at him in concern but he was smiling at her. She breathed a sigh of relief.

"I really thought you were cross with me for speaking out of order," she said.

"I think you should be a little more careful how you express yourself. It can give a wrong impression. Now leave the files with me and ask Barry to come and see me when he is free."

About half an hour later, Barry arrived at Adam's office. He was looking a bit flustered as he came in.

"What a morning," he said as he sat down. "There was a glitch in the computer system and I have been trying to sort it out."

"Is it okay now?" asked Adam. "Or do we need to get someone in?"

"It should be okay. I'll keep an eye on it for the rest of the day."

"You could do with a coffee," said Adam and he asked Sally to bring in two coffees to his office. When she arrived, she put them on the desk.

"Thank you, Sally," said Adam and she left the room.

Barry gave Adam a surprised look.

"Sally was rather subdued," he said. "Is she alright?"

"She did speak out of turn this morning and I had to have a word with her. She'll get over it."

Barry did not fancy being reprimanded by Adam and he made a mental note to be careful what he said.

"Did you have a good weekend, Adam?"

"I had a most interesting weekend. I met my son Peter and his two children; I saw a property I might consider buying. I learned some facts about my other children and I had a disagreement with Leah."

"Goodness," said Barry. "You certainly packed it full of activity. Has Leah recovered from her cold?"

"Oh yes, she is fully recovered and by the way, we did make it up and we are still good friends."

"Thank goodness for that."

"Now, let's get down to business," said Adam, firmly. "How are you getting on with the job I asked you to do?"

"It's nearly completed. I've prepared the document to transfer the house to Leah's name. It just needs your signature. The standing order has been cancelled as from the beginning of October and a direct debit has been arranged from your accounts; that also needs a signature. I now have to work out the total of the payments you want to make and I hope to do that today."

"Well done, Barry. Hopefully, you will have it all ready for me tomorrow morning."

"Yes," said Barry. "Unless we get any unexpected problems."

"Don't say that," said Adam, sharply "A remark like that got Sally into trouble."

Barry looked at him and wondered what was on his mind that was making him so unusually sensitive.

"I know something is bothering you," he said. "Can I help?"

Adam looked at Barry. He felt a real need to share his thoughts with someone and Barry seemed to be the obvious person. He knew Barry would keep it confidential.

"You know most of what happened last week," he said. "But you don't know what Mr West said to me as he left."

Barry was surprised. He couldn't imagine what had upset Adam so much. The meeting with Mr West had been business-like but conducted in a very civil way.

"Are you going to tell me what was said?"

"It doesn't seem so strange now that I have had time to think about it," said Adam. "But these were his words to me as he was leaving: I'll be in touch. It may be sooner than you think. Those were his exact words."

Barry sat and thought about what Adam had just told him.

"I can't see anything wrong in that," he said. "I don't understand why it affected you so badly."

"It was the phrase 'sooner than you think' that tipped the balance. It could have been a sort of threat but of course, I knew that was not the case. My immediate reaction was that I was no longer in charge of my own life. That was when my mind went blank. It was a frightening experience for me too and although I've recovered my senses, I still wonder exactly what he meant."

"Did you tell Leah how you felt?"

"No," replied Adam, quickly. "You are the only person I've told. Let me tell you, Barry, I've had enough of not knowing my direction in life. I really want to have stability and I hoped that this job would provide that."

Barry felt sorry for Adam. He was obviously going through a crisis of confidence. Barry had read about the effect this could have on a man and he was determined to do what he could to help him.

"Listen to me," said Barry. "I am speaking as a friend, not an employee. Your move to Oxford has started a chain of events which will ultimately give you the stable environment you so desperately want. You have a respected position in a brand-new office and a loyal staff who enjoy working for you. You are inevitably going to be more in the picture when it comes to Head Office and area managers because you are a very successful manager. Publicity can be the price you have to pay for success. On top of that, you have renewed your relationship with Leah and your children and I'm sure you are happy about that. You have only been here five weeks and so much has happened. You must feel that your feet have hardly touched the ground. But it is early days and things will settle down. There will be changes along the way but I know you will face any challenges with determination and that you will succeed." Barry finished speaking and faced Adam. "I hope I shan't suffer the same fate as Sally for speaking out of turn," he said, solemnly.

"A friend is free to speak his mind at any time," smiled Adam. "I need time to digest your words. You'd better go back and check your computer and take these coffee cups with you."

Adam looked at his diary. His next appointment was at 3 o'clock. Time for some fresh air he thought and he informed Sally that he was going out for an hour.

"Make sure you hold any phone calls until I get back?" he said with a smile.

He went out and bought a coffee and sandwich at a brasserie in the High Street. As he sat there, he noticed a jeweller's shop opposite and decided to have a quick look before going back to the office. He crossed the road and looked in the window. There were some beautiful diamond rings glinting in the sunshine but none of them had prices attached. He realised he would need a couple of hours to go into the shop and choose, so he walked back to his office.

Business was brisk and there were queues at most of the tills. Adam made a mental note to tell Barry they needed some standby staff to open extra tills at times like these. As he walked past Sally's office, he called through the door:

"All quiet on the Weston front, Sally?"

"There have been no phone calls while you were out," she replied.

"Can you come into my office? There are some letters I'd like you to type up. It is important that they are posted today."

She went to his office for the letters.

"I have half an hour before my final appointment," he said. "I need to make some personal calls but I will be finished by three o'clock."

Sally left the room and Adam picked up the phone. He took the brochure out of his briefcase and dialled the number of the estate agent.

"Can I speak to the manager please?" said Adam.

The manager came to the phone and Adam introduced himself.

"Ah yes," said the estate agent. "You are the gentleman who looked at the Marina apartment yesterday."

"That is correct," Adam replied. "I am very interested in it and would like to have a second viewing."

"When would you like to come?"

"It would have to be at nine o'clock one morning."

"I could meet you there at nine o'clock tomorrow morning," said the agent.

"That will be fine," said Adam. "You have all my details."

Adam had finished all his business for the day by 4 o'clock. He cleared his desk and took a couple of files home with him. On the way out, he called in to Barry's office. He spoke to him about the queues at the tills and Barry said he would have a word with the training department and see what could be arranged.

"I'm just completing your figures," he told Adam. "It should be ready tomorrow."

"That reminds me," said Adam. "I shan't be in the office until after ten o'clock tomorrow morning. I have an appointment in Swanton at nine o'clock and it will depend on the traffic as to what time I get here."

"Right," said Barry. "Let's hope that the computers behave themselves in the morning. I'll see you then."

Adam left the building. He wanted to do a bit of shopping on his way home. His cupboards were pretty empty and he needed milk and bread. He stocked up on ready meals and bought some more of his favourite beer. Back home, he heated up a macaroni cheese, put it on a tray and took it into the lounge to eat it. He switched on the television and watched the six o'clock news. He felt quite content; this was the sort of life he was used to. For the first time, he felt happy in his home and he knew he would sleep well that night.

He was up early the next morning and by 8.30 was on his way into Swanton. He had been seriously thinking about the apartment. Actually, he liked it very much when he first saw it but he wasn't going to admit that to Leah. The traffic was horrendous and he arrived five minutes late. Mr Flack, the estate agent was waiting and introduced himself.

"Sorry I'm late," said Adam. "The traffic was bad."

"Ah yes," said Mr Flack. "It's the school run every morning. It will be quieter later on."

They went inside and Adam had a quick look around.

"I like this place very much," said Adam. "But I need some more information before I make a decision."

Mr Flack looked at Adam intently. He could tell he was a hard-headed businessman and hoped he wouldn't ask too many difficult questions.

"First of all," said Adam. "These houses are built very close to the river. What guarantee is there that they won't be affected by flooding?"

"The builders have worked very closely with the local council. The houses are built on concrete posts which are set into the ground. This means that they are well above any rise in the water level."

"Is there a written guarantee for that?" Adam asked.

"The specifications are written in the deeds."

"I see that most of the properties are occupied. Have there been any problems in obtaining a mortgage?"

"Not that I am aware of," replied Mr Flack.

"What about ongoing costs?"

"There is council tax, of course," said Mr Flack. "And the usual utility bills. There is also an annual ground rent."

"And what does that cover?"

"It covers the costs of keeping the communal areas clean and tidy and the upkeep of the outside of the buildings."

"That's unusual," remarked Adam.

"Well, it is quite an exclusive development and the builders want it maintained to a high standard."

"I understand that the sale includes everything that the apartment has in it. What value would you attach to the contents?" asked Adam.

Mr Flack was not expecting that question. He took a minute or two to consider his answer.

"I can't give you an exact figure," he said. "But I do know that everything is top quality, even the towels and bed linen and the soap in the bathroom."

"I would like to register my interest with you regarding this property," said Adam. "If I decide to go ahead, I will make you an offer before the end of the week. In the meantime, please keep me informed if there are any developments. You have my telephone number."

He thanked Mr Flack and went back to his car. Mr Flack stood at the door and watched him go. Wow, he thought. I wouldn't want to be interviewed for a job by him."

It didn't take long for Adam to get back to work. He called Sally into his office.

"Are there any messages or phone calls?" he asked.

"I've made two appointments for you tomorrow and there have been no important phone calls," she replied.

"Thank you, Sally. I shall have some letters for you later."

Adam then called Barry to tell him that he was back in Oxford.

"I have some papers for you to sign," said Barry. "Shall I bring them in?"

"Yes, please and bring some coffee as well."

Barry was there within five minutes and he put a folder on Adam's desk.

"The details you need are all in there," he said. "They just need your signature."

Adam opened the folder and took out the two top pages. He read them through and then signed both of them.

"Thank you, Barry," he said. "I'll take the folder home tonight and check your figures with mine, then I can decide what action to take. By the way, I went to view a property this morning, that's why I was late into work."

"Where was it?"

"It was in Swanton at a place called the Marina."

"That's a new development down by the river, isn't it? I've heard that it is very nice but expensive."

"It is an apartment which has been the show house," said Adam. "It is being sold with all furniture and furnishings included."

"Did you like it?"

"Yes, I did," said Adam. "Actually, it was Leah who found it in the local property pages. We both went to see it on Sunday and she fell in love with it but I felt she was pushing me into it. That's what the disagreement was about."

"Are you saying that Leah is thinking of moving out of her house?" said Barry in surprise. "You've just changed it into her sole ownership."

"No, I'm not saying that," replied Adam, emphatically. "Leah has no intention of moving out of her house or of me moving in."

It took Barry a while to absorb this information.

"You mean you are going to live in separate homes?" he said, finally. "And not live together?"

"That is Leah's idea and as usual she explained it very clearly to me."

"Well, I don't understand it," sighed Barry. "How can you live together in two different places?"

"I found it hard to accept but I'm beginning to see her point of view. We are still man and wife, whatever that means, but for the past twelve years, we have been living single lives. That is the pattern we have become used to and it seems to suit both of us. Actually, we are very lucky, we can have the best of both worlds: companionship and privacy."

"Well, good luck to you both. So, are you going ahead with the apartment?"

"That depends on how the money situation resolves itself but I would like to put in an offer by the end of the week. Please don't tell Jen about this. I don't want Leah to know until the deed is done."

"I won't say a word," said Barry. "I couldn't explain it to her anyway because I don't understand it myself. I feel as if I need a lie-down," he muttered as he left the room.

Adam smiled to himself. He wondered if Barry would ever be able to understand it. He put the folder in his briefcase with the figures which he had worked out. In the afternoon, he had two appointments. One of the clients was a solicitor and when they had concluded his business Adam said:

"I may need your services soon. I am looking to buy a house near Oxford."

The solicitor took a business card out of his pocket and gave it to Adam.

"You are welcome to use us at any time," he said as he left.

Adam put the card away in his drawer, thinking that might be a useful contact.

That evening, he sat on his settee and took out the folder which Barry had given him. He had done a very thorough job, he thought, as he leafed through it. He found the paper with the final calculation on it and compared it with his own set of figures. They were very similar and Adam breathed a sigh of relief. Now he could seriously consider his financial state. He had the money from the sale of his flat in Leden and he earned a good salary. His living expenses had not been extravagant so he had some savings as well. He added it all up then took away the cost of repaying Leah's mortgage. He was pleasantly surprised by the amount he had left. Now he had some serious thinking to do.

Firstly, he considered his options. He could pay off Leah's mortgage and not have any monthly mortgage payments. Or, he could increase the monthly payments so that it was all paid up in five years. But if he wanted to buy that apartment, he would have to take out a mortgage on that anyway and did he want to be paying two monthly payments? He wanted to keep it as simple as possible so decided on the first option. Obviously, there would be a bit more work for Barry to do but he wouldn't have to go far to get all the information he needed. He decided to speak to him tomorrow.

On Wednesday, Adam went into work as usual. It was already getting busy and he went straight into his office. He said good morning to Sally and told her to ask Barry to see him as soon as he was free. It was half an hour before Barry appeared.

"Sorry, I've taken so long," he said. "I've been trying to organise some extra tills but there was only one trained member of staff available."

"I've been thinking about that," said Adam. "We have a lot of spare spaces on the first floor. At first, I thought it could be made into a flat but I think I've got a better idea. Why don't we use some of it as a trainee department for potential staff and for those sixteen-year-olds who are sent out from the schools on job experience? There are some very good schools in this area and we would have the first choice of the brightest students."

"That sounds an excellent idea," said Barry. "But it will take some organising."

"Maybe it is one of those challenges you were talking about the other day," smiled Adam. "But it is certainly worth considering in the future. Now let's concentrate on the present."

He took the folder from his briefcase and looked at Barry.

"I'm very impressed with what you have done for me but I've changed my mind."

"Changed your mind?" asked Barry in amazement.

"Don't panic," he said, laughing. "It is only a minor detail. You can cancel my direct debit on Leah's mortgage. I intend to settle it up completely."

"You do wind me up," said Barry with a sigh of relief. "I can do that without any problems."

"Good. Our figures agree on the outstanding amount and I will transfer the money this morning. You must let me know what costs are involved."

"Are you sure about this?" Barry asked in a hesitant voice.

"Yes, I am sure," answered Adam. "It is my way of trying to compensate for all those years when Leah was coping by herself."

"I understand," he said. "Is there anything else?"

"Yes, one more thing," replied Adam. "I have decided to put an offer in for the apartment and I shall need a mortgage. I want you to tell me the amount I can borrow based on my salary."

"But you could work that out for yourself," said Barry in surprise.

"I'd rather not arrange my own mortgage. I wouldn't feel comfortable giving myself the money."

"Of course, I will do it. When are you going to make the offer?"

"I thought I'd do it when you have gone. It will be considerably less than the asking price and I wouldn't want to embarrass you."

Adam had kept a very straight face while he spoke but then he burst out laughing.

"Barry, your face is a picture!"

"I'm just glad it won't be me on the other end of the phone," said Barry with feeling. "That estate agent doesn't know what is going to hit him," and he left the room chuckling to himself.

Adam composed himself and then picked up the phone.

"Good morning, Mr Flack," he said in his best business voice. "This is Mr Richards."

"Good morning to you Mr Richards. How can I help you?"

"I'd like to make an offer on the apartment you showed me yesterday."

This man is no time waster, thought Flack.

"I hope we can do business," he said.

Adam then informed him of his offer and heard a gasp on the other end of his phone.

"I shall have to consult the vendors," said the startled estate agent. "I assume you are open to negotiations?"

"I'm always interested in other people's opinions," replied Adam, primly. "Negotiation is certainly one option."

"I'll be in touch when I have some news," said Mr Flack.

"Thank you. I should like an answer before the end of the week," and he ended the call.

Adam stood up. It had been a satisfying morning he thought and now it was time for some fresh air and a sandwich. He walked up to his favourite café and sat inside with his coffee and a ham roll. His eyes kept straying to the jeweller's shop across the road. He looked at his watch and decided that he had enough time to go into the shop to find out about the prices of the rings in the window. He crossed the road and rang the bell. It was the sort of shop that kept its front door locked and he knew they must be guarding a small fortune.

The door was opened by a man dressed in a smart suit.

"Good morning, sir," he said. "Can I be of assistance?"

Adam explained what he was looking for and he was invited into the shop.

"I only have a limited amount of time today," Adam said. "I am looking for a diamond ring for a friend. I would need much longer to choose one but I wondered what you have to offer?"

"We have a large selection to choose from," said the assistant. "Have you a particular setting in mind?"

"Not really," said Adam. "I shall know it when I see it."

The assistant opened a glass cabinet and took out a small tray of rings.

"This will give you an idea of the different styles which are available. The weight of the diamond determines the price and the settings are all eighteen-carat gold."

Adam looked at the rings and tried to imagine which one Leah would prefer. It was not going to be a simple choice but one ring, in particular, caught his eye. It was a solitaire diamond of medium size with a smaller diamond either side of it. He pointed it out to the man behind the counter who picked it up and gave it to Adam. This is the one, he thought, beautiful but practical, just like Leah. He gave it back to the man.

"I like this one but I really haven't time to make a decision now. I will leave you my card and return as soon as I can."

"It would be advisable to check the size to make sure it will fit the friend's finger," said the assistant.

"That's not a problem," replied Adam. "I already know the size. I must be going. I'm already late back."

The man looked at Adam's business card. Then shook Adam's hand.

"Thank you, Mr Richards. I look forward to seeing you again."

He unlocked the door and Adam walked briskly back to his office. He didn't like being late. It was not a good example for the rest of the staff. There were only one or two customers waiting to be served and he went straight back to his office. No sooner had he sat down than Sally burst in.

"Where have you been?" she cried. "I've had two phone calls from Head Office. Mr West wants to speak to you. I said you would speak to him as soon as you came back."

Adam took a deep breath. He was determined not to panic.

"See if you can contact his secretary, please Sally and I'll speak to him as soon as he is available," he said.

It had been a quiet week so far but he had the feeling that it was just about to change. His phone rang.

"Mr West wishes to talk to you."

"Thank you, Sally," said Adam and almost immediately Mr West's voice came down the phone.

"You are a very elusive chap," he said, lightly. "I've been trying to reach you for the past hour."

"I'm sorry, I went for a breath of fresh air and got side-tracked."

"That happens to all of us from time to time," replied Mr West. "But now down to business. There is to be a disciplinary hearing for James Brown on Friday and I would like you to be there. It starts at eleven-thirty; can you be here by then? It will also be an opportunity for you to meet some of the other directors. Let me know what time your train arrives and I will arrange for someone to pick you up at the station. Don't worry about it. It is highly unlikely that you will come in contact with James Brown. You will be able to watch the proceedings via a video link."

"Do I need to bring anything with me?" asked Adam.

"No, just bring yourself. I think you will find it very interesting. When it is over, I'd like to take you to lunch at my club. It will be a chance to have a chat. I look forward to seeing you on Friday."

Adam put the phone down and called Sally. When she came in, she looked at him expectantly.

"Cancel my appointments for Friday," he said. "I shall be in London at James Brown's disciplinary hearing."

"You won't have to meet that dreadful man, again will you?" she said, looking at him in horror.

"I don't think I shall need to see him in person. Apparently, I can watch the proceedings via a video link. Now ask Barry to come to my office."

When Barry came in, he found Adam sitting in his chair deep in thought.

"What's happened?" asked Barry.

Adam told him about the phone call.

"I don't understand why Mr West wants me there. I shan't do anything during the hearing, just watch what is going on."

"You can learn a lot by just watching," Barry said wisely.

"But why did he say I should meet some of the other directors?" persisted Adam. "And why does he want to take me out for lunch at his club?"

Barry looked at Adam. He really does not know he thought. Well, I'm not going to scare him by explaining it. Instead, he said:

"I should think it will be a most interesting day. You will learn a lot about how the other half lives. Just go with the flow and enjoy it."

"Is there anything you want to tell me, Barry?" asked Adam, sharply.

"I don't know anything more than you," he said as he left the room.

Adam was not convinced by Barry's answer but he decided to accept it for now. He had too many things to think about before Friday.

That evening he phoned Leah. He checked that she was alright then he said:

"I have to go to London on Friday and I don't know what time I'll be back. I won't be able to come over on Saturday."

"That's okay," said Leah. "I shall be busy in any case. I was going to ask if you would like to come for lunch on Sunday? It is my birthday soon and we usually have a Sunday lunch to celebrate it. Peter will come with his family and Alice might too."

"I'd love to come. Can I do anything to help?"

"No, thank you. I'm quite used to organising it by myself. We shall eat at one o'clock so come when you are ready."

"It's not your birthday on Sunday is it?"

"My birthday is next Tuesday," she said. "But Sunday is the most convenient time for us to get together."

"I shan't bring your present on Sunday," he said. "You will have to wait until Tuesday. By the way what number should be on the card I buy?"

"Don't be cheeky!" Leah said. "You should never ask a lady her age."

"I'll have to guess then," he laughed. "I'll phone you at the weekend and I'll see you on Sunday."

Leah put the phone down and wondered why Adam was going to London, obviously something to do with work she decided. She would be busy anyway and didn't need any distractions.

Adam sat down and thought about the things he needed to have completed by Tuesday. He hoped Barry could give him the deeds of Leah's house by then. It would be good if he could agree on a price for the apartment and most importantly, he wanted to buy that ring. The first thing he did on Thursday morning was to get Sally to find out the time of the trains to London.

"There is a train at ten past and twenty to every hour," Sally told him. "Most of them go to Paddington but you can change at Reading for Waterloo."

"I think I need to go to Paddington," said Adam. "How long is the journey?"

"About forty-five minutes."

"I'll take the 9.40 from Oxford," he said. "That should get me there in plenty of time. Mr West said that he would send someone to meet me at the station. Can you please phone his secretary and tell her what time

I shall be arriving?"

When Sally left, Adam looked at his diary. He had two appointments later in the morning and one in the afternoon, leaving him no time to go to the jewellers. He would have to go on Monday. He made a note to tell Sally not to make any arrangements after one o'clock on Monday. Then he called Barry into his office and told him about Friday.

"I am leaving you in charge," he said. "Sally will work with you and I have every confidence that you will do a good job."

"We'll manage without you for one day," he said solemnly. "But I don't know if we could cope for any longer than that."

Adam glared at Barry.

"Are you trying to wind me up?" he demanded.

"On the contrary," said Barry. "I'm doing my best to keep you relaxed." and they both laughed at each other.

There was a knock at the door and Sally came in.

"There's a Mr Flack on the phone, Adam. He wants to speak to you."

"Thank you, Sally. Put him through."

Barry stood up to leave but Adam gestured for him to stay.

"Listen and learn," he whispered. "Good morning Mr Flack," he said in his best business voice. "How can I help you?"

Mr Flack had a very strident voice and Barry could hear the conversation quite clearly.

"I've had a word with the vendors, Mr Richards and they are not happy with your offer, not happy at all. They want another ten Grand."

"That is out of the question," Adam said firmly. "I will meet them halfway and raise my offer by five thousand."

"I will tell them that," said Mr Flack. "But that may not be enough."

"It is more than enough from my point of view," said Adam. "I consider the offer to be a fair one so now it is up to you to negotiate with the vendors. Good day, Mr Flack."

Barry was sitting on his chair laughing to himself.

"I assume that was the estate agent?" he asked.

"Yes, it was," said Adam. "Full of his own importance but just had his wings clipped. He will certainly have earned his money if this deal goes through. Talking of money, have you transferred the money to pay off Leah's mortgage?"

"It is all ready to do. It just needs your authorization."

"I'd like to finalise that today," said Adam. "You set it up on your computer and I'll come and do it in your office."

"Right," said Barry. "I'll let you know when it is ready."

That's one thing I can tick off my list, thought Adam and hoped he'd hear back from Mr Flack today; that would be another tick.

He called Sally and asked her to get him a coffee and a sandwich for his dinner. Then his thoughts began to turn to tomorrow. He still didn't understand why Mr West wanted him there. Maybe it was because of the reports which they had written. Mr West had certainly seemed impressed when Adam had first shown them to him. He really couldn't think of any other reason. He felt like he was being treated like royalty; a car to meet him at the station, dinner at an exclusive club, meeting the directors. Mr West was a real gentleman so maybe this was just the result of good breeding and impeccable manners. His thoughts were interrupted by a knock on the door and in came Sally with his coffee and sandwiches.

"Thank you, Sally," he said. "Did you speak to Mr West's secretary?"

"Yes," said Sally. "We are getting to know each other quite well. It is all arranged for you."

The rest of the day passed quietly but before he went home, Adam went to Barry's office to complete the transfer of money to pay Leah's mortgage.

"Good luck tomorrow," said Barry. "Enjoy your day in London."

"I don't know about enjoying it, I still have a feeling that there is something unusual about it," he replied.

"Are you seeing Leah this weekend?"

"Leah has a birthday lunch on Sunday with Peter and his family. She has invited me to it. I'm really looking forward to it."

"Hold that thought," said Barry.

There it was again, that comment from Barry, thought Adam, puzzled.

"Have you any plans for the weekend, Barry?"

"I've been told that the garden needs tidying up before the winter. My plans are made for me," he sighed.

"Hard luck," said Adam, sympathetically. "If I get that apartment, I shan't have any gardening to do but I suppose I can always help Leah. I'll see you on Monday morning, all being well."

Barry watched Adam go out of the main door. He looked composed enough, he thought and enigmatic as usual.

Adam spent the evening tidying up his kitchen before getting himself something to eat. He took it into the lounge and sat on his settee. He was getting used to the place now. Some of his furniture was still piled up against the wall and some boxes were stacked in a corner. He suddenly realised that he would have a problem when he moved. The apartment was fully furnished with furniture which was designed for the place. His own pieces would be totally unsuitable for a modern apartment. He wondered what on earth he would do with it all. He thought about it for a while and decided he would first of all offer it to a charity shop and the pieces they didn't want would go to a second-hand dealer or to the dump. But getting rid of his faithful old settee, felt wrong and he hoped Leah would find room for it in her conservatory.

He went upstairs, had a shower and got ready for bed. He was beginning to feel anxious about the next day and hoped he would get to sleep before becoming too restless. One thing was for sure, tomorrow would be a most unusual day. He put out the light and pulled the duvet over him, wishing Leah was there with him, with her calming influence. He went to sleep thinking about her and slept all night long.

Chapter Eleven

He woke early on Friday morning and lay there thinking about the day ahead. He consoled himself that it was just another day, as he got dressed. Why should he think it would be any different from the days that had gone and the days still to come? He had a good breakfast and was soon on his way to the station. He parked his car and bought his return ticket. He didn't have to wait long for the train and he was soon speeding his way towards London. The train arrived on time and Adam disembarked. Almost immediately a man in a chauffeur's uniform approached him.

"Mr Richards?"

"Yes, that's me."

"I am Mr West's driver. The car is waiting and I will take you to Head Office. Please follow me."

Adam went out of the main exit and there was a large black limousine parked outside. The rear door was opened for him and they were soon driving along the London streets. The traffic looked horrendous to Adam and he felt glad not to be a part of it. But the chauffeur was effortlessly weaving his way through it all and Adam had to admire his driving skills.

"Here we are," said the driver and held the door open for Adam to get out.

"Thank you," said Adam. "I do admire your driving skills."

The chauffeur looked pleased.

"It's my job," he said modestly and he drove away.

Adam stood and looked at the building in front of him. It was large and imposing. A uniformed doorman was standing at the top of the steps. As Adam reached the door he stepped forward.

"Mr Richards, I presume?" he said.

"Yes, that's me."

"We have been expecting you, sir," said the doorman. "I have orders to take you straight to Mr West but first you will need your identity disc."

He took Adam over to a large desk in the middle of the marble hallway. The girl at the desk smiled at Adam.

"Here is your identity disc, Mr Richards. You must wear it at all times inside the building."

"Thank you," said Adam and hung it around his neck. He looked closely at it and it said: Adam Richards - Visitor.

"You can leave Mr Richards with me now," she said to the doorman then she turned to Adam. "I will tell Mr West that you are here and he will send someone to collect you."

She phoned through to Mr West's office and was given some instructions. Before long a young man came down the corridor and said to Adam:

"Please come with me, sir. Mr West will see you now."

"That is what the dentists say before they pull your teeth out," smiled Adam.

"I assure you it will be far more pleasant than a visit to the dentist," he said with a smile.

They walked along carpeted corridors with beautiful paintings on the walls until they arrived at an office door with Mr West's name on it. The young man knocked on the door.

"Come in."

The young man led the way and Adam followed him. As soon as Mr West saw Adam, he rose from his chair and went to greet him. He shook his hand warmly.

"I'm glad you could make it. It is good to have you here. I am looking forward to chatting to you over lunch. But now there are more pressing matters. The inquiry is due to start in fifteen minutes. You will not be needed in the room itself but you can watch it all from the ante-room via a computer link. Jack, here," and he indicated the young man who had met him in the hall. "Will sit in with you and answer any questions you might have."

There were two other gentlemen in the room and Mr West said:

"Before you leave us, allow me to introduce you to two of my fellow directors."

Adam shook hands with them and the first said:

"Very pleased to meet you, Mr Richards."

"Good to have you onboard, my lad," said the other man.

Adam noticed the warning look Mr West gave to the elderly man.

"If you will come this way, sir, we will make sure that the video link is working properly," Jack said and he led the way into a small office with two comfortable chairs in it and a great deal of technical equipment.

"My goodness," said Adam. "Is all this electrical gadgetry even used?"

"It is becoming more and more important to be able to protect ourselves against cyber-attacks," replied Jack. "This is nothing compared to what is in other parts of the building."

He switched on a large screen as he was speaking and now there was a picture on it. It was the room where the hearing would take place.

"It looks like a courtroom," said Adam with a shudder. "It is quite intimidating."

"I suppose the way in which it is conducted is similar to a court appearance," Jack said. "But there are no policemen present and no judge or jury. Mr West will have discussed the case with other Board Members and our lawyers. In this case, the evidence is quite overwhelming so they know what the verdict will be already."

"That seems a strange way to me but I suppose it spares the defendant hearing all the evidence made public," said Adam.

"None of this will be made public," said Jack. "That is why we have this form of disciplinary hearing."

Adam was watching the screen intently. He could see several lawyers in their black gowns but he couldn't see Mr James Brown.

"Where is Mr Brown?" he asked.

"He will be escorted in when the bell rings," Jack said.

A moment later, he heard the tinkle of a bell and Mr Brown was brought in accompanied by a security guard. He sat down next to his lawyer and had a good look round the room. He seemed to be looking for someone. Adam shivered, thankful that he was out of sight.

"Are you alright?" asked Jack. "I think I'll order some coffee and biscuits."

"That would be most welcome," Adam said. "It seems a long time since breakfast."

He was watching the screen and he heard a voice say: "everyone, stand" and Mr West came in followed by the two directors. He was carrying the file which Adam had first seen in his Oxford office. He opened it up and took out some papers.

"Mr James Brown," said Mr West. "Please stand and confirm your name."

Mr Brown did as he was asked and Mr West continued.

"Mr Brown, it has come to our notice that you have been discharging your duties in an unacceptable way. You have created a great deal of anxiety, particularly among the female staff in the offices you have visited. We have received many complaints about your suggestive behaviour. In the most extreme cases, this has amounted to sexual harassment. How do you plead?"

"Not guilty," replied Mr Brown, definitely. "It is all lies."

"I do not think this file is full of lies," said Mr West, sternly.

"You haven't got one piece of solid evidence against me. It is all fake information made up by your office," said Mr Brown.

"I do have very solid evidence from a visit you made recently," Mr West said quietly. "I have it here," and he produced the three notes from his folder. "Shall I read them out for everyone to hear?"

Adam held his breath while he waited for the answer to that question. He didn't want Sally and Barry involved in the proceedings. He could see Mr Brown having a long discussion with his lawyer. Finally, the lawyer stood up and said:

"My client accepts responsibilities for his actions and wishes to change his plea to guilty as charged."

Adam let out a huge sigh of relief.

"Thank goodness for that," he said. "I didn't want to have my secretary and assistant manager mixed up in this sorry business."

There was a knock on the door and a secretary came in with a pot of coffee and some biscuits.

"Would you like me to be Mum?" she said with a smile.

"Yes please," said Adam and he smiled back at her.

What a charming man, she thought as she left the room and wondered if he was married.

Adam was completely oblivious to his effect on women.

"What happens now, Jack?" he asked.

"Mr Brown will leave the room while Mr West and his co-directors make a final decision. It shouldn't take long because they already know the verdict."

Adam was grateful for the cup of coffee and the biscuits and by the time he had finished them, everyone was back in their seats.

"Mr Brown, please stand," said Mr West.

Mr Brown stood nervously behind his chair. Adam could see him shaking.

"Mr James Brown," said Mr West in a formal tone. "You have been found guilty of severe dereliction of duty and of bringing the name of this company into disrepute. You will be dismissed immediately and will leave these premises by two o'clock this afternoon. You are required to take all your belongings with you. Your pension will be paid in full when it is activated but your monthly salary will be terminated as from today. Finally, if you contact any of your former colleagues or connections, I shall hand the file over to the police and then no doubt it will be made public. You may now leave."

Mr West and the directors left the room and Mr Brown was helped out by his lawyer.

"That is a pretty harsh verdict," Adam said.

"No more than he deserves," answered Jack. "This has been going on for years but the three notes from your office were vital pieces of information needed to complete the evidence."

"Was that why Mr West asked me to come?" asked Adam.

"It was part of the reason," said Jack. "But I know he is also looking forward to chatting to you. Now we had better go and find him. I know he will be wanting his lunch."

He took Adam back to Mr West's office and knocked on the door.

"Come in."

Jack opened the door. Mr West was talking to his secretary and passing some files over to her.

"I've almost finished," he said as he gave her the last instruction. "Jack, will you please arrange for the car to be ready in ten minutes? Adam, Jack will take you to the front hall and I'll meet you there. Then we can go and have a good lunch."

As they walked along the corridor, Jack pointed out the different departmental offices.

"How many people work here?" asked Adam.

"About six hundred," Jack replied. "But it can increase to a thousand when there is a crisis."

"Does that happen often?"

"Not very often, thank goodness. I have only experienced one since I have been here and that was pretty scary."

Adam's thoughts turned to his own office in Oxford and thought what small fish they were in a very large sea. When they reached the front hall, Adam stood and looked around.

"This is a very impressive place and a very impressive organisation," he said. "And is Mr West the man responsible for all of this?"

"Mr West has a Board of Directors to help him but ultimately he is the man in charge," answered Jack.

Adam was beginning to feel a little uneasy. He was not used to all this opulence and power. Those nagging doubts were creeping back into his mind. What was he doing here and why? This did not feel like his world at all. His thoughts were interrupted by a voice behind him:

"Ready for lunch, Adam?" and he turned to find Mr West standing behind him. "You were miles away then."

"I'm sorry. I was just soaking up the atmosphere. It is very different from what I am used to."

"We are all working towards the same goal," said Mr West with a smile. "Now my immediate goal is lunch. The car is here so let's go."

"I thought the traffic in Oxford was bad but this is something else," said Adam, as the chauffer once again skilfully negotiated the traffic.

"I would never drive in London," said Mr West. "I would be a nervous wreck. My chauffeur is an essential part of my staff."

By now they were outside Mr West's club.

"Good afternoon, Mr West," said the doorman. "We are expecting you."

"Thank you, Bernie," said Mr West and at that moment the head waiter came bustling up.

"Your table is ready sir," he said with a bow.

"I have a visitor with me today. This is Mr Richards."

"You are most welcome, sir," said the waiter, bowing to Adam and he led the way into the restaurant.

There were several other diners already seated and they greeted Mr West as he walked past. They were taken to the table in a secluded section of the restaurant. Adam looked around and discovered that they were the only two people in that area. Mr West noticed this.

"I personally asked for this table because there is something important that I want to discuss with you. But first things first. I think I need a stiffener after this morning's events. What would you like?"

"I'll have a whiskey and soda," said Adam. The waiter had been hovering in the background and Mr West gestured him to come over.

"Two whiskeys and soda please, Bruno," he said. "Now what are you going to eat?"

"It is difficult to choose," Adam replied as he looked at the menu. "What would you recommend?"

"I like the garlic-infused lamb shoulder with roasted vegetables."

"I'm not a fan of garlic," Adam replied. "I think I prefer the roast salmon with Hasselback potatoes."

I like a man who is not afraid to state his preferences, thought Dominic West.

The waiter came back with their drinks and Mr West ordered the food.

"How did you find this morning's proceedings, Adam?"

Adam considered before his reply.

"It was not a pleasant experience to see a man brought to his knees but I acknowledge the fact that it was self-inflicted. Under the circumstances, I thought it was handled in a very straightforward manner and on reflection, I think the verdict was a fair one."

Mr West looked impressed by Adam's answer.

"You have the ability to condense a situation into a concise way of looking at it. That is a good asset," he said.

Adam thought of Leah. She was able to explain a problem in a clear and forthright manner but he had never thought that he had that ability too. Adam saw the waiter coming with a trolley and their lunch was put on the table in front of them.

"Would you like anything further?" asked Bruno.

"No, thank you," said Mr West. "This looks delicious."

Adam had not realised how hungry he was. During the meal, the conversation was quite casual.

"Would you like a dessert?" asked Mr West.

"No thank you," said Adam.

Mr West turned to Bruno and ordered two Irish coffees. Bruno cleared the plates from the table and he was soon back with the coffees.

"That will be all, thank you, Bruno."

The two men were left facing each other across the table.

"I expect you have been wondering why I asked you here today?"

"Yes, it has been on my mind," said Adam. "I assume it was because of the James Brown business?"

"That is partly the reason. I wanted you to see how we conducted an internal investigation because I was interested to hear your assessment of it. But there is something else I want to discuss with you."

Adam took a sharp breath.

"I had a feeling that it was not a casual invitation but I have absolutely no idea of any other reason."

"That's good, very good."

Adam looked at him curiously but didn't say a word.

"You heard the verdict on James Brown. That means that his post as area manager is now vacant. I would like to put forward your name to fill it but I need to have your permission to do that."

Adam was speechless. It took him a couple of minutes to take in what he had heard. When he did find his voice, he said:

"But I've only been in my present post for five weeks. I really don't want to leave the Oxford office so soon. I'm very happy there and I've made up my mind to settle in that area."

"The area manager's job is in the West Midlands, so you could quite easily be based in Oxford. The first floor of the building could be converted into the area office. You would still keep your present position as general manager but since the area job involves more travelling, I would suggest that your assistant manager is promoted to manager so that he could supervise the day to day work of the branch." Mr West stopped talking and looked at Adam expectantly. "Of course, I don't want your answer immediately. You can have a week to think about it before you make a decision."

"Of course, I would be interested in the post but I do have other commitments in my life I need to consider," Adam said.

"Yes," said Mr West. "I understand you must consider your family."

"My family," said Adam, faintly. "What do you know about my family?"

"Forgive me, Adam. I had to find out more about your background before I could make you an offer. I know you are married and have four children. I know why you moved to Leden and how you coped with the bad times. I know how hard you studied and I have had glowing reports from the area manager up there. I know that you have always maintained your dignity in all circumstances. I know that as a result of your move to Oxford you have been seeing Leah and that you are working hard to renew your relationship with her. You have overcome many problems in your life and you deserve the success which is available to you. You are quite capable of success at the highest level."

Adam was lost for words.

"But how did you get all this information?" he stammered.

"There are ways and means," smiled Mr West. "I have always found that if you are honest with a person, they will give you honest answers." He looked at his watch. "Time I was getting back. I have enjoyed your company, Adam, and I look forward to hearing from you before next Friday."

"Thank you for your hospitality," Adam said as he shook Dominic's hand. "I have a lot to think about."

"Would you like a lift to the station?" asked Mr West.

"No, thank you. I'll find my own way back. The fresh air will do me good."

Adam went down the steps and out into the street. Mr West watched him stride off down the road. What an interesting man, he thought. So capable and yet so modest.

Adam had no idea where he was in London so he just kept on walking. He needed to clear his head before the train journey home. He noticed a Costa Coffee shop on the corner of a busy street. He bought a coffee and carried on walking along the street. This is my world, he thought to himself, good fresh air and coffee in a cardboard cup.

He walked on until he felt calmer, then he stopped and looked around him. This was his first time in London and he had no idea how to get to the station. He hailed a taxi.

"Paddington Station please."

It was getting dark and judging by the amount of traffic it was also the beginning of the rush hour. The taxi stopped at the main entrance to the station. Adam got out, paid the driver and went inside. It was heaving with people rushing about.

All he wanted to do was get out of there and went towards the information boards. He saw that the next train to Oxford left in ten minutes. He hurried towards the platform and found the train waiting. He boarded it and was lucky enough to find a seat. Two minutes later, it pulled out of the station. Adam breathed a sigh of relief to be on his way home.

He leaned his head on the back of the seat and thought about the events of the day. He felt exhausted but there was one thing that troubled him most. How did Dominic West know about Leah? There were only two people who knew that Leah was his wife: Jen and Barry. Jen had never met Mr West but Barry had. The penny began to drop, only Barry could have told him. Then Adam had another thought. Barry had denied knowing anything when he had asked him; he would have some explaining to do on Monday morning.

When the train arrived in Oxford, Adam went to find his car and drove home. It was only when he was inside his house that he finally relaxed. He pulled the curtains and closed the blinds. He made himself a nice cup of tea and went to sit on his settee.

"I've had enough of today," he said out loud. "I want to be alone in my own little nest." As he said these words he thought of Leah and how she had said that they were used to living single lives. She's right, as usual, he thought. Tonight, he wanted to be alone. Tomorrow he knew he would feel differently and want company. We can work it out, he thought. Right now, he was exhausted and went for a good, hot shower to wash away the grime of London.

Half an hour later, he was ready for bed. As he lay there, he thought of the chauffeur-driven car, the thick carpeted offices and corridors, the bowing waiter at the private club. That was not his life, he decided. He liked to meet real people who treated him as an equal, not some kind of deity. He felt relieved that he had reached this conclusion. The other problems could wait until tomorrow. And he drifted off into a contented sleep.

Chapter Twelve

When Adam woke on Saturday morning, it was quite late. He looked at his watch and was surprised to find that it was nearly ten o'clock. However, he had no need to rush and was looking forward to a day to himself. He got dressed and went to the kitchen to make a cup of tea. He took it into the lounge and sat on his settee. The events of yesterday were slowly drifting back into his mind. He remembered the noise of the traffic and the crowds of people all living their lives at breakneck speed. He thought of the contrast with the hushed silence of the Head Office and the controlled behaviours of its staff. He thought of the homeless young people he had noticed on the streets and the lavish hospitality which he had enjoyed. He thought of Dominic West and wondered what sort of a family background he had.

This last thought made Adam sit up. How on earth did Mr West know about Leah and his family? He must have known why Adam left Leah twelve years ago but it didn't seem to have affected his opinion of him. In fact, he appeared to believe that he had redeemed himself in some way. Adam knew he would always feel guilty about what happened but now surely was the time to move his life forward? And so he decided to accept Mr West's offer but it would have to be on his own terms.

He knew he had to speak to Barry. It wouldn't be easy to do that on Monday so, he decided he couldn't wait any longer, he would have to phone him right now. He dialled the number and Jen answered.

"Hello Adam," she said. "Did you enjoy your trip to London?"

"Enjoy is not the best word," he replied. "Let's just say it was interesting. Can I speak to Barry?"

"He is in the garden. I'll call him in."

Adam heard Jen calling Barry's name and before long he picked up the phone.

"Hello Adam," he said. "How was your trip?"

"It was very interesting," said Adam with a touch of sarcasm in his voice. "I need to talk to you. Can you be released from your gardening duties and meet me at the pub?"

"I could do with a break," he said. "I could be there by twelve-thirty?"

"That's fine by me. I'll see you there," said Adam.

Barry turned to Jen and told her that he had to go out.

"Where are you going?" she demanded. "The garden is only half done. Why can't you stay and finish it?"

"I'll finish it when I get back," he said. "Adam says he needs to talk to me. So, I said I would meet him."

"So, it's a pub meeting is it?" Jen said in a resigned voice. "You men are all the same. Stick together at all costs."

"I don't know what he wants to talk about or why it couldn't wait until Monday," Barry said patiently. "It must be important to him so I feel I must go."

He went upstairs to the bathroom, washed his hands and changed out of his gardening clothes. He said goodbye to Jen and was on his way to meet Adam.

Adam was already seated at a table in the corner when Barry arrived. He had two pints of lager in front of him; he pushed one of the glasses to Barry.

"You managed to get excused from duty then?" he said with a smile.

"Yes," said Barry. "But she wasn't too happy about it." He supped his lager and looked at Adam. "I can't help wondering what you need to talk about."

"It's funny you should say that because I felt exactly the same when I was summoned up to London yesterday. But after being primed with a lavish lunch I soon found out. I think you know the answer already."

Barry looked directly at Adam with a frown on his face.

"I don't know what you mean," he said at last. "I have no idea why you were asked to go to Head Office. I assumed it was to do with the James Brown business and you thought that too."

"It was partly that but I always had the feeling that there was more to it and I was right. From the minute I stepped off the train, I was treated like royalty. I knew there was another reason and it was only after a first-class lunch that I discovered it."

"I still don't understand why you think it has anything to do with me," Barry repeated.

Adam looked at Barry. He seemed to be genuinely surprised at what he had heard.

"After lunch, Mr West offered me the post of area manager," Adam said. "He also told me that if I accepted it, you would be promoted to manager of the Oxford Office but that I would remain as General Manager. He went on to say that he had been making enquiries about me and he knew everything about my background and about my family. He even knew Leah's name."

Barry had been listening in amazement. He sat there with his mouth open but couldn't find the words to speak.

"There are only two people who know that Leah is my wife," Adam continued. "You and Jen, so one of you must have told Mr West. As far as I know, Jen never met the man but you have, so how do you explain it?"

Adam sat back and waited for Barry to answer. He didn't feel at all comfortable quizzing Barry like this but he needed to know the truth.

After a long pause, Barry spoke.

"Mr West did phone me to ask if you had a wife and family. I was in a tight spot between telling him and being loyal to you. I think he realised my dilemma and assured me that anything I told him would be in the strictest confidence. I had to take a chance and accept his word on it. I told him that you were married but had been living apart from Leah for the past twelve years. I said that since you had been in Oxford, you had been in contact with her and that you wanted to try to get back together. I said that you had four children and four grandchildren. That is all I told him."

"But how did he know about my time up north?" Adam said.

"I know nothing about your life up there. I couldn't tell him anything about that."

Adam thought back about his time in Leden. He never had any close friends up there. The only person he had sometimes confided in was the area manager.

"I think I know how Dominic West learned about my time in

Leden," he said. "The only person I ever talked to about personal matters was the area manager. Mr West must have spoken to him too."

"I'm sorry if you feel I have let you down," Barry said. "You know yourself that it is difficult to say no to a request from Head Office."

"I can see you were in a difficult position. I always felt that there was something you weren't telling me. I'm glad that it is now sorted."

"So am I," said Barry "I've not been happy keeping it from you but I honestly didn't know why Mr West wanted such information. Is there something else that is bothering you?"

"There is one other remark made by Mr West which I can't get out of my mind. He said that I was capable of success at the highest level," replied Adam.

Barry looked at Adam, realising that he still didn't know.

"Perhaps he is lining you up as his successor?"

Adam looked absolutely horrified.

"I assume that's a joke?" he said abruptly.

Barry just shrugged his shoulders.

"I would never in a million years want his job," said Adam, emphatically. "All that bowing and scraping and tipping of hats."

"Are you saying that you would refuse it if it was offered to you?" Barry asked in surprise.

"I most certainly am saying that."

"But what about the area manager's job?"

"I think I will accept that but it will be on my terms. How do you feel about the manager's role?"

"I know I could do it," said Barry. "And you would still be around. I've learnt a lot in the past five weeks."

"You must be a very quick learner. I have every confidence that you will make a success of it. There is one proviso though."

"What is that?" Barry asked nervously.

"That you do not keep any secrets from me," Adam said firmly.

"I promise."

"That's settled then," Adam said. "I'm glad we had this chat and cleared the air. Now I can look forward to my weekend and you can go back to your garden."

As Barry drove home, he was thinking about the conversation which had just taken place. It had all been a complete surprise to him. He was glad that he had been able to tell Adam about Mr West's phone call. He knew that Adam was an honest, straight-talking person and he had hated having to keep the secret from him. He knew he could take on a manager's role but he hadn't expected it to happen so quickly. He decided not to tell Jen until it was formally offered to him.

Jen was in the kitchen when he got back. She was cooking dinner and the smell was delicious.

"I'm back," he said and kissed her on the cheek.

"What was that for?" she asked in surprise.

"It's a thank you in anticipation of that dinner I hope is nearly ready. I'll finish the garden tomorrow."

Jen couldn't help thinking what a good man she had married and wondered what he and Adam had talked about in the pub.

When Barry had left, Adam went up to the bar and ordered another pint.

"The wanderer returns," said the barman with a smile.

"I'm glad to be back," said Adam. "And I am looking for a good dinner. What can you offer me?"

"Take your pick," said the barman indicating a board on the wall with five choices written on it.

Adam looked at it and thought of the menu he had been shown yesterday. At least it is all written in plain English and I shall know what I am eating. He chose cod, chips and peas then went back to his table and waited for it. He was deep in thought when a voice said:

"Your dinner, sir."

Adam looked up and saw a young waitress in front of him holding a plate.

"Thank you very much," he said and smiled at her.

The girl blushed and smiled back.

"No problems," she said and went back into the kitchen.

Adam tucked into his meal and soon the plate was empty. I really enjoyed that, he said to himself. Better than salmon and Hasselback potatoes.

When he got home from the pub, he lay down on his settee and was soon fast asleep. He was woken by the sound of his phone ringing.

"Hello?" he said, sleepily.

"You sound half asleep," said Leah.

"I was asleep," said Adam, struggling to sit up.

"Did you enjoy London?"

"Not much. It was too noisy and too dirty and too crowded. What have you been doing today?"

"Shopping and cooking ready for tomorrow," she answered. "I'm tired out but at least I can expect an undisturbed night in my own bed."

"You'd better make sure you lock the back door," Adam said with a laugh. "I've got a front door key anyway."

"I shall put the chain on the door," replied Leah. "I shall only take it off after ten o'clock to-morrow morning."

"Spoilsport. I'll be waiting on the doorstep at one-minute past ten. I'll see you then."

He was up early the next morning. I hope Leah had a good night's sleep in her lonely bed, he thought with a smile. It didn't take him long to drive to Leah's house and he looked at his watch as he arrived. It was exactly ten o'clock. I wonder? He thought as he went up to the front door. He tried his key in the lock but the door only opened an inch or two. He closed it quietly then bent down to the letterbox and shouted through it.

"The time is one-minute past ten."

The door was opened immediately.

"Be quiet," she said indignantly. "What do you think you are doing?

Whatever will the neighbours think?"

She closed the door behind him and turned to go back to the kitchen but he caught hold of her arm.

"Just a minute," he said. "I haven't said good morning to you," and he took her in his arms and kissed her lips.

"I've missed you," he said.

"I've missed you too," said Leah and kissed him back.

He held her close to him and whispered in her ear:

"I love you. Did you sleep well in your lonely bed?"

She looked at him and smiled.

"It took me a while to get warm. I missed the double duvet."

Adam laughed.

"I've been called many names in the past but never a double duvet."

He followed her into the kitchen. It was remarkably tidy.

"I was expecting to see lots of preparation in here but it is very tidy."

"I did all of the preparing yesterday," said Leah. "With some help."

"Who came to help you?" I did offer you know."

"Do I detect a hint of jealousy?" asked Leah in a surprised voice. "It was Tesco of course. You can buy most things ready to go in the oven. I wish Tesco had been around when we were first married. I could have avoided so many cooking disasters."

"What are we having today?" asked Adam.

"Roast chicken with stuffing, Yorkshire puddings, roast potatoes, carrots and peas and gravy of course."

Adam looked thoughtful.

"I remember your gravy," he said. "It always had lumps in it."

"There will be no lumps today," Leah said firmly. "It comes out of a pot".

"Is there anything I can do to help?"

"You could lift the dinner plates from the top shelf of the cupboard," she said. "They are quite heavy and they don't get used very often."

"How many shall we need?"

"Six large plates and two smaller ones for the children," she said. "I'll go and get a meat dish and the electric knife from the utility area."

"I don't like the sound of an electric knife," said Adam with a shudder. "I would prefer the old-fashioned carving knife and fork."

"Peter always uses an electric knife. It carves the meat so much more efficiently" said Leah.

"I must make sure he carves the chicken then," Adam said.

"I'm going to make some coffee," she said. "The chicken is already in the oven and the rest can be done quite quickly. The only thing I must remember is to put the roast potatoes in on time. I'll bring the coffee into the lounge."

Adam walked through the dining room on his way to the lounge. The table was laid ready for the meal and the chairs were arranged around it. She has been busy, he thought. And she has done it all by herself. He was looking forward to seeing Peter again and meeting his wife. He was impatient to see his grandchildren and wondered if they would remember him. He was standing at the back of the lounge looking at the conservatory when Leah brought the coffee in.

"It is not very nice weather today," he said. "The children won't be able to go into the garden."

"This is when the conservatory is so useful," she said. "All their toys are kept in the cupboard and they can play indoors."

He went and sat beside Leah and they drank their coffee.

"Tell me about Peter's wife," he said. "What is she like?"

"Quite pleasant and a good mother to the children."

Adam was quite surprised by the short answer and he detected a note of caution in it.

"What time will they be here?" he asked.

"They usually arrive about twelve-thirty," she replied. "We eat at one o'clock and they leave around two-thirty."

"That is a pretty tight schedule," said Adam. "Why do they leave so early?"

"Janet's parents live in the south of the town and she likes to visit them too. She doesn't drive so Peter has to take her." Leah looked at the clock. "I must put those roast potatoes in," she said. "And check on the chicken."

Adam followed her into the kitchen.

"I'll lift it out of the oven for you," he said.

He put on the oven gloves and lifted the chicken onto the table. He removed the foil which was covering it and stuck a fork into the meat.

"I think it is cooked," he said. "Shall I put it back in the oven?"

"Yes please, but leave the foil off then the skin will crisp up."

"Anything else?" asked Adam.

"There is a bottle of wine on the table which needs opening. The children will have coke. Janet won't approve but she knows better not to argue with me."

There it is again, thought Adam. He couldn't mistake the disapproval in her voice.

Leah was busy in the kitchen when the knocking started on the front door. Adam waited in the lounge while Leah opened the door. Then he heard:

"Granny Leah, Granny Leah!"

Benjie was holding a large bunch of flowers.

"Happy Birthday!" he shouted as he handed over the flowers.

"Happy Birthday," said Lucy as she gave Leah a box of chocolates.

Leah hugged them both and gave them each a big kiss. Adam smiled to himself. He sat on the settee and waited. The children bounced into the lounge and then stopped when they saw Adam.

"You're not asleep," said Benjie.

"No," said Adam. "I'm very much awake."

Lucy looked at him carefully.

"You're Adam," she said. "You're Granny Leah's friend".

"That's right," said Adam.

Lucy was still looking intently at him.

"You look like my Grandad Bob," she decided. "I shall call you Grandad Adam."

"That would be very nice," Adam replied wondering if Lucy was aware of what she had just said.

The children went through to the dining room and into the conservatory. They were taking the toys out of the cupboard and playing quite peacefully. Adam stood up as Peter came through the door.

"Hello Dad," he said and shook hands with his father.

"Hello, Peter. Good to see you again," said Adam.

"This is my wife, Janet," Peter said as she walked into the room.

"I'm very pleased to meet you," Adam said and he held out his hand. She looked at it uncertainly and then offered a very limp handshake.

"Peter said you are now working in Oxford. Do you live there?"

"Yes, I do," Adam replied. "It's good to be back in a familiar area."

Janet looked at him curiously

"Oh. of course," she said. "You lived here before you moved up north."

He felt it was a very pointed remark and decided she might be quite a hard nut. They were interrupted by a small voice.

"I've built a house. You promised."

"Yes, I did," said Adam. "I'll come right now".

"Dinner will be ready in a minute," said Janet sharply.

"We won't be late for dinner, shall we Grandad Adam?"

"No, we mustn't be late for Granny Leah's birthday dinner."

He went into the conservatory with Lucy. They sat together on the floor and Lucy never stopped talking. Adam was really enjoying himself, especially when Lucy put her arms around his neck and said:

"I like you, Grandad Adam".

"Come along, Lucy and wash your hands," said a sharp voice. "It's time for dinner."

Adam stood up and Janet glared at him. She must have heard what Lucy did and heard what she said. He went to the kitchen to wash his hands and found Leah surrounded by plates and serving dishes. Adam was relieved to see Peter carving the chicken using the electric knife. Some of the dishes had vegetables in them.

"Shall I take these in?" asked Adam.

"Yes please," said Leah. "And could you come back for the plates?"

Adam fetched the plates and took in the other vegetables. Peter put the meat dish full of chicken in the middle of the table. Finally, Leah brought in the Yorkshire puddings and roast potatoes.

"Now help yourselves," she said and sat down at the end of the table. Peter served up Benjie's dinner and Janet looked at Lucy. Adam noticed that Janet had already helped herself to a glass of wine so he topped it up. He poured a glass for the other three adults and Leah poured some coke into the children's glasses. Adam raised his glass.

"Here's to the cook and all of her hard work to provide us with this meal!"

They all clicked their glasses and the children thought it was great fun.

Leah was relieved it had all gone smoothly. She cleaned away the dirty plates and removed all the dishes from the table. The kitchen looked like a bomb had hit it. She brought in the dishes for dessert.

"There is a trifle in the fridge and warm apple tart with ice cream," she said.

"I'll get it," said Adam quickly.

"I'll get the ice cream," Peter said. "I know where it is".

The children had a small helping of ice cream and then they were full up.

"Can we get down?" Benjie asked.

"Please" added Janet forcefully. "It's Granny Leah's table, you must ask her."

"Granny Leah may we get down please?" they asked most politely.

"Yes, you may," said Leah. "You can go and play in the conservatory. It will be Christmas and you might have some new toys."

"I'm going to write a letter to Father Christmas this time to tell him what I want," said Benjie.

"What you would like," his mother corrected him. "We can't always have what we want."

"How will Lucy tell Father Christmas what she would like?" asked Adam.

"She can't write yet," Benjie said. "She'll have to draw pictures or perhaps I could write a list for her."

"That would be a very kind thing to do for your sister," Adam said.

The children went into the playroom and the adults sat around the table.

"How is work going, Peter?" asked Adam.

"It's okay," said Peter. "The contract finishes in two months so I shall soon have to start looking for a new contract. Have you had a good week?"

"Mixed," said Adam. "Quiet beginning to the week but a frantic end."

"We all get weeks like that," said Peter. "I don't like tempting fate."

"A chip off the old block," smiled Adam. "I feel exactly the same."

"I'll go and make some coffee," said Leah, standing up.

"We must be going soon," said Janet. "I need to visit my parents. I'll go and help the children clear up their toys. I know Leah likes the place to be clean and tidy."

Adam and Peter were left sitting at the table.

"Janet seems a bit prickly," said Adam.

"She lacks confidence," said Peter. "It's her way of coping when there are new faces around. She has a chip on her shoulder that we lived in a house like this and she lived in a council house in the south of town. We live in a perfectly adequate house near Reading but she is always wanting new furniture, new clothes, the latest washing machine. She is never satisfied."

Peter sounded quite frustrated by the time he had finished and Adam felt sorry for him.

"Mother and Janet don't like each other much and I have difficulty keeping the peace sometimes. The children adore mother but I find it hard to bring them down as much as she would like."

"Maybe now I am around, they could come and stay here for a couple of nights. I am sure we could manage them together and it would give you and Janet a break. You sound as if you could do with one."

Peter was about to reply when Janet said:

"All cleared up. Time to go."

Just then Leah came in with the coffee.

"We'll drink our coffee, first," said Peter. "Then we will go."

The adults took their coffee into the lounge and the children started tinkering on the piano.

"Do you still play the piano, Leah?" asked Adam. "You played the church organ too."

"I certainly don't do that now," she said, so firmly that it surprised him and he made a mental note to ask her about it later.

They drank their coffee and then said their goodbyes.

"Have a think about my suggestion," Adam said quietly to Peter.

"Goodbye, Granny Leah!" Benjie shouted.

"Happy Birthday!" Lucy said. "Goodbye, Grandad Adam."

When they were safely in the car, Janet turned to Peter.

"Did you hear what Lucy said?"

"Of course, I heard," he replied, irritably. "After all, he is her grandad."

"He must have told her," fumed Janet. "That is out of order."

"He did not tell her," he said emphatically. "No one told her. She worked it out for herself."

For once, Janet was lost for words and Peter was glad of the silence which lasted the entire journey.

After waving the children off, Leah closed the front door. She went back into the lounge and collapsed on the settee.

"Thank goodness that went smoothly," she said. "I think everyone enjoyed their dinner."

Adam sat down beside her.

"I'm sure they did," he said soothingly. "It was all delicious and the children were very well behaved."

"It's not the children who worry me. They are delightful," she said. "It's Peter's wife. She can be difficult."

"I noticed that she didn't lift a finger to help you. Peter helped clear the table but she never moved."

"She never offers to help, not even at Christmas when there are usually nine of us around the table," Leah said. "She is pretty strict with Benjie and Lucy, whereas Peter is much more easy-going with them. She is a good mother and their house is always spotless. I wonder if their marriage is heading for trouble."

He put his arm around her and told her of his suggestion to Peter.

"That would be fun," she said. "But I doubt if Janet will allow it."

"Let's wait and see," he said. "I'll help you clear up then we can sit and relax."

They worked together to clear the table and do the washing up. The pans in the kitchen were washed up and put away in the cupboard and the leftover food was in the fridge.

"That's it for now," said Leah thankfully. "It makes such a difference having someone to help."

"Your wish is my command. Now we'll go and sit down and finish off this bottle of wine."

He found two clean glasses, picked up the bottle and followed her into the lounge. Leah curled up on the settee and Adam put his arm around her.

"I shall sleep well tonight," she said.

Adam kissed her on the forehead.

"I could improve that," he whispered. "But I haven't brought my overnight bag."

"Perhaps you should keep a spare one here?" Leah said in an innocent voice. Adam looked at her and laughed.

"You've done it again," he chuckled. "Solved a problem with a simple answer. I might just take your advice."

They sat in silence, each with their own thoughts until Adam said:

"I don't understand why your answer was so sharp when I asked you about the church organ."

"I never go to church now," she said. "I haven't been inside the place for the last ten years."

Adam was shocked at hearing this.

"But you have always been to church from when you were a child," he said. "Whatever happened?"

"It's a long story," said Leah. "But I'll cut it short for you."

She paused before she answered, then she said:

"After you left, I tried to carry on my life as before and that included playing the organ every Sunday. But as time went by, I started to lose interest and it almost became an intolerable burden. And then there was quite an influx of re-located people from London and the whole atmosphere of the church changed. It became evangelical with the emphasis on what they called 'outgoing' and I felt they were more into this than addressing the needs of the current church members. They never offered me any support through a difficult time and I became very disillusioned with the whole set up. I tried to figure out what was upsetting me until one day I realised that I didn't need to sit among a group of strangers and pretend to be one of them. I wrote a letter resigning my church membership and I never even received an acknowledgement of my letter."

"But you were brought up in a church. It was always an integral part of your life" he said in amazement.

"I know but funnily enough my background has been my strength. I was raised as a Christian and that will never change but for the first time, I recognised the true meaning of faith. You don't have to be preached at every Sunday or to be made aware of the needs of others, even if they are starving in Ethiopia, or homeless in London. Faith is always with you, it is inside you at all times and it is up to the individual to recognise it and use it wisely."

"It sounds as if it could be a life-changing experience," Adam said thoughtfully.

"I know it was. For the first time, I felt free to be myself. I could make my own decisions and not have to worry about conventional criticisms. I am lucky because I had the confidence to do it but it may not work for everyone."

"Did you talk to anyone about how you felt?"

"No, you are the only person I have told."

Adam was struggling to make sense of what he had heard. It was so unexpected and so unlike the Leah he had married.

"This is another example of how we have developed as individuals," he said. "There is so much I need to learn about the new you."

"There is so much we need to learn about each other," she said with a smile.

"I am a simple person," he said. "It won't take you long to learn everything about me."

"Don't underestimate yourself. I think you are quite a complex character and it will take me a while to work you out, but I'll get there in the end," she said confidently.

"Will that be when we are very, very good friends?"

"Most probably," said Leah and kissed him.

"I suppose I'd better be going," said Adam in a sad voice. "There's no room at this inn tonight."

"I'll make a quick cup of tea," she said, getting up off the settee. "Then your breath will smell like tea rather than wine."

She disappeared into the kitchen and soon came back with two mugs of tea.

"I've been thinking," Adam said. "I had a watershed moment a few nights ago. I suddenly started to think about the blessings in my life and I began to make a list of them in my mind."

"What is strange about that?"

"For a long time, I couldn't see anything good in my life," said Adam. "And then suddenly I realised that things were getting better and I thought of that song 'Count your Blessings' and I felt much happier after that." He drank his tea. "I really must go. Lots to do this week. What time will you be finished on Tuesday?"

"I've rearranged my lessons," she said. "I'll be finished by six o'clock."

"I'll be here on the dot. Just you and me on Tuesday. I won't forget your birthday present." He kissed her goodbye and turned to go. "I won't forget the spare overnight bag either!"

Leah waited until she heard the car drive off then she put out the lights, made sure the back door was locked and went to bed. She was so tired that she couldn't even think about the day's events. Soon she was fast asleep.

Adam went home thinking about what Leah had told him. He was astounded by her admission about the church. Ever since he first knew her, she had been closely involved in all church activities. It was because of her that he had become a church member too. Their children had attended the Sunday School and the whole family had been regular church-goers. He suddenly realised that it was years since he had even thought about the church or anything to do with religion. Once again, he reminded himself how selfish he had been, wrapped up in himself and his problems when all the time Leah had so much to cope with by herself. She must have a very strong inner strength, or faith as she calls it. He was really looking forward to making her life less stressful and that should start on Tuesday.

Before he went to bed, he rummaged through some of his boxes and found his old overnight bag. It was full of old clothes and other bits and pieces. He tipped it all into a plastic carrier then took the empty bag into his bedroom. He put it on the floor where he could see it clearly. Must not forget to take that on Tuesday, he thought.

Chapter Thirteen

Adam knew that the next week was going to be very busy. As soon as he reached his office, he called Sally in.

"Have you sorted out my appointments for today?"

"Yes," she replied. "You have two meetings this morning and none after lunch."

"Thank you, that's fine. There is something that I must do this afternoon. Now could you please ask Barry to come in when he is free?"

It was half an hour before Barry arrived.

"Sorry to have taken so long," he said. "The computers were playing up again."

"Call the engineers and get them to check the whole system," said Adam. "This is happening too often."

Barry made a note of that order, then asked:

"How was your weekend?"

"Sunday was an interesting day. There was a family lunch to celebrate Leah's birthday. I get on very well with Peter but I found his wife hard work. The children were delightful. Lucy is only three years old but she decided to call me Grandad Adam."

"You don't look old and wrinkled enough to be a grandfather," Barry said with a laugh.

"Thank you very much," Adam said wryly. "Flattery will get you nowhere. Now down to business. Have you completed the transfer of Leah's house?"

"Yes, it is all ready for you. The deeds are in my office."

"Can you bring them to me? It is Leah's birthday tomorrow and I want to give them to her as part of her birthday present."

Part of her present? Thought Barry, wondering what else Adam was giving her.

At that moment, Adam's phone rang and Sally said:

"There's a Mr Flack on the phone. He wants to speak to you."

"Good morning Mr Flack," said Adam.

"Good morning to you Mr Richards," he replied in a cheery voice. "I have some good news for you. The vendors have accepted your revised offer but they require a ten per cent deposit in order to confirm the deal."

"That can be arranged," said Adam. "My solicitor will contact you in the next day or two. He will deal with all the necessary paperwork. Thank you very much, Mr Flack." He put the phone down. "That's another thing to tick off my list," he said in a satisfied way. "I have no appointments this afternoon and I shall be out of the office for a couple of hours. I have some shopping to do. I'll let you know when I am back and you can bring me the deeds then."

"Right," said Barry and stood up, looking straight at Adam. "I'm still a bit confused about our conversation at the pub. Did you say that you would accept the area manager's job and I could be promoted to manager?"

"That's exactly what I said but it is all confidential information at present. I have until the end of the week to let Mr West know my decision and I'll probably phone him on Thursday. Please don't say a word to anyone about this, not even Jen."

"I can keep a secret," said Barry.

"I know. I discovered that on Saturday."

Barry gave him a sheepish look and left the room.

Both of Adam's clients arrived on time and their business was soon completed. When they had gone, he took the solicitor's card out of his drawer. He dialled the number and asked to speak to Mr Truscot. Adam told him that he intended to buy a house and asked if he would do the conveyancing for it. Mr Truscot agreed and he arranged to meet on Wednesday morning at eleven o'clock. Adam asked Sally to write that in his diary and then sat back in his chair. It had been a busy but fruitful morning. He had the feeling that the pieces of his life were beginning to fit together like a jigsaw puzzle.

He left his office and told Sally that he would be away for the next two hours. He tapped his coat pocket to make sure that he had his notebook with him. He sat in the window seat of his favourite café where he had a good view of the jeweller's shop. The staff in the café were beginning to know him. One of the girls came over and said:

"The usual, Mr Richards?"

Adam smiled at her.

"Yes please," he said. "What's your name?"

"It's Bridget," she replied. "I come from Holland."

She went off to get Adam's order and soon came back with the coffee and ham roll.

"Thank you, Bridget," he said with a smile and she looked pleased.

When he had finished, he crossed the road and rang the bell on the door of the jeweller's shop. The same young man came to unlock it.

"Good afternoon, Mr Richards. Please come in."

Adam entered the shop and the assistant took his place behind the counter. He took out the small selection of rings which he had shown Adam previously.

"Would you like to see a further collection, sir?"

"No, I don't think so," said Adam. "I really like the solitaire I saw the other day."

He pointed it out. The assistant picked it up and handed it to Adam.

"If you take it to the door, you will see how the sunlight sparkles on the different facets of the stone."

Adam stepped into a patch of sunlight and immediately the stone sprang into life, convincing him beyond doubt that this was the one. When he told the assistant, he replied:

"Very good, sir, but we need to find out if it fits your friend's finger."

"Of course," smiled Adam.

He took out his notebook, opened it at the appropriate page and showed the assistant the picture of the outline of the ring.

"I will just check the size of this particular ring," he said. "Then I can check the size against your sketch. The size is marked R," he continued. "This is an average size for a lady's engagement finger. I will check it with your picture."

He placed the ring on top of Adam's diagram. It fitted exactly.

"Would you say that is a good omen?" smiled Adam.

"It is indeed fortuitous," the young man said seriously.

Adam looked at the ring again. He imagined Leah wearing it and he felt confident that it was the right one. The only thing he hadn't looked at was the price.

"That ring is eight hundred and eighty-five pounds but with the ten per cent discount, it will cost eight hundred."

About eight times as much as her first engagement ring cost thought Adam but she is worth every penny.

"I'll take it," he said and paid for it with his credit card.

"Would you like it gift-wrapped, sir?"

"Yes please."

"That will take five minutes, sir," said the young man. "That gives us time to complete the paperwork."

Ten minutes' later, Adam left the shop. The ring was safely in his pocket. Only one more thing to get, he thought and headed to the nearest card shop. He remembered that Leah would be fifty-one but decided not to risk it and chose a card with a mother cat lying on a rug while her four kittens were bouncing around her.

Barry saw Adam return to the office and noticed that he was not carrying any parcels or packages and wondered if he hadn't found what he was looking for. He decided to go and get the deeds so that Leah would have one nice present at least. He collected the deeds which were in a large brown envelope and took them to Adam.

"I've brought the deeds," he said. "Would you like me to gift wrap them?" he added with a grin.

"I don't think that will be necessary," said Adam. "I think it is much more intriguing to have a big brown envelope as a birthday present rather than something wrapped in shiny paper."

"I'm beginning to feel sorry for Leah even though it is her birthday," Barry said. "Imagine her reaction when she is presented with a brown paper parcel?"

"Don't you think that giving her a house is a good enough present?"

"I think it is a superb present," Barry said quickly. "But I also know how ladies expect their presents to be expensively wrapped with all the trimmings."

"Then perhaps she will like this?" Adam said and produced a small package from his pocket. It was beautifully wrapped and tied with a gold ribbon.

"That's exactly what I mean," Barry said enthusiastically. Then he stopped and stared at Adam. "Is that what I think it is?" he said hesitantly.

"It depends what you think it is," teased Adam. "But you won't know until after Tuesday."

He put it back in his pocket and Barry left Adam's office thinking to himself how lucky he was to have such a good boss who was also his friend.

Adam spent the evening in a reflective frame of mind. It had been a most satisfactory day and he was beginning to understand what it meant to count one's blessings. Leah talked about her faith and perhaps he was beginning to feel his faith in the future returning.

On Tuesday morning, Adam was up early. He wanted to phone Leah before she went to work. He pressed her number and she answered almost immediately.

"I just thought I would give you a good start to your special day," he said cheerfully. "Happy Birthday Leah, from your very good friend who loves you very much."

"Thank you!" Leah said with a laugh. "I'm really lucky to have a very good friend like you. I love you too and I can't wait until six o'clock comes."

"I'll bring your present with me."

"That will be nice," said Leah. "But you are my present. Just bring yourself."

"I'll be there," he assured her and ended the call.

Fortunately, he was busy all that morning with clients but when things quietened down after lunch he sent for Barry.

"Did you contact the technical department about the trouble with the computers?" he asked.

"Yes," said Barry. "They are sending someone to look at it tomorrow morning."

"I've been thinking," Adam said. "If the first floor is going to be turned into an office for me then we shall need a lot more technical equipment. When you meet this guy make some casual enquiries about upgrading the whole system to include extra offices upstairs."

"I'll do that but I think I need to go and have a look up there first."

"Why don't we both go and have a look right now? I'll just tell Sally where I shall be for the next half an hour."

"I'll tell my secretary," Barry said. "And I'll meet you at the bottom of the stairs."

Before long, they were climbing the stairs to the first floor.

"Have you had a look at what is up here, Barry?"

"When we first moved in, I had a quick look but I haven't been up since."

They stood at the top of the stairs and looked around. The whole floor was open in front of them; none of it had been divided up into smaller sections. There were quite a few old boxes in one corner but otherwise, it was quite empty.

"A proper blank canvas," Adam said. "The planners should have no trouble in converting it into whatever we want."

"Have you any ideas about that?"

"I haven't given it much thought yet," Adam replied. "I shall need an office and a variety of small offices for secretaries, storerooms, staff rooms, etc. I should also have a comfortable communal area where visitors can relax."

"If you do accept the job when would you expect to start it?"

"Almost immediately I suppose. The first thing I would have to do is go up to Birmingham and sort out the offices up there. I assume James Brown's secretary is still employed. I certainly hope so because I have a feeling that everything is in a bit of a mess."

Barry thought for a moment.

"Does that mean that I shall be promoted at the same time?"

"I am not sure how it will be organised but if I have anything to do with it, the answer is yes," Adam replied.

"We shall need a new assistant manager."

"I suppose we shall. Have you anyone in mind?"

"Not really," said Barry. "But I'll have a think about it."

"We should be able to manage between ourselves for a few weeks," Adam said. "I should only be away for the odd day or two. There's no reason why we can't continue as we are now. The only difference is that you will be earning a manager's salary."

"That will certainly help to pay the mortgage," Barry said with a grin.

"Talking of mortgages, I am seeing a solicitor tomorrow morning. He is doing all the paperwork regarding my apartment. I will give him your name as the contact for the mortgage and can you let me know how much I can borrow."

"Does Leah know you are buying that apartment?" Barry asked.

"No, and I'm not telling her. I'm keeping it as a surprise."

"I hope Leah hasn't got a dodgy heart," Barry said. "All these surprises could give her heart failure."

"She'll get over it," Adam said confidently. "But I'll let you know in the morning if she has survived."

They went back down the stairs.

"I'm going home early today, Barry. I have an important date this evening."

"Good luck, Adam. Wish Leah a happy birthday from me."

On the way home, Adam called in at the shop and bought two bottles of wine. He packed his spare overnight bag and put the deeds and the birthday card in it. He checked in his pocket that he had the ring and left the house.

He arrived at Leah's house just as she was saying goodbye to her last student. He waited in the car until the other car was driven off then he collected the wine and his bag and went to the front door. He let himself in with his key and put the wine on the hall table.

Leah heard him come in and she came out of the kitchen. Adam clasped her in his arms.

"Happy Birthday, Leah! I love you more than I can say."

Leah looked at him with tears in her eyes.

"This will be my best birthday ever because you are here."

"I'll make sure of that," he said and kissed her.

Just at that moment, the phone rang.

"I'd better answer it," Leah said and picked it up. "Thomas!" she cried. "How lovely to hear from you."

Adam left her talking to their son and carried his bag up to the bedroom. He found the brown envelope and Leah's birthday card and took it downstairs and put it on the coffee table. Leah was still on the phone so he moved the wine from the hall table and put it in the fridge. Then he went into the lounge and looked at the birthday cards which were displayed on the mantlepiece. There was one from Jen and Barry and several from people he did not know. Benjie and Lucy had each made their own cards. Peter and Janet had sent a card and there was one other which he noticed. He took it down and looked inside it. It said 'Happy Birthday Mum. With love from Alice.'

Adam found it rather odd that there was no mention of her children or husband. He realised that Leah had said very little about Alice and he wondered why. Then he heard Leah put the phone down and she came into the room looking happy.

"That was Thomas," she said. "And Harriet was there as well. It was lovely to talk to them and say thank you for the flowers they sent me."

She sat on the settee next to Adam and he picked up the birthday card and gave it to her.

"Another one to add to your collection," he said with a smile.

Leah opened it and after she had read it, she looked at Adam.

"That is not the sort of message I usually have in my birthday cards," she said in a stern voice.

"I am not the sort of visitor you usually have on your birthday I suspect."

"My friends' cards all say Happy Birthday or Have a good day. I've never had a card from a very, very good friend. I can't imagine what it means," she said thoughtfully.

"I am sure we can work it out between us," he replied.

But Leah wasn't really listening. She had picked up the brown envelope and was looking at it curiously.

"Where did this come from?"

"It's your birthday present," Adam said casually.

"My birthday present? In a brown paper envelope?"

"It is a recycled brown paper envelope."

Leah was turning it over in her hands. It felt quite bulky.

"What is inside it?" she asked.

"Why don't you see for yourself?"

She opened the envelope and pulled out a wad of papers. The top one had a sort of inscription on it which started with the words 'Herein are legal deeds for the owner of…'

Leah stopped reading at that point and looked at Adam in disbelief.

"What does it mean?" she stammered.

"It means that you will have no more mortgage payments because this house now belongs to you."

Leah was completely lost for words.

"I know exactly how much you have paid over the last twelve years so I decided to make things right. I have paid off the mortgage and the house is in your name only."

"But you can't do that," Leah stammered.

"I have done it," Adam said firmly. "It will give you security and it has eased my conscience."

"It must have cost you a lot of money."

"You are worth every penny," said Adam as he kissed her.

"Thank you, seems perfectly inadequate," Leah said slowly. "But I do thank you from the bottom of my heart."

She could feel the tears welling up inside her and she buried her head on Adam's shoulder.

"I don't really know what to say," she sobbed.

"You don't have to say anything. You've said thank you and that is enough."

"I think I am suffering from shock. I can't stop shaking."

"I know the cure for that," he said. "You just stay there."

He went into the kitchen and came back with a bottle of wine and two glasses. He poured it out and gave one glass to Leah.

"A birthday toast," he said. "From one very good friend to another."

Leah drank her wine and looked at Adam.

"That was not an act of a very good friend," she said softly. "Only a very, very good friend could do what you have done."

Adam was stunned.

"Do you mean that?" he asked.

"I think the fuse has reached its destination and is about to light the flame," Leah answered. "That's how I feel but I don't know how you feel about it?"

This time it was Adam who couldn't find the words. He sat and looked at Leah with tears in his eyes.

"Does that mean that you can forgive me?" he asked, eventually.

"It is not a question of forgiveness. The past has gone by. It is more acceptance of the present and of the way we have both changed. I loved you as you were when we were first married. I wasn't sure if I loved the new you, that's why I needed time. Now I am certain that I love you as much, if not more than I did then," and she put her arms around him and kissed him.

Now it was Adam's turn to find the right words. He swallowed hard before he spoke.

"I have always loved you but I was never sure of your reaction after the way I treated you. But you have been so gentle and kind. You have listened to me and helped me understand how to move forward in my life. I haven't enough words to say how much I love you but I will do everything I can to make you happy. You are the most precious thing in my life." He put his arms around her and they sat there in perfect contentment. It was Adam who broke the silence.

"I think it is time for another birthday gift," he said.

"What do you mean by that?" Leah asked. "You've already given me my present."

Adam reached into his pocket and brought out the gift-wrapped box. He gave it to Leah.

"This comes with all my love."

Leah took the box and undid the ribbon; then she removed the wrapping paper. She looked at the small black box which was lying in her hand. She knew exactly what was in it. Adam was watching her closely. He could wait no longer.

"Open it."

She opened the box and gasped.

"Adam, it's beautiful!" she said.

He lifted the ring out of its box and took hold of Leah's hand. He slipped the ring on to her finger and it fitted perfectly.

"This is our new beginning," he said with a voice full of emotion. "Now we can look forward to spending the rest of our lives together, even if it is in different houses," he added with a smile.

"Adam you are too good to me and too generous. How can I ever repay you?" she cried.

"You have already repaid me. We are now very, very good friends and that opens up the opportunity for many different kinds of presents."

Leah was looking at her ring and finally said:

"I've never had a ring like this before. It is about five times as big as my original engagement ring. I shall always treasure it."

"That's because I love you five times as much," Adam said as he kissed her. "I think another toast is called for," and he refilled their glasses.

"My turn," said Leah as she raised her glass. "A toast to my kind and generous husband for making this such a special day."

They drank the toast and then Adam said in a surprised voice:

"Do you know that is the first time you have called me your husband?"

"I guess that's because tonight is the first time that I have recognised the new you as my husband. I have thought of you as a friend while I have been trying to understand you. I don't think you realise how much you have changed."

"I don't think you have changed much," he said. "You were always a confident and capable wife and mother. Even as a teenager, I know you did amazing things. I think the biggest change for you is your calmness and positive attitude to life whatever it throws at you."

"What you see on the surface doesn't always reflect what is happening underneath," she said. "You get into the habit of hiding your real feelings of loneliness and frustration when there is no-one to share them with."

Adam put his hands around Leah's face.

"Look at me?" he said. "And promise that you will share everything with me, even your darkest thoughts."

"I promise," said Leah. "But you must promise me the same."

"I promise," he said and he kissed her. "Let's finish the bottle and drink to that," he said as he filled their glasses.

Leah lay back in Adam's arms and yawned.

"I'm feeling a bit woozy," she said. "I'm not used to the combination of wine and excitement. Time for bed I think."

"You go up and I'll make sure the back door is locked and the window is shut. We don't want any unexpected visitors tonight," he teased.

Leah went upstairs and got ready for bed. She went straight into the back room. I don't think I need to make any excuses for being here tonight, she said to herself. She heard Adam come up and go into the bathroom. When he came through the bedroom door he pretended to be surprised.

"What are you doing in my bed?" he asked.

"Waiting for my husband to join me," Leah replied coyly.

"I can't disappoint my wife," Adam quickly said and slid under the duvet.

"Now what happens?" Leah asked in an innocent voice.

Adam thought for a moment then he said:

"I've got a good idea. It is still your birthday, so why don't I give you a third present?"

Leah turned towards him.

"I think I would like that," she whispered.

He clasped her to him as if uniting their very souls.

"I'm there with you," he said.

The flame has been well and truly lit, he thought and felt he was now the happiest man in the world.

Chapter Fourteen

The next morning Adam was up early. He needed to go home before he went into work. Leah woke as he was getting dressed. He kissed her and said:

"I'll ring you this evening."

"Yes," murmured Leah as she turned over and went back to sleep.

Adam left quietly and was soon back in his own house. He made himself a cup of tea and sat on his settee to think about the events of last evening. He had enjoyed surprising Leah with her presents but the third present was the biggest surprise of all. That was not something he had anticipated; it had put their relationship on an entirely different level. They had accepted each other in a way, they had both changed and now they could support each other and move forward together.

He arrived at work in a very cheerful mood. Barry saw him arrive and followed him into his office. He looked at Adam and laughed.

"You look like the cat that got the cream," he said, "Did Leah enjoy her presents?"

"Yes, she did," Adam said with a grin on his face. "We both enjoyed the presents."

Barry just managed to stop himself asking Adam what he meant by that comment. Instead, he asked:

"And was the ring the right size?"

"Of course, it was," Adam said. "I measured it before I bought it. Would you like to see a picture of it?"

He showed Barry a photo from the jeweller's catalogue.

"That's a solitaire diamond!" Barry said in amazement. "No wonder Leah was pleased with it. By the way, I have been instructed to invite you for supper on Saturday. Jen is going to speak with Leah." He looked at the photograph again. "I look forward to seeing the real thing then."

"Thank you for the invitation," Adam said. "I'm sure we will both be pleased to accept it. Now down to business. Have you worked out how much I can borrow? I am seeing a solicitor this morning and shall need to give him some figures."

"Yes, I have it here," Barry said and handed him the paper.

"That's a very generous amount," Adam said. "I don't think I shall need all that."

Barry looked at him in surprise.

"You are the first person who has ever said that to me. Usually, people expect a larger offer."

Adam looked at Barry and smiled.

"Thank you for working it out," he said. "It is good to know that I shall be solvent after I've paid for the apartment."

Barry stood up to leave but then he said:

"Don't forget that as an employee you will get a special discount."

"Every little helps," Adam replied with a straight face.

Barry left the office chuckling to himself. Sally saw him pass her office. The boss must be in a good mood this morning, she thought, wondering what he did at the weekend. Just then Adam's voice came over the intercom:

"Can you come into my office, Sally?"

She collected her notebook and diary and knocked on Adam's door.

"Come in," he said and Sally entered.

"I have an appointment for eleven-thirty at my solicitors," he said. "His office is just up the road, so I shouldn't be long. What else have I booked in for today?"

"You have an appointment at ten o'clock," she said. "And there is someone coming at eleven-thirty about the computers."

"Barry will deal with that," he said. "But it might be a good idea for me to join in the conversation. Tell Barry that I will join them when I get back from the solicitor. What about this afternoon?"

"You have two appointments but you should be finished by three-thirty."

"Good. Tell Barry I want to see him in my office at a quarter to four.

How are you getting on with sorting out those old files?"

"I'm slowly getting them done," Sally answered.

"I think you had better make it a priority. We may need some extra office space quite soon."

"Very well," Sally said. "Could I have one of the junior staff to help me?"

"Yes, of course, you can. Arrange it with Barry"

"Thank you," she said and went back to her office.

Five minutes later the phone rang.

"Your client is here," she said. "I'll bring him in."

Adam spent half an hour discussing a business transaction and when the man had left, he decided to go to the staff room to make himself a cup of coffee. There were two other members of staff in there and they were quite surprised to see him.

"Good morning Mr Richards," said one. "We don't often see you in here."

"No, my secretary usually gets my coffee but she is busy. Now how do I work this machine?"

The girl smiled at Adam.

"Would you like me to do it for you?"

"That is very kind of you. Milk and one sugar please?" he said with a smile.

He sat down at a table with the two girls and they all chatted together. Suddenly one of the girls looked at her watch and gasped.

"Look at the time. We should have been back ten minutes ago. Mr Wilson won't be pleased," and stood up to leave the room.

"Tell him you were talking to me," Adam said with a glint in his eye. "That should make it alright."

"He's nice," said one girl to the other.

Adam returned to his office and told Sally that he was going to see his solicitor.

"I shall be about half an hour. Did you tell Barry that I would join him when I get back?"

"Yes," Sally answered. "He said he would probably be upstairs. I've never been up there."

"It's just a big empty space at present. We are exploring different possible uses for it."

He collected his papers he needed and walked up the street to Mr Truscot's offices. The solicitor was waiting for him and they soon got down to business.

"It all seems quite straightforward," Mr Truscot said. "Have you a date in mind for completion?"

Adam thought for a minute.

"I have to give one month's notice on the place I am renting. I think I will do that next week. I do have somewhere to stay if necessary but I would like to be in before Christmas."

"I understand the property is vacant," Mr Truscot said. "And that there is no chain. Assuming that the legal side does not encounter any problems, I would expect it to be completed early in December. In the meantime, I will keep you informed about developments."

"Thank you very much," Adam said as he shook his hand. "It is a pleasure to do business with you."

As he walked back down the street, he thought he would have to tell Leah soon and ask if he could stay with her for a couple of weeks if necessary. He returned to his office and checked with Sally in case there had been any phone calls.

"Just one," said Sally. "Head Office has been on the phone. Mr Dominic West wanted to speak with you. I said that you would ring him when you were back."

"Thank you, Sally. Give me five minutes then see if he is available."

Five minutes later, his phone rang.

"I have Mr West on the line."

"Put him through," said Adam. "Good morning, Mr West."

"Good morning, Adam. This is just a quick call to ask if you have thought about our conversation last Friday?"

"Yes, I've thought about it and fully intended to phone you tomorrow to give you my decision. If the offer of area managers post is still available, I would like to accept it. But I would like to have further discussions with you regarding certain details."

"That's good. That's very good. I am pleased with your decision. I know you will do a first-rate job. Your most immediate problem will be to sort out the mess in the Birmingham office."

"There is one important thing which I need to know, Mr West and that is the date when the appointment begins?"

"As far as I am concerned, it starts today," Mr West replied. "But I suppose there will have to be paperwork involved, contracts etc… I will get my secretary to do that at once. It should be completed by the end of this week."

"I would prefer to wait until it is all signed and sealed," Adam said. "But in the meantime, I do need to have a clearer picture of what it entails and I need to think about the new offices we shall have here."

Mr West thought for a minute, realising this man drives a hard bargain.

"We need to arrange a meeting to iron out the details. I could do with leaving the noise and smoke of London for a few hours. I will come to Oxford on Friday at 2 pm. Is that convenient for you?"

"Yes, that's fine," Adam said. "I look forward to seeing you."

On his way upstairs, Adam called in to see Sally.

"I hope I have no appointments from two o'clock on Friday," he said.

"No, Friday afternoon is free," she said, looking at the diary.

"Good. Mr West will be coming to see me at two o'clock on Friday. Make a note of that please."

Sally wrote it in the diary and then looked enquiringly at Adam.

"We have some business to discuss and I will tell you about it next week," Adam told her and he went off to find Barry.

Sally wondered what was going on. Obviously, something important for the chairman to visit them twice in two weeks.

Adam found Barry upstairs with the computer engineer.

"How is it going?" he asked. "Have you reached any conclusions?"

"I've given Geoff a rough idea of how we might use this space but I'll leave him to explain the technical details," Barry said.

"Let's go down to my office and talk about it over a cup of coffee?" said Adam and the other two men agreed.

"Three cups of coffee please, Sally," Adam called out as they passed her office.

When the coffee had arrived, Adam turned to Barry.

"What are we going to need if we turn that floor into an office suite?"

"I've given Geoff an idea of the number of offices we would like to turn it into, but he can explain the equipment we should need."

"I have had a good look at the computers which your main office is using at the moment," said Geoff. "And taking into account the amount of business you do in this branch, they need an urgent update and a complete reorganisation of the internal communications systems. With regards to offices on the first floor, I can't be sure what you will need until I see the plans. All I know at this stage is that it will be a major undertaking."

"Would it be one system for the two floors, or would there be separate systems?" Adam asked.

"That would depend on the use of the new offices. If it is simply an extension of the current work of the branch then one system would be sufficient. But if the new offices are to be used in a way which needed extra security, then it would need a completely different system. I will send you my report by the end of this week."

"Thank you," said Adam.

He and Barry shook the man's hand and he left the office.

"That was a useful meeting," said Barry. "There was a lot of technical jargon which I found hard to take on board so it will be really helpful to see it written down."

"Talking of boards," said Adam. "I've had a phone call phone from

Dominic West. I told him that I would accept the job and he is coming here on Friday at two o'clock to discuss the way forward."

"Two meetings in two weeks plus your meeting in London? He doesn't waste time, does he?"

"I mustn't waste time either," Adam said decisively. "We must get together and make a list of what we need. If we do it together, we shall be less likely to forget anything important."

"I'll see you at quarter to four," Barry said. "We can make a start. By the way, two of the girls were late returning from their coffee break this morning. I asked them the reason and was told that they had been chatting to you. I hope you are not going to upset the smooth running of this establishment by chatting up the female staff?"

"Sorry," said Adam with his tongue in his cheek.

He called Sally and asked her to go and buy a sandwich for his lunch.

"You'd better check that we have the right sort of biscuits for Friday, too," he added.

His first appointment wasn't until two o'clock and he was looking forward to having a quiet hour when he could start to think about the offices upstairs. Sally came back with his lunch and Adam told her that he didn't want to be disturbed for the next hour.

He was determined to get a clear idea of what the layout of the new office would be. Being upstairs, they would need a disabled access, possibly a lift. He would need an office space big enough to take files from a large number of branches since he would be responsible for the West Country plus Devon and Cornwall. He paused as the enormity of the job suddenly hit him. It was going to be a mammoth task and he could see himself doing a great deal of travelling. He would need an efficient secretary and he hoped that would be Sally. If they had a receptionist in the communal area, that would take some pressure off her and he knew he would need extra office staff to deal with general correspondence, not to mention a coffee machine in the new staff room. He smiled to himself. What a challenge, he thought but he knew he was ready for it. He thought of Leah when she had said there would be challenges ahead and she was right as usual but he didn't think she had this particular challenge in mind. He knew exactly how he was going to approach it but first, he would have to convince Dominic West that he was confident of success.

He paused again. Three months ago, he wouldn't even have considered it, but since Leah had come back into his life, he felt capable of anything with her support. However, he still felt nervous about telling her he was buying the apartment.

"Your first client is here," said Sally over the intercom.

"Show him in please, Sally," said Adam, quickly tidying his desk.

Adam was busy for the next hour and a half but all the business was concluded without any problems. He passed the relevant files to Sally for her to complete the paperwork and before long, there was a knock at the door and Barry came in carrying two cups of coffee and a brand-new file.

"You look as if you mean business," said Adam.

"I have a feeling this file will soon be bulging with information," he said. "So, I thought I would get it started this afternoon."

"Have you written anything in it yet?" asked Adam.

"Just one or two thoughts," Barry replied. "I didn't have much time to sit and think. The office has been so busy."

"We are going to have to consider taking on more staff, Barry. But the most urgent thing is this meeting on Friday. We only have one and a half days to make a list of questions which need to be answered and we mustn't miss anything out. I have started to think about it," and he showed Barry the observations which he had written down.

"That's a good start," Barry said. "With regards to the dimensions of the offices, the planners will decide that."

"Yes, they will," Adam said. "But I shall make it clear that I don't want any poky little places. I want as much light and space as possible."

"It might be possible to look at the downstairs offices at the same time in order to make them more open?" Barry said. "I see you are hoping to keep Sally as your secretary. Does that mean that I shall be able to offer a promotion to my secretary?"

"If you think she can do the job, I see no reason why you can't offer it to her."

"She's very competent and we work well together. I'm sure she could do it." Barry replied.

"Remember this is all confidential until it is officially signed and sealed so be careful not to drop any hints," said Adam. "I haven't told Sally about it yet."

"The other burning question is when do these promotions take effect, Adam?"

"Mr West told me that the paperwork should be completed by the end of this week so maybe he will bring it down with him on Friday. So, it could start as early as next Monday. I shall have to use my office for the area manager's work as a temporary base, so most of the files in here will have to come to your office. Will you have room for them?"

"It will be a tight squeeze but we will manage."

"If this building work goes ahead as we want it to there is going to be a lot of disruption. When everything is finalised then we will tell the staff what is happening and ask for their patience and co-operation. I think that is enough to think about for now. We will meet again tomorrow and probably add more questions to the list."

"It is nearly closing time," Barry said. "I'll just go and check that everything is okay. I'll see you in the morning."

Adam didn't leave the office immediately. He sat in his chair and thought about how conscientious Barry was and that he would make a good manager. However, he wondered if Barry realised just how much extra responsibility he would have? It seems that he would be out of the office quite a lot so Barry's workload would increase. Adam made a mental note to support him and not dictate to him.

He collected up his papers and put them in his briefcase. It had been a busy and eventful day. He decided to phone Leah this evening but not tell her about the apartment until the weekend. On the way home, he stopped to buy himself some bread, milk and a few microwave dinners. He had been so busy all day that he hadn't had time to think about food. He also bought some more beers and after eating his dinner, he settled down on the settee. He had a lot of thinking to do but the first thing on his mind was to phone Leah. He dialled her number and she answered almost immediately.

"That was quick," Adam said. "Were you sitting on the phone?"

"No, I was sitting by the phone," she said. "I've just finished teaching and I was having a rest."

"Have you had a busy day?"

"No busier than usual," she said. "The most difficult thing was coming down to earth after the excitement of having a birthday."

"You needn't have just one birthday a year you know," Adam said with a laugh. "I'm sure there will be plenty of opportunities for more presents and surprises. You'll just have to get used to them."

"I'll do my best but I hope you have some surprises for you, too. By the way, Jen has invited us for supper on Saturday evening. She said that Barry was going to mention it to you."

"He has asked me and I told him that I was sure we'd be delighted to enjoy Jen's home cooking," Adam said. "Will you let her know?"

"Yes, I'll tell her," she said. "In spite of your loaded slur on my efforts."

Adam laughed.

"I'll be with you on Saturday afternoon. I love you."

"I love you too," she said and put the phone down.

Adam settled down to think about the implications of his new job and the visit of Dominic West. He knew he had to have a clear idea of the alterations needed to the office upstairs. He felt grateful that he could have a purpose-built office suite and he wouldn't forget the improvements on the main floor. The communication system within the building would be greatly improved and they would all have to get used to the latest technology. His first problem would be sorting out the Birmingham office and transferring all the files down here. Then he would need a list of all the branch offices he would be responsible for and send them all details of how they could contact him. Sally was going to be kept busy with all of that and she would need some help. Barry's secretary could deal with all the business side of the office but it looked like they would have to recruit more staff. It promised to be a very busy time and on top of all that, he was moving house.

He needed a drink and went to the kitchen for a beer. When he returned to the lounge, he rested his head on the back of the settee and closed his eyes. He went to sleep and woke up half an hour later with a stiff neck. He rubbed it with his hand and thought how he wished Leah was there. He remembered he would have to tell her about the apartment at the weekend and decided Sunday would be best.

He thought all its modern furniture wasn't quite his style. He preferred a bit of comfort, surrounded by familiar things. He would definitely need Leah's help. His decision to donate his own furniture to charity might need to be reversed. The solicitor would check that the building was in good order but now he felt he needed to take a closer look at the furniture and would arrange that for next weekend when hopefully Leah could come with him.

Chapter Fifteen

As Adam drove into work the next morning, he anticipated another busy day ahead but the priority was to confer with Barry about the way forward. The main office was quiet when he arrived and he went straight to Barry's office.

"We need to talk," he said. "Can you come to me as soon as possible?"

"I'll just check that everything is running smoothly," Barry answered. "Then I'll be with you."

Adam spoke to Sally as he passed her office.

"Barry will be coming down to see me in a few minutes. Do I have any appointments this morning?"

"You have one at eleven o'clock and two this afternoon," said Sally.

"Can you hold any calls until we have finished and tell Barry's secretary to do the same?" he said and walked on into his office.

Sally knew something secret was going on. Adam had assured her he would explain everything next week and she could tell it was important. She spoke to Barry's secretary but she knew nothing either.

Barry came into Adam's office.

"Everything is okay," he said. "But I think we may soon need to take on more staff."

"I have already thought of that," Adam said. "And that is one of the first things we must do as soon as everything is confirmed."

He then explained to Barry the thoughts which he had the previous evening.

"I want to be absolutely clear in my own mind what I need to discuss with Mr West. Is there anything more you have thought about?"

"There is one thing, Adam. It is a question about the appointment of a new assistant manager. Should we promote within the branch or should we advertise in the company magazine?"

"My feeling is that we should advertise it. If there is anyone who already works here, they would be at liberty to apply. The staff here all work together in a very professional way so we would have to be careful to appoint someone with the same work ethic."

"Would it be possible to appoint on the basis of a three-month probation period?" Barry asked.

"I don't think that is general practice but I see no reason why it can't be done that way. The decision will ultimately be yours."

"But you would have to okay it," said Barry.

"I could have an input if you wanted me to but you would do the interviewing and make the recommendation," Adam said. "There is one more thing which is on my mind. A couple of weeks ago we mentioned the possibility of having a training department for the sixth form students."

"Yes, I remember, but you said that it was something for the future."

"Well, I suppose this is for the future from when we first talked about it," Adam said.

"Are you saying that you consider two weeks difference to constitute a future?" Barry asked in amazement. "You're surely not thinking of organising that right now?"

"I'm not thinking of doing anything about the academic side of it right now, but I did wonder if it might be possible to include a small lecture room in the plans for upstairs. It would also double as a conference centre for area managers to meet together to discuss any problems and put forward new ideas."

"I think it is an excellent plan," Barry said with enthusiasm. "Are you going to run it by Mr West?"

"Yes, I am," said Adam. "If he agrees it will be the first of its kind in the country. I am going to ask for everything that we have discussed, Barry. I feel confident that our ideas will be good for the company as a whole and it will be interesting to see if they fit in with the thoughts of some of the elderly Board Members."

"It will be an exciting time but it will also mean a lot of hard work. It will be a tremendous challenge, but you obviously feel up to it," Barry said.

"Six months ago, I wouldn't even have dreamed about it," said

Adam. "But the fact that Leah and I are together again has woken me up to what life can offer. I must admit that I feel confident about the future but I am relying on you to stop me if I get too cocky."

"I think that we will both rise to the challenges which face us and we will succeed."

At that moment the phone rang and Sally said:

"Your eleven o'clock appointment is here."

"Barry is just leaving," he said and he turned towards him. "One more discussion tomorrow morning and by the end of the day we shall know."

Adam was busy for the rest of the morning and at lunchtime, he decided to get some fresh air. He walked up to his favourite bistro and ordered lunch from Bridget, the waitress. On the way back, he called in the market and bought two pots of hyacinths which should flower at Christmas time, one for Jen and one for Leah. The rest of the afternoon passed quickly and by five o'clock he was on his way home.

He spent the evening thinking about tomorrow's discussion with Dominic West. He decided to make a note of the main points which he wanted finalised. He may be the Chairman, he thought but we must respect each other's views. He prepared himself not to expect him to agree with everything they were asking for.

On Friday morning, he was up early ready to face the challenges ahead. When he arrived at work, he left his briefcase in the office and went up the stairs to the first floor. He looked around him at the big empty space which was exactly the same size as the office downstairs. He pictured it as a totally different area. He wanted it to be a friendly place as well as a business place. He stood there imagining what it would be like until his thoughts were interrupted by Barry.

"There you are. I saw your briefcase in the office but couldn't find you anywhere."

"I was daydreaming," he said. "A last flight of imagination before I find out what the future could be like."

"Let's go and have a cup of coffee?" Barry said soothingly.

Adam looked at him and smiled.

"I said you might have to bring me down to earth," he said. "But I didn't think it would be so soon."

They went downstairs and Barry went off to get the coffees. Adam said good morning to Sally and asked her about his appointments for the morning.

"You have two clients," she said. "One at eleven o'clock and the other forty-five minutes later."

"I should be finished by twelve-thirty then," Adam said. "That will give me time for a sandwich before Mr West arrives."

"I'll go and get your sandwiches soon," said Sally. "And I'll make sure the coffee and biscuits are ready."

"Thank you, Sally," he said.

Barry came back and the two men disappeared into Adam's office. They sat facing each other across the desk.

"Are you feeling nervous?" asked Barry.

"I'm not nervous about meeting Dominic West," Adam said. "In fact, I am relieved that it is here and not in Head Office. I find that place quite intimidating. I am just hoping that we haven't been too ambitious in our plans for this place."

"Nothing ventured, nothing gained," said Barry. "I think the plans which we have discussed could have very positive results, not only for us but for the company as a whole."

"I absolutely agree with you but it will all have to be ratified by the Board Members and some of them are quite elderly and may not like these modern ideas."

Barry paused for a moment.

"I think Mr West is the key to success. If he approves, I am sure he can persuade the doubters."

Adam agreed with Barry's point of view.

"There is one more thing I think we should add to the list. I would like to have a sprinkler system installed in case of fire."

"That should certainly be a priority," Barry said. "No doubt it will be part of Health and Safety regulations."

"I don't know how long our meeting will last," Adam said. "But at some point, I would expect you to join us so you had better be on stand-by for the afternoon."

"Right," Barry said. "Good luck. I am sure you will succeed."

Adam was glad to be busy for the rest of the morning and the time passed quickly. Soon it was nearly two o'clock, so Sally went to the main entrance to meet Mr West. He arrived promptly and she stepped forward to greet him.

"Good afternoon, Mr West," she said.

"Good afternoon, Sally," he replied and shook her warmly by the hand.

She led the way through the main customer area to Adam's office. She knocked on the door and it was immediately opened by Adam. The two men shook hands and Sally returned to her office.

"Did you have a good journey?" Adam asked.

"I drove myself," Dominic answered. "It was a pleasure to drive through the countryside."

"I expect you are ready for a coffee," Adam said. "I'll ask Sally to get it for us."

"Have you told Sally about the changes which will take place soon?" asked Mr West.

"No, the only person I have discussed it with is Barry, my assistant manager."

"I hope to see Barry while I am here," said Mr West. "I owe him an apology for putting him in a difficult situation."

"We have sorted it out," Adam said. "And it certainly proved that Barry could keep a secret."

There was a knock at the door and Sally came in with the coffee and the biscuits.

"Shall I pour it?" she asked.

"Yes please," Adam said.

"Milk and one sugar I think?" she said, putting Dominic's cup on the desk in front of him.

He looked at her and smiled broadly.

"You have a good memory," he said. "You are very observant."

"Thank you, Sally," Adam said and he noticed how Dominic's eyes followed her out of the door.

Mr West opened the file which he had taken out of his briefcase.

"Let's get down to business," he said. "I have had the necessary papers drawn up which confirm your appointment as area manager. They just need your signature. I also have the confirmation that you will remain as general manager of the Oxford branch and finally the appointment of your assistant manager to become manager of this office."

"You have done all that in two days?" he said, amazed.

"There is a legal team working at Head Office," Mr West said. "And when I give them an explicit order, I expect it to be done."

Adam just looked at him in wonder.

"That will all be settled this afternoon and you will both take up your new posts on Monday," Mr West said firmly. "Now I want to hear your thoughts on the way forward."

Adam took a deep breath before he spoke.

"The first thing is to go up to Birmingham and sort out the mess left by James Brown. I am hoping that his secretary is still available to help me. I shall bring all his files and business details down here. Then I shall get a list of all the smaller branches in my area and notify them of the way they can contact me if necessary. Obviously, I intend to visit all of them but that won't happen until next Spring. It is going to mean some re-organisation of staff and space and we will need to take on extra help."

Dominic West had been listening intently to what Adam was saying and he nodded his head in agreement.

"Don't forget that you will have the authority to make your own decisions without contacting us. Now, I understand that you want to convert the first floor of these offices into the area manager's office? I'd like to see the space you have available."

"We can go upstairs now," Adam said. "I'll just ask Sally to bring us some more coffee when we come down. Barry and I have discussed plans for upstairs so would you mind if he joined us?"

"Not at all," said Dominic. "Three heads are better than two".

Adam told Sally to ask Barry to join them and the two men went up the stairs. Mr West was surprised to find such a large empty space.

"This is crying out to be made useful," he said. "It is like a blank canvas."

"That's exactly how I felt when I first saw it," Adam said. "But the more I have thought about it, the clearer the plan has become in my mind."

Barry came up the stairs and shook hands with Mr West.

"I owe you an apology," said Dominic West. "But I hope I am forgiven?"

"It was a bit awkward," said Barry. "But Adam and I have a good relationship and we were able to sort it out."

"Now, I want to know how you are going to use all this beautiful space? No doubt you have plans for it?"

"We haven't anything written down," said Adam. "But in my mind, I know exactly what I would like."

He proceeded to tell Dominic about his office, the communal area with reception desk, the additional offices and storerooms and finally he outlined his plans for a lecture room for sixth form students and area conferences.

"We shall also need a lift for disabled access and a sprinkler system as a precautionary measure," he concluded.

Barry then explained about the new computer system and an advanced system for the new offices. Both Adam and Barry had spoken with such enthusiasm that Dominic West was taken aback by the detailed thought which had gone into the enterprise.

"Let's go back to the office and recover with a nice cup of Sally's coffee. You have obviously put a lot of thought into this project and I need to consider each part of it," he said. "Will you join us for a coffee, Barry?"

"I will just check everything is running smoothly," Barry answered. "Then I would be pleased to join you."

The two men went into Adam's office and before too long Sally came in with the coffee and Barry joined them.

"Thank you, Sally," Adam said and again he noticed Dominic looking at her.

They sat around the desk and discussed in more detail the proposals Adam had made.

"I will arrange for our company architects to draw up detailed plans and costings. However much it costs, I think it would be money well spent, but of course, it will have to be confirmed by the Board. The slight problem is that most of the members are elderly and near retirement. They tend to want to hold on to traditional values," said Dominic.

"I respect tradition," Adam said. "But time does not stand still. We have to be prepared to accept innovation and modern business practices if we want to maintain a healthy reputation. Do you think the Board will object to our plans?"

"Most of the Board will be retiring at the beginning of next year and I want to replace them with younger members. I know how to handle them if they start to make noises. A couple of gin and tonics, a slap-up meal and finish with at least two glasses of port. By then they are too comatose to refuse and the job is done."

Adam and Barry looked quite shocked but Dominic just laughed.

"Please forget I said that."

"If you will excuse me," said Barry. "I must get back to my office. It is nearly closing time."

"Before you go, I need your signature," Dominic said as he pulled some papers out of his files. "These papers confirm your appointment as office manager, starting next Monday."

Barry signed the papers and shook hands with Mr West.

"Thank you very much, sir," he said. "I can't imagine a better boss than the one I have."

"You will make an excellent manager, Barry. You have the best mentor and I know you will be successful. Don't forget to keep in touch in case I have any more secrets for you to keep!"

The three men burst out laughing.

After Barry had left, Dominic put the other papers on the desk and invited Adam to sign them. Adam put his signature on each document and handed them back. Dominic put them in his briefcase and closed it up.

"All the official papers are signed so now you are able to move forward. Would you mind if I asked you a personal question?" Dominic West said with hesitation.

"I don't mind," Adam said. "You already know more about me and my family than anyone else in this office, with the exception of Barry. His wife and Leah have been best friends for many years so we have a common bond."

"How is your relationship going with Leah? Is it making progress?"

"Our relationship is back, on a husband-and-wife footing but we don't live in the same house. We have recognised that we got very used to living our own individual lives for twelve years and that it would be a terrific strain on both of us to co-exist in the same house. So, Leah's house now belongs to her and I am buying an apartment by the river. But our relationship couldn't be better."

Dominic West looked at Adam with sad eyes.

"I really admire you," he said quietly. "You made a mistake but you overcame it with great determination. I think you would be the first to admit that you deserve the success which has come your way and I know there is a lot more for you if you want it." He stopped talking for a minute or two and then he said: "I've made a mistake too. My wife and I live apart and I hardly see my children. I had a letter from her solicitor at the beginning of the week asking for a divorce on the grounds of adultery. I shall go along with it because I don't love her anymore but I know there will be arguments over the custody of the children."

"My children are all grown up," Adam said. "The arguments of custody have all been overtaken by their problems. Leah has been a one-parent family through their formative years and my problem is getting to know my own children."

"I am seriously thinking about early retirement," Dominic admitted. "I have private means and there would be a generous pension. I want to get out of London to a nice house in the country built next to a golf course," he said dreamily.

"I have always found that if you plant the seed of desire in your heart it will develop to your advantage," Adam said.

"That is an interesting thought," Dominic said. "What you are saying is that you must let the seed grow slowly and naturally and it will eventually provide the answer to its own problem."

There was a knock at the door and Sally came in.

"Can I clear the coffee cups?" she said. "It is past closing time."

"I'm sorry but I didn't realise it was so late," Adam said. "Does this mean you have missed your bus home?"

"There will another one in an hour," Sally assured him.

"I am driving my own car. Will you allow me to drive you home?"

"It is not on the way to London," Sally said. "In fact, it is quite the opposite direction."

"That's no problem," Mr West said. "I would be pleased to help you out."

"Thank you. I'll just take these cups to the kitchen then I'll be ready."

Sally went off and Mr West turned to Adam who was looking at him with a strange expression.

"Don't forget Sally is my secretary," Adam said firmly. "No poaching," and he wagged his finger at Dominic West.

"Scouts honour."

The two men shook hands.

"I'll start the ball rolling on the plans next week," said Dominic. "I'm really looking forward to seeing it come to life. I shall keep in close touch with you and will do my very best to make sure that all of your plans come to fruition."

"Thank you very much. It is good to know that we can move forward with confidence," Adam said.

"One more thing," said Dominic. "I hope I shall have the pleasure of meeting your wife in the not too distant future. I intend to take a personal interest in the developments here. I do enjoy coming to visit you."

There was a light knock and Sally opened the door.

"I'm ready," she said.

Adam escorted them both through the empty building to the front entrance.

"I'll see you on Monday, Sally."

He wished Dominic a good evening and a safe journey home. As he stood at the door and watched them walk away towards the car park, a strange thought hit him. I wonder, he said to himself.

"Did I just see Sally leaving with Mr West?" said Barry, coming up behind him.

"You certainly did," Adam replied. "Sally missed her bus and he offered to take her home."

"You sound a bit concerned," Barry said. "I'm sure Sally will be quite safe with him."

"I'm sure she will. I'll just fetch my briefcase then we can go home."

He locked the main door and switched on the security system.

"We will see you and Leah to-morrow evening," said Barry.

"Yes, we're looking forward to it. I think we can tell them our news and make it a celebration."

"It will probably surprise them so much that they will be speechless!"

"That will be a first," Adam answered and they both laughed.

Adam was glad to be going home. It had been an exhausting day and he was beginning to feel the effects of it. He realised that he had only eaten a sandwich at lunchtime and he was hungry. He noticed a fish and chip shop in the shopping precinct; just what he fancied. He stopped to buy cod and chips. He took it home and sat on his settee to eat it out of its paper wrapping. Feeling a lot better, he threw the empty paper in the bin. He found a can of beer in the fridge but there was very little food in there so he decided to go shopping in the morning, making a mental note, to buy some wine.

He phoned Leah. She did not answer immediately and he was just about to try again later when she said:

"Hello, Adam."

"I thought you might be out," he said.

"I was out," she answered. "I was sound asleep."

"Are you alright? It's not like you to sleep in the daytime."

"It's been a particularly busy week," Leah said wearily. "Several teachers were away at school and I had to cover for them as well as my evening lessons. And I have had Alice on the phone every day in a distressed state. I'm just worn out."

"What has caused Alice's problems?" Adam asked.

"It would take too long to tell you over the phone. I'll explain it to you at the weekend," she said.

"I have to do some shopping in the morning but I'll come straight over once I've finished. I shall be there about twelve o'clock and I'll bring some sandwiches for lunch. Now go to bed and have a good night's sleep and treat yourself to a lie-in tomorrow morning," he said decisively.

"I'm not used to being ordered about," Leah said shortly. "But on this occasion, I might just obey instructions."

"Good. You are beginning to learn your lessons," Adam said sternly. "I'll see you to-morrow. There's one more thing I need to tell you; I love you" and he put the phone down.

He sat back on his settee and thought what a momentous day this had been for him and Barry. It looked like they were about to get everything they'd hoped for. It would take some serious organising and a lot of hard work. They'd draw up an initial plan of action on Monday and tell the staff about all the changes on Tuesday.

His thoughts turned to the conversation he had with Leah, particularly the news about Alice. They had hardly mentioned their eldest daughter but he did remember Leah saying there were problems with her husband and children. He was determined to find out more because Leah obviously needed some support. It was getting late so he switched on the television to hear the latest news. It was mainly about disasters and civil disobedience which were the last things he wanted to hear about, so he switched it off and went to bed.

As he lay in bed, Adam's thoughts turned to Sally and Dominic West. He was sure he had detected more than a hint of interest from Dominic's side but Sally seemed totally unaware of it. He wondered why

Dominic had confided in him about his marriage and thought it might be wise to find out more about his boss, if only for Sally's sake.

Chapter Sixteen

"I don't mind waiting for the next bus if you prefer to go back to London, Mr West?" said Sally, as they walked down the street together.

"We are not in the office now," he said. "Please call me Dominic."

"I'll try to remember," she said.

He took her arm protectively as they crossed the busy street and into the car park.

"You are going to have to give me directions," he said, once they were in the car.

"It is quite straight forward. If you go south on the A34 I will tell you when to turn off. I live in a village called Steventon."

"Do you live by yourself or have you a partner?" asked Dominic.

"I have lived alone since my divorce three years ago," she replied. "That's when I moved to the village so that I could be on a bus route into Oxford."

"Don't you have a car?"

"The car was not part of the settlement," Sally said. "And in any case the traffic is bad and there is very little parking in Oxford. It is expensive too." She was carefully watching the road. "Take the next exit, then we are nearly there."

"Is there anywhere we could eat around here?" Dominic asked. "I'm really hungry."

"There are a couple of pubs but the food is not brilliant." She thought for a minute. "There is a fish and chip shop in the village. They do a good cod and chips. We could eat it at my place if you don't mind?"

"Can we eat it out of the paper?" he said, eagerly. "It is years since I did that."

Sally laughed.

"Of course, we can. It will save on the washing up. You can see the shop now, just across the road. I'll go and get it."

"You stay right there," he said. "This is my treat."

He soon came back with two hot parcels which he gave to Sally to hold.

"My house is about a hundred yards further on the left-hand side," she said. "There is a good parking space at the front so you won't have to park on the road."

"Here we are," Sally said as the car stopped.

She got out quickly and unlocked the front door. Dominic followed her as she put the lights on and led the way into the lounge. She found a couple of paper serviettes which she placed on the coffee table, then they both sat down and opened up their supper. The smell was delicious and the food tasted just as good.

"That beats gourmet lunches every time," Dominic said happily. "I really enjoyed that."

"I'll make some coffee," Sally said. "There is a cloakroom near the front door if you would like to wash your hands."

She went into the kitchen and a couple of minutes later Dominic wandered in.

"I'll make some coffee seems to be your mantra," he said with a smile.

"It is a very important part of a secretary's job," she said lightly. "It keeps the boss happy." She carried the coffee into the lounge. "Milk and one sugar?" she joked.

The lounge was quite small and cosy. There was a flame-effect electric fire glowing in the hearth. Sally sat down on the settee next to Dominic. He rested his head on the back and closed his eyes.

"Are you feeling tired?" she asked quietly.

"Yes, I am. It's been a long and busy day. Sometimes I get tired of life itself."

"What do you mean?" she asked with concern.

Dominic opened his eyes and looked at her.

"Don't worry I'm not suicidal. Sometimes I feel trapped in a place where I don't want to be. I get tired of the rat race and the responsibilities that go with it. That is one reason why I enjoy coming to Oxford. It is such a pleasure to talk with Adam, the way in which he has turned his life around is so inspiring."

"I know nothing about Mr Richard's private life," she said. "All I know is that he is a good person to work for. He is very fair and honest in everything that he does. He is ambitious but he would never be ruthless. I know that he and Barry are planning something but I have no idea what it is."

"It is actually a very exciting project. I feel sure he will tell you about it on Monday." He looked at his watch. "It's getting late but I don't want to move. This is the first time I have felt relaxed in months," he said with a sigh.

"But isn't there anyone at your house who will be expecting you home?" she said anxiously.

"There is no one at home. I live alone in a big empty place which used to be filled with love and children's laughter."

She didn't know what to say. She looked at Dominic in amazement.

"I'm sorry," he said as he stood up. "I didn't mean to burden you with my problems. It's time I was off."

"Sit down for a minute," she said. "Do you honestly live alone?"

"Yes, I honestly do. I have a housekeeper who does my washing and keeps the house clean and tidy but most of the time I am there by myself. If I feel I need company, I drive to my parent's house or stay at my club in London."

"But I've heard you speak about your children, where do they live?"

"They live with their mother and her new partner. My wife had filed for divorce on the basis of her adultery."

"That is very unusual," she said. "It is more often the man who commits adultery and then wants a divorce."

Dominic took Sally by the shoulders and looked straight into her eyes.

"I swear on my life I have never been unfaithful to my wife. I do not love her anymore but I would not commit to anyone else until I am a free man. I shall not contest the divorce but there are a number of outstanding legal matters to do with property and custody of the children."

"But why are you telling me all of this?"

"I didn't mean to but I couldn't help myself. The peaceful atmosphere of this house and the easy way in which we have been talking seemed to overcome me. I am so sorry to upset you, that was the last thing I wanted to do. I have so enjoyed your company this evening."

She wanted to put her arms around him and comfort him but she suddenly remembered the difference in their social standing.

"You haven't offended me in any way," she said. "I am upset for your sake. I don't like to see anyone as unhappy as you seem to be. It is quite a surprise because you have always appeared to be in complete control of your life."

"That is what a public-school education does for you," he said in a resigned way. "It gives you the veneer of self-assurance which covers the real you. I have carried on the family tradition in business with all its trappings of wealth but I have nearly had enough of it. The time is coming when I want to make some life-changing decisions and that is why I need to talk to people I trust. I know that I can talk to Adam or Barry and I am asking you if you will be my friend too?"

"Of course, I'll be your friend," Sally said resolutely. "I'll always be there if you want to talk and I'll do whatever I can to help you."

He stood up and put his arms around her.

"Thank you," he said. "You have no idea how much that means to me," and he hugged her tightly.

Sally looked at the clock on the wall and then she looked at Dominic.

"It's very late and I don't want to seem too forward," she said. "But I have a spare room if you would like to stay for the night?"

"That's very kind of you but I wouldn't want to impose on you."

"It's my turn to be assertive," she smiled. "The bed is already made up and it would be no trouble at all. It will be easier for your journey back in daylight."

"In that case, I will accept your kind offer. I do feel emotionally drained and I would probably have stopped the car in some layby and gone to sleep."

"I expect I can find you a spare toothbrush," she said as she led him up the stairs.

She settled him in the bedroom and said goodnight then she went back downstairs. She tidied up the lounge and switched off the lights. Then she went upstairs, cleaned her teeth and was soon ready for bed. As she lay there, she thought about the events of the evening. It had all been quite unexpected and she was having trouble making sense of it. Hopefully, she'd understand it better in the morning, she thought as she drifted off to sleep.

Chapter Seventeen

In spite of his concerns about Sally's welfare, Adam slept well. He was up early the next morning and was soon off to the shops. He stocked up on food for the week and then bought two bottles of champagne. He went back home and unloaded his car. He put the food in the fridge and the champagne on the table ready to go to Leah's house. He remembered the two pots of hyacinths which he had bought earlier. Finally, he phoned Barry.

"I am just about to come to Swanton. I've got two bottles of champagne and a present for Jen. Can I drop them off on my way?"

"Jen is out shopping but I'll be here," Barry said. "I'll see you soon."

Adam loaded the car and he was soon on his way. He stopped off at Barry's house and put the champagne in the fridge. He left the hyacinth in the kitchen.

"We will tell them this evening," Adam said. "Make sure you have the glasses ready."

"Can't wait to see their reaction," chuckled Barry.

Adam drove on to Leah's house and arrived just as she was unloading shopping from her car. He helped her to carry it in and she shouted:

"Put the kettle on. I'll put my car in the garage."

He boiled the kettle and made coffee and suddenly remembered that he had promised to bring the sandwiches for their lunch.

"I've forgotten the sandwiches," he said. "I'll pop to the shop when we have had our coffee. Did you sleep well?"

"Yes, I took your advice and I feel much better this morning. I'm looking forward to seeing Jen and Barry this evening," she said.

"So am I," Adam said with a grin. "It is going to be very interesting. There might even be some surprises."

"What do you mean by that?" Leah asked uncertainly, "I've had enough surprises recently to last me for a very long time."

"These are nice surprises," Adam said and tapped the side of his nose.

"Now you have made me nervous. You are a sly old fox."

"Not so much of the old," Adam said and kissed her.

"I must go and put the shopping away," she said, standing up.

"I'll go and get some sandwiches," Adam said. "Then we can have a nice relaxing afternoon."

He was soon back with two packets of sandwiches and after they had eaten their lunch they retired to the lounge and made themselves comfortable on the settee.

"How has your week been?" Leah asked.

"It's been okay," he said sleepily.

Leah looked at him and thought it's no good trying to have a conversation with him, so she lay back and closed her eyes. It was more than two hours later when she woke up. Adam was still fast asleep. I'll put the kettle on she thought and then I am going to have a shower and get myself ready for this evening. It was already dark outside, so she closed the curtains before she went upstairs. She looked in her wardrobe to find something to wear and finally decided on a pair of grey trousers and a deep pink cashmere jumper which was a Christmas present from last year. She put on the pearl necklace which Thomas had given her and then took the diamond ring out of its box. She slipped it on to her finger and it sparkled in the light. She was standing there admiring it when she heard Adam calling her name.

"Leah, where are you?"

"I'm just coming down," she said as she put out the light.

"I woke up and you had disappeared," Adam said.

"You have been asleep for nearly four hours," Leah told him. "You must have been very tired."

"It has been an exhausting week but I'll tell you about it later." He looked at her closely. "You look very smart," he said. "Have you got a special date?"

"Only with my husband. He seems to think there is something special about it but he won't tell me," she added with exasperation in her voice.

"You'll find out soon enough," he said. "Now I need a wash and brush up before we go out."

"I'll make a cup of tea," Leah said as she went into the kitchen.

She noticed the hyacinths on the worktop and she picked them up and took them into the dining room. Adam soon came downstairs and they took their tea into the lounge.

"It is quite a while since I enjoyed Jen's cooking," Leah said. "I'm really looking forward to it."

"So am I; her cottage pie was delicious."

"I wish I was a better cook," Leah said wistfully. "But I've never been interested in it."

"You are a better teacher," Adam said. "You can't be good at everything."

"What do you think you are good at?"

"I am good at giving out surprises," he said with a grin as he touched the ring on her finger.

"Your surprises have a habit of creating a shock in the receiver," she said with a wry smile. "I have a feeling that you have something up your sleeve for this evening."

"Time to go," he said.

Leah put on her coat and Adam locked the door behind them. It was only a short drive to Barry's house and they were soon ringing the front doorbell. Jen opened the door and kissed them both.

"Come on in out of the cold," she said. "Barry won't be long. He is just talking to his mother on the phone."

They went into the lounge where the fire was burning brightly. On the coffee table, there were some crisps and a bottle of wine with four glasses. Barry came bustling in.

"Sorry about that," he said. "My mother is a real chatterbox."

Jen raised her eyebrows and smiled.

"Excuse me," she said. "I must check the oven."

Barry poured out the wine and Leah picked up two glasses.

"I'll take this to Jen and see if she needs any help," she said.

"Have you said anything to Jen?" asked Adam in a low voice, when she was gone.

"No, I haven't said a word, but I get the feeling that she is a bit suspicious. What about you?"

"I haven't told Leah anything, but I did say that it could be an interesting evening with one or two surprises. I can't help teasing her and I know she is a bit jumpy."

"We will eat first and try to behave as normally as possible at the supper table," said Barry.

Leah had taken Jen's wine into the kitchen. They looked at each other and Jen said:

"They are up to something. I can feel it in my bones and look what I found in the fridge?"

She opened the door and showed Leah the two bottles of champagne.

"Champagne!" I don't know what could possibly deserve a champagne celebration." She gave Jen a strange look. "You're not pregnant, are you?"

"Certainly not," Jen replied. "Are you?"

"No way!" said Leah and they burst out laughing.

"Supper is ready. Will you tell those two sly creatures in the lounge?"

Leah and Adam took their seats at the table and Barry helped Jen to carry the food in. When they were all seated Adam asked in an innocent voice:

"Did you two enjoy your chat in the kitchen? We heard you laughing didn't we Barry?"

"We certainly did," Barry said just as innocently. "We were hoping to share the joke, weren't we Adam?"

"It was a private conversation between two ladies," Leah said pointedly.

"There was no joke," added Jen.

The two men looked suitably abashed.

Jen had made a smoked salmon and asparagus quiche with salad and new potatoes.

"That was delicious," Leah said when they had finished.

"It was a real treat," said Barry. "I don't get fed like that every day."

Jen gave him a stern look.

"I'll pour you another wine, dear," he said. "And I'll help you to clear the table."

Adam and Leah both laughed. Jen brought in the dessert which was chocolate and orange tart with double cream. Barry poured out more wine and everyone was happy.

"I'll clear the table later," Jen said. "Let's go and find some comfortable seats."

They moved into the lounge. Leah and Adam sat on the settee while Jen and Barry sat in the chairs on either side of the fireplace. They were all feeling very full up and rather sleepy. No-one said a word but there was definitely an air of expectation in the room. Eventually, Adam looked at Barry who took the hint.

"I'll just clear these dirty glasses," he said as he stood up.

Leah and Jen glanced at each other but didn't speak.

Barry returned with a tray of champagne glasses in one hand and a bottle of champagne in the other. Leah and Jen remained silent.

"I think a celebration is called for," Adam announced.

"What are we celebrating?" asked Leah.

Barry had been struggling to open the bottle and suddenly the cork popped out with a loud bang. It shot across the room and ended up under the table. Barry quickly filled the glasses and handed them around. He turned to Adam.

"Your turn now."

Adam stood up and cleared his throat.

"Barry and I have new jobs. Barry is being promoted to manager of the Oxford branch and I will be general manager there. I have been promoted to area manager for the whole of the west of England. Now let us drink to our success!"

They all raised their glasses and drank a toast. Leah and Jen had been listening to Adam with their mouths open but still, neither of them spoke. At last, Leah said:

"You've done it again, haven't you? Turned a surprise into a shock."

"Aren't you pleased for me?" Adam pretended to be hurt by her apparent indifference.

"Of course, I'm pleased for you," she stated firmly. "I knew you were hiding something. And I am very pleased for Barry too." She went over and kissed him. "Congratulations! And you'd better go over to your wife. I think she is still in shock."

Barry quickly went over to Jen and put his arms around her.

"It's alright," he said quietly to her. "Why don't you sit down?"

"I know it is good news for both of you," she stammered. "But it was so unexpected."

"Adam has been negotiating it for the past week and it was all confirmed yesterday afternoon. We start our new posts on Monday," Barry said.

"It doesn't mean we have to move, does it?" Jen asked anxiously.

"No, nothing changes. Adam made sure that he could run the area office from Oxford and the whole of the first floor will be made into his area office."

"I shall appreciate it more when I have got over the shock," Jen said.

"You both stay where you are," Barry ordered Leah and Jen. "Adam and I will go and make some strong coffee."

"Well, that surprised me," said Adam as they went into the kitchen. "I think Jen was genuinely shocked and Leah sounded a bit cross."

"Leah is used to you and your surprises," Barry said. "But Jen and I don't usually have secrets from each other. She hasn't got Leah's strong constitution."

"She will be alright, won't she?" Adam asked anxiously.

"Once she has got used to the idea, she will be fine. But I shall probably get told off for keeping it a secret."

"I'm going to tell Leah about the apartment tomorrow," Adam said thoughtfully. "That will be another surprise for her."

"I admire your courage," Barry said shortly. "I know I shall need some time to restore normal relations."

They carried the coffee into the lounge and set it down on the table. Jen had moved from her chair and was sitting next to Leah on the settee. She was holding Leah's ring in her hand.

"It's beautiful," she said. "May I try it on?"

"Of course, you can," Leah said.

She slipped it onto her finger. It was slightly too big for Jen and she said to Leah:

"It fits you perfectly. How did Adam know your size?"

"He wouldn't tell me," Leah replied.

Barry and Adam had been listening to this conversation.

"I have my methods," Adam said and kissed Leah on the forehead.

As they drank their coffee, Leah ventured to ask some more questions about the news they had just heard but Jen remained mainly silent. Adam and Barry answered in a non-committed way.

"I told you it could be a very interesting evening, didn't I, Leah?" said Adam.

"Yes, you did," replied Leah. "And as usual, you were right."

"It's getting late," Adam said. "We had better be going."

"Yes," said Leah. "I'm looking forward to a few words in private with you."

Adam looked at Barry and raised his eyebrows.

"I hope to see you on Monday, Barry, even if it is with two black eyes."

Barry laughed.

"In that case, I promise I will back up your story."

"Thank you for a lovely evening, Jen," said Leah, kissing her. "I'll phone you early next week."

Adam followed her and whispered in Jen's ear:

"Don't worry. Everything will be alright. Barry and I will make sure of that."

"Are you sure you are fit to drive?" said Leah, as they got to the car.

"Never felt fitter," he answered. "I'll get you home safely."

Leah made sure she had her seatbelt on as he sped off. Five minutes later he had parked on Leah's drive and they went into the house.

"I'm ready for bed," Leah said, yawning.

"You go on up and I'll make sure the back door is locked," Adam teased her.

"I'm not in the mood for jokes," Leah said. "Or surprises."

"Tomorrow is another day," Adam said wisely. "Who knows what it might bring."

She just looked at him and went on up the stairs. She really is in a bit of a huff, he thought. There will be no more presents tonight. He turned off the lights and climbed the stairs. As he went into the bedroom, Leah said sleepily:

"Did you lock the back door?"

"Of course, I did," he said. "I don't believe in nasty surprises."

He kissed her goodnight and lay down beside her. The news hadn't been greeted with as much enthusiasm as he expected. Women, he thought, so unpredictable and he turned over and went to sleep.

Adam woke the next morning with a slight hangover. He went to the bathroom for a drink of water and then decided to go and make a cup of tea. It was too early for the heating to come on and the house felt cold. He carried two cups back to the bedroom and stood Leah's cup on the bedside table. He quickly slid back under the duvet and sat up in bed to drink his tea. He leaned over to Leah and said:

"I've brought you a cup of tea."

Leah just grunted and turned over. Looks like I'm going to drink both cups, he said to himself and reached over for the second cup. He put his empty cup in its place and pulled the duvet around him. Five minutes later, Leah stirred and reached for her tea but the cup was empty.

"I thought you said you had brought me a cup of tea?" she said in an aggrieved voice.

"I thought you were asleep, so I drank it."

"Typical man," Leah shot back. "Always impatient."

"I'll go and make you another one."

"No, thank you. I've gone off the idea."

Adam looked at her closely.

"Why are you so prickly this morning?"

"I'm not prickly."

"Oh! Come on," Adam said. "What's the matter? You are like a bear with a sore head. Why are you so cross with me?"

"I don't know," sighed Leah. "I think it is all these surprises that you keep springing on me. My life used to be organised and fairly predictable. Now it is ever-changing and I can't get used to it. I feel quite confused."

Adam looked at her with genuine concern.

"I had no idea you felt like that," he said. "I never meant to put any pressure on you. The fact is that things have been happening so rapidly at work that Barry and I have been carried along in the flow. Perhaps we need to slow down and temper our enthusiasm."

"I know you think it fun to surprise me," she said. "But it makes me quite nervous. I am used to a well-organised life and these constant changes really upset me."

Adam took hold of Leah's hand and looked directly at her.

"There is one more thing which I need to tell you," he said in a hesitant voice. "I shall be moving house before Christmas."

Leah looked at him in amazement.

"You have it all arranged in secret," she said, "without breathing a word about it?"

"I was going to surprise you," he said apologetically. "But I couldn't do that now, in view of how you feel."

"It is your house and your choice," she said. "But are you going to tell me where it is?"

"It is in Swanton about a mile from here and you have already seen it," Adam answered.

"You haven't bought that apartment by the river?" she gasped.

"That's the one, although I may want to make some alterations in the furniture."

"But you didn't seem at all interested in it when we were there?"

"I told you that I felt I was being pushed into it. I went there and had a second viewing because I wanted to be sure that it was my decision."

Leah was silent for a minute or two.

"You are a very independent person and I must try and remember that in the future. Of course, I'm pleased about your promotion at work and your new house but I hope there aren't too many other secrets lurking in that mind of yours."

"Am I forgiven?" he said and kissed her.

"I don't say that I forgive you, but I do understand you a little better."

"That's good enough for me," he said holding her close as he kissed her and this time, she kissed him back.

It was much later when they finally got dressed and went downstairs. Leah made some coffee and they took it into the lounge.

"Are you hungry?" she asked.

"Not really," he said. "I'm still full up from last evening."

"I hope Jen is alright," said Leah, looking worried. "She is not as used to your little surprises as I am."

"She'll be fine. I'm sure Barry knows how to handle the situation."

"You two seem to have been very busy planning this new venture. Are you able to tell me about it, or is it another of your secrets?" she asked.

"It had to be a secret until the appointments were confirmed on Friday afternoon," he said. "We shall make a plan of action tomorrow and then tell the staff about it on Tuesday. Mr West has promised to get things moving as quickly as possible."

"Who is Mr West?"

Adam proceeded to give Leah an outline of what was planned and of Mr West's role in it.

"It sounds like a lot of extra work and upheaval," she said.

"I shall be travelling quite often as the area manager and it is quite a big area to cover. Barry will be a full-time manager and I have every confidence in him. I shall be the general manager of the branch and will be available to support him if necessary."

"And in the middle of all that you say you will be moving house? It's unbelievable!"

"I have to give one months' notice on the house I'm renting," Adam said. "And I shall do that this week. So, I will have to move out on November 30th. The solicitor says that it should be completed by the second week of December, so I could be homeless for a couple of weeks," he said sadly.

"You are the limit!" she laughed. "I'll get my violin and start playing it."

"You are a hard woman," he said pretending to cry. "But your heart is not made of stone, it is pure gold."

"You flatter me and seduce me in order to get your own way."

"Well, it has worked so far," he said as he put his arm around her.

"I sometimes wonder if you just say you love me in order to take advantage of my good nature," she said primly.

"Well, I don't give diamond rings to every woman I meet and I have already shown you how much I love you once today. What more can I do?"

"You are doing very well," she said as she kissed him. "And I couldn't bear to think of you sleeping under a bridge in the cold. Of course, you can come here but what are you going to do with all your furniture and belongings?"

"It will have to go into storage until the apartment is ready," he said. "But I would be really grateful if you could help me to decide what to keep and what to give to charity?"

"Of course, I'll help you. But I don't even know where you're living at present."

"I could take you there one weekend," he said. "It won't take long to decide."

"Let me know in good time which weekend it will be. It is getting towards Christmas and I am quite busy."

"I promise," he said. "And I promise not to give you any more deliberate surprises, although I am allowed small surprises, aren't I?"

"The smaller the better," Leah answered and she picked up the coffee cups and took them out to the kitchen.

When she returned to the lounge, Adam was sitting with a frown on his face.

"The other day you said that you had been having a lot of phone calls from Alice. Are you going to tell me what is troubling her?" Adam asked.

Leah sat down and thought for a while.

"I have already told you what I think of her husband and the behaviour of her children but until recently she has assured me that she is coping. I haven't seen her for the past four months and she won't let me visit her at home. But when I spoke to her last week, she was in floods of tears and really didn't want to talk. I honestly think that she is on the edge of a breakdown and I don't know what to do."

"Does she know we are back together?"

"I haven't told her and I don't think Peter has either."

"It sounds pretty serious to me," said Adam. "It is obvious that she needs help."

"The trouble is that it is possible to easily cover up the truth over the telephone. I'm sure that things are much worse than she makes out. I really need to go and see for myself, but I don't want to upset her even more," Leah said sadly.

"How long does it take to get there?"

"About forty-five minutes, assuming the traffic keeps moving."

"So, we could easily go this afternoon," Adam said. "Why don't you phone her and see how she is today but don't say anything about us going to see her."

Leah looked a bit dubious at this suggestion.

"It is Sunday today; her husband might be there."

"All the better," said Adam. "I'd like to meet him."

Leah was still unsure but her concern for her daughter was too strong and she picked up the phone. When Alice answered it, all she could hear was loud music in the background.

"Whatever is that racket behind you?" asked Leah.

"The kids have a few friends here and they are having a party," she said in a tearful voice.

"How are you feeling today?" Leah asked anxiously.

"I don't like all this noise, I can't think," Alice said. "I must go. William will be here soon," and she put the phone down.

Adam had been listening to the conversation.

"That's it," he said. "We are going to see what is happening up there."

Leah knew there was no point arguing with him so, she found her coat and they were soon on their way. During the journey, she gave Adam more details of what had been happening over the past three years.

"When Jonathan was a baby, she used to bring him down to see me every week. They would be with me for three or four hours but during that time her husband would ring her at least twice with some paltry excuse."

"He sounds like a control freak," Adam said.

"That is true but I think his problem goes deeper than that."

When they arrived at the house, Adam parked the car on the drive. There were no other cars, just a number of bicycles scattered about. The music was still blaring away inside the house as they went through the front door. Leah led the way into the kitchen and found Alice sitting at the table with a glass of wine in her hand. She immediately put her arms around her daughter.

"Oh Alice," she cried. "What has happened to you?"

Alice did not answer. She was looking at the figure standing in the doorway.

"Dad?" she said slowly and looked at her mother. Leah nodded at her and Alice repeated: "Dad."

Adam stepped forward and hugged his daughter. She burst into uncontrollable tears. He held her close for a few minutes.

"It's alright Alice," he said. "I'm not going to leave you again." Then he looked at Leah. "I'm just going to find where this dreadful music is coming from."

He walked towards the lounge and opened the door. The room was a complete mess with empty beer cans and bottles and a distinct smell in the air. He went over to the record player and pulled the plug out of the wall. Everyone turned to look at him and one of the boys come up to him and said in a menacing tone:

"Who the hell are you?"

"I might ask you the same question," said Adam.

"I'm Jonathan Rankin, and I live here."

"And I am your Grandfather, Adam Richards."

"You can't be," Jonathan laughed rudely. "He went away years ago and I know nothing about him."

Adam drew himself up to his full height.

"I am not in the habit of telling lies," he said firmly. "Your mother is my daughter and that is a fact. Now I suggest that you and your friends clean up this room before they leave. I will see you again in fifteen minutes."

The other boys had been listening to this conversation and started to pick up all the rubbish. Jonathan slunk away to find some black bin bags and Adam returned to the kitchen. Leah had boiled the kettle and was making a cup of tea. Adam sat down next to Alice and put his arm around her.

"I can't believe it's you," Alice said weakly. "Are you and Mum back together? I've tried not to worry her too much but it's been hard, very hard."

"Mum has told me all about what has been going on but she doesn't know everything. You will need to talk to us so that we know how best to help you."

Alice looked at him and the tears started to roll down her cheeks.

"I can't tell you anything," she wept. "I dare not."

Adam was shocked.

"Are you frightened?" he asked urgently. "What are you afraid of?"

But Alice would say no more. Adam noticed that most of the boys were now leaving. He told Leah to stay with Alice and he went back to the lounge. Jonathan was standing there with two black bags full of rubbish. All the boys had gone but one girl was talking to him. She went up to Adam as he entered the room.

"Jonathan says that you are our Grandfather. I'm Jessica, his sister. I don't believe him of course. My dad says you went off with some floozy years ago."

"Do you believe everything your father tells you?" Adam asked.

"Of course, we do," Jessica answered. "It's no good asking Mum anything. She is usually half sloshed. So, tell us who you really are."

"I have already told you," Adam replied coldly. "Now I suggest you go up to your rooms. Your mother needs to be in the lounge."

As the two children turned to go out of the room, Jessica said over her shoulder:

"Our Dad will be home soon. He will sort you out."

"I look forward to meeting him," Adam said sweetly.

He returned to the kitchen.

"Alice, the lounge is clean and quiet now. Why don't you go and sit in there?"

"I'll spend some time in here," Leah said. "I'll try to clear the table and wash up."

Alice allowed herself to be led to the lounge. She sat on the settee next to Adam and looked around.

"It is a long time since I was in here," she said. "I usually sit in the kitchen all day."

"Do you go out shopping or visiting friends?" he asked.

"I go to the local shop for cigarettes and wine every day," Alice said.

"How do you do your food shopping?"

"I don't do that," she answered. "William does it and he does the cooking for the children."

"Do you go and visit friends?"

"I have no friends," Alice said sadly. "It is just me," and she burst into great sobs.

"Do you still love your husband?" Adam asked. "Please tell me the truth."

"I suppose I do but he is not really my husband. He is the father of my two children and they don't love me very much. They ignore me all the time and will only listen to their father. I know he is seeing another woman and he has introduced her to the children. I don't know what to do."

"Don't worry, Alice, we will work something out," said Adam. "I think you need to get away from this house for a while."

"William will never allow it. I know he won't let me," Alice said in panic.

"William will not be able to stop you. I will make sure of that."

"But you have never met him. You don't know what he is like!" she said, rapidly becoming hysterical.

"You must trust me," Adam said soothingly. "I have met plenty of awkward people in my time."

Just then Leah came into the lounge and drew Adam to one side.

"A car has just driven up. I'm sure it is William," she said quietly.

"You stay with Alice and try and get her to talk," said Adam. "I'll deal with William."

He went into the kitchen and started to dry the cups and glasses which Leah had washed.

"Who the hell are you and what are you doing in my kitchen?"

Adam put the cloth down and held out his hand.

"I'm Adam Richards, Alice's father. You must be William Rankin, Alice's husband?"

"Too right I am," William said rudely, ignoring Adam's outstretched hand. He looked around the kitchen. "Where is she? Where's Alice?"

"Alice is in the lounge with her mother," Adam said smoothly.

"In the lounge?" sneered William. "She never goes into the lounge. She always sits at the kitchen table with a glass of wine in one hand and a cigarette in the other. I thought you had disappeared off the face of the earth. When did you reappear?"

Adam decided to ignore these insults.

"You don't seem to have a very high opinion of your wife. Have you no respect for her?"

"How can you respect someone who is an alcoholic and a chain smoker? It started soon after we married and has got steadily worse."

"That is interesting," Adam said in a cool voice. "Do you think there is any connection between the marriage and the subsequent deterioration of her mental health?"

William gave him a stony look and nearly exploded with anger.

"Are you blaming me for her shortcomings? I've provided her with everything she needs, money, a big home, a car, jewellery, she has had it all," he fumed. "And what has she given me in exchange? Nothing but trouble!"

"She has given you a son and a daughter," Adam said.

"A lot of use that has been," William said nastily. "She has never been a proper mother to them. They have no respect for her."

"That makes three of you then," Adam said calmly. "I understand you have already introduced them to your new lady friend?"

"You seem to have been busy poking your nose into other people's business."

"My daughter's welfare in my business," Adam answered sharply. "And I shall be looking into it very closely."

"Are you threatening me?" demanded William.

"Why would you feel threatened? You said yourself that you have no guilty feelings."

William looked at Adam warily. He was not used to anyone questioning him. He usually managed to have the last word but he was beginning to feel a bit uncomfortable. Adam sensed this.

"I need to go and speak with Alice," he said. "Then I shall come back and inform you what has been decided. It might be a good idea if you asked the children to join us so that they are fully aware of the situation."

William was about to object but Adam had already left the kitchen. He went into the lounge and spoke to Leah.

"Take Alice upstairs and help her to pack a case and make sure she puts all her jewellery in it. She will be coming home with us tonight."

"I can't do that," Alice said in a terrified voice. "He will come after me, I know he will," and she began to shake with fear.

Adam went over and steadied her.

"He won't come anywhere near you. I give you my word on that."

Leah put her arm around Alice and helped her up the stairs. They went into the bedroom and closed the door behind them. Adam went back into the kitchen where William and the children were waiting impatiently. He stood at the table in exactly the same place where Alice usually sat.

"Alice will be coming home this evening with her mother and me. She will be with us for the foreseeable future. Her physical and mental health will be assessed by a doctor and if she requires any specific treatment, I shall expect you to pay for it."

Jonathan and Jessica looked at each other in horror.

"Who is going to look after us!"

"You've already told me that your mother doesn't look after you, so it looks as if you are going to have to make other arrangements," Adam said firmly.

William stepped right up to Adam and pointed his finger at him.

"You can't do this!" he said angrily. "You can't just remove my wife from her own home. I'll take you to court."

Adam didn't flinch.

"Now who is doing the threatening?" he asked, and William took a step back. "I wouldn't do that if I were you," Adam went on. "You may open Pandora's box."

Leah came to the kitchen door.

"We're ready," she said quietly and took Alice out to the car.

"There's one more thing," said Adam, facing William. "Do not attempt to contact Alice in any way. We will keep you fully informed about her progress."

He walked out of the kitchen leaving William red with anger and the two children totally confused.

The drive home took place in almost total silence. Alice cried softly on her mother's shoulder for most of the way. When they arrived at the house, Adam helped her out of the car and carried her suitcase. The house was nice and warm as they went into the lounge. Leah put the kettle on and made them all a cup of tea. She brought the biscuit tin in as well and offered it to Alice but she shook her head.

"When did you last eat, Alice?" asked Leah.

"I can't remember."

"I'm starving," Adam said.

"So am I," said Leah. "We haven't eaten all day. I suppose I could manage beans on toast."

"That's fine," Adam said. "You can share mine if you like, Alice."

She gave a little smile.

"That's better," he said. "That's more like my little girl."

Leah soon came back with their suppers on two trays.

"I did you half a slice," she said to Alice. "In case you change your mind."

"Thanks, mum. I'm not used to anyone waiting on me."

"Your mother and I will soon change that," Adam said. "She can't stop herself helping other people."

Adam finished his supper and stood up.

"I really must go," he said. "I've got work tomorrow."

Alice gave Leah an enquiring look.

"It's alright, Alice," she said. "Your father has his own house but he also spends some time here. The arrangement suits us well and we are quite happy with it but I will explain it to you later."

Adam kissed Alice.

"Now you be a good girl Alice," he said, kissing her. "And do what your mother tells you. We will soon have you feeling better."

Leah went to the door to see him off.

"I'll try and come over mid-week," he said. "But I'll keep in touch by phone. Get her to the doctors as soon as you can. I'm sure he can give her some pills to help her." He took her in his arms and whispered, "I love you. Don't worry, we will sort this out for Alice."

"I love you too," she said. "And thank you for doing something practical about her problem."

She went back into the lounge where Alice was sitting with her eyes closed.

"Are you tired?" Leah asked softly.

"I am weary of struggling through each day," Alice answered. "It is so quiet here. I haven't felt so peaceful for a long time."

"You need complete rest of the body and of mind," Leah said gently. "And I'm sure the doctor will be able to give you something to help you relax."

"Are you pleased that Dad has come back?" Alice asked.

"It was quite unexpected and a bit of a shock at first. We are not the same people as when he went away and we have had to get to know each other all over again. But we love each other very much and we have an arrangement that works for both of us."

"I'm glad you are happy. You have not had an easy time," and Alice gave her mother a kiss.

"Time for bed, I think," Leah said. "I can keep you company in the big double bed or you can have your own little room."

"I think I'll have my own little room," she said. "I don't want to disturb you all night." Then she looked at Leah in amazement. "I made a decision," she cried. "I actually made a decision for myself."

"That's good," Leah said. "I'll carry your case up for you. I'll make some space in the wardrobe tomorrow and we'll sort out your washing."

Leah went to the bathroom cabinet and found some paracetamol. She gave two to Alice.

"Take these tonight, tomorrow we'll get something from the doctor."

Alice did what she was told and was soon tucked up in bed.

"You will have to go to school tomorrow," she said anxiously. "What if William comes while you are out?"

"Your father gave him explicit instructions not to contact you. I don't think even William will ignore that. In any case, I intend to take two days off school to help you settle in here."

"It is good to be home," Alice said sleepily and before long she was fast asleep.

Leah went downstairs to make sure all the doors were locked and the lights were out. She felt exhausted but also relieved that Alice had been rescued from a harmful situation. She knew she could never have done it by herself. William had such a chauvinistic attitude he would never have listened to her.

Adam was very tired after such a weekend. He felt glad to have finally met William, although he had no desire to be in his company. He felt sure they would cross swords again at some time in the future but right now all he needed to concentrate on was getting a good night's sleep, ready for the start of his new job. He had a good hot shower and was soon in bed. Just before he fell asleep, he reminded himself to ask Sally in the morning how she got on with Dominic West.

Chapter Eighteen

When Adam arrived at work the next morning, the first thing he did was to call Sally into his office. He needed to explain to her what had been going on and to ask her if she would take on the job of secretary to the area manager.

"Dominic said that you would tell me about it on Monday morning," she said. "Yes, I accept your offer and I'll continue to be your secretary."

Adam looked at her and raised his eyebrows.

"Dominic said that, did he? What else did Dominic say to you at the weekend?"

Sally blushed.

"It was all perfectly innocent. He drove me home, we had fish and chips at my house, we talked a great deal until very late so I suggested he stayed the night and he went home the next morning."

"And you say that all that is perfectly innocent," Adam gasped. "Fish and chips for the managing director, I don't believe it!"

"He said it was the best food he had eaten in ages, better than a gourmet meal," Sally replied, quite unmoved by Adam's comments. "And we ate it out of the paper," she added.

"You said that he stayed the night?"

"I do have a spare room. I always keep the bed made up in case my mother comes to stay."

Adam sat back in his chair and looked hard at Sally.

"I still can't believe it," he said.

"Well, it is the truth," she said, shortly. "He is actually a very lonely man despite his exalted position. He just wanted to talk like any normal person who is lonely."

"Did he tell you about his wife and children?"

"He told me a lot of things. In confidence."

Adam took the hint and changed the subject.

"I think I can hear your phone. You'd better go and answer it. Maybe it's Dominic?" he added playfully. "And ask Barry to come into my office as soon as he is free."

Sally gave him a piercing look and left the room. Soon after, Barry arrived.

"Is Jen alright?" Adam asked.

"Yes, she is okay. It took the whole of Sunday to pacify her but she is over the worst of the shock and already making plans for a new kitchen. How was your weekend?"

"Pretty hectic," said Adam. "I told Leah about the apartment and she took it quite well. I've promised her there will be no more big surprises but just little ones. Then I had to ask her about staying there if I become homeless. She didn't say I would have to sleep on the street."

"It sounds like you had fun," Barry said.

"You haven't heard the rest yet," Adam sighed. "Leah had told me that she was very worried about Alice, our daughter, so she phoned to see how she was. It was very obvious that she was in a worrying mental state so we decided to visit her on Sunday afternoon to see for ourselves what was happening. I won't bore you with all the details but I had a very unpleasant encounter with her husband and as a result, we brought Alice back home with us and Leah is looking after her. She urgently needs to see a doctor because she is on the edge of a complete breakdown."

"What did her husband say when you told him you were taking Alice away?"

"He was totally objectionable and threatened court action but he is just an overinflated windbag."

"What about the children?"

"Their father will have to look after them," Adam said firmly. "Now, let's get down to business. We must arrange a staff meeting to let them know our plans. When do you suggest we hold it?"

"We are too busy all day," Barry said. "I think the best time would be before we open in the morning."

Adam nodded his head in agreement.

"Tomorrow morning at nine-fifteen. It won't matter if we open up five minutes late."

"I will organise a memo for every staff member to tell them about it," Barry said.

Adam looked at him and laughed.

"This is your first job as manager of this office," he said. "Don't forget it is Monday morning and you are in charge."

"This role reversal will take a bit of getting used to," Barry said.

"It will be easier tomorrow because I shall be getting to grips with my new role too. I intend to go to Birmingham as soon as possible to sort out that office."

"Have you told Sally what is about to happen?" Barry asked.

"Yes, I told her this morning and she has agreed to carry on as my secretary," Adam said. "She also told me that Dominic West slept at her house last Friday night."

"What did you say?!" Barry spluttered.

"She said it was all very innocent," Adam said with a grin. "And of course, I believe her."

"He doesn't waste much time. I'm sure Sally can look after herself."

"I'm sure she can," Adam said with conviction.

"I'd better go and get this memo organised before you hit me with any more surprises," Barry said as he stood up. "You and your surprises," he muttered to himself as he went out the door.

Adam now turned his attention towards the area manager responsibilities; a trip to Birmingham was the first priority. He called Sally into his office.

"I want you to contact the Birmingham office and see if James Brown's secretary is still working there. If you can get hold of her, I'd like to speak with her. Don't forget that from today Barry will be the manager here. I shall be fully occupied with the area manager's business but of course, I will be available for any real problems."

"Who is going to be Barry's secretary?" Sally asked.

"He hopes to promote his present secretary but he hasn't asked her yet. He will do that after tomorrow's meeting," Adam said. "Have you finished sorting out those old files? We are going to need space in both our offices."

"I've nearly finished," Sally replied. "One of the junior staff has been helping me."

"If you feel that she is reliable, you can offer her a promotion to under-secretary. You are going to have a busy time helping me to sort out this mess and it will be good experience for her."

"Do you want to interview her?"

"No, I trust your judgement. Just make sure you notify the salary department."

Sally went back to her office thinking about what Adam had said. This is going to be a very interesting project and she felt quite excited. She found the number of the area manager's office in Birmingham and picked up the phone. A woman's voice answered and Sally asked if she was James Brown's secretary.

"Yes, I was until a week ago," she replied.

Sally introduced herself and explained about Adam's appointment.

"Thank goodness for that," said the woman. "I've been trying to find out what was happening but nobody seemed to know."

"Mr Richards will be coming to Birmingham on Wednesday and he would like you to be available in the office help him sort things out," said Sally. "Could I have your name please?"

"I'm Louise Bell and I'll make sure I am here."

"Thank you," Sally said. "Would you hold the line? Mr Richards would like to speak with you."

Sally buzzed Adam and told him who was waiting to speak with him.

"Put her through," he said.

He had a long conversation with Ms Bell.

"I need the details of every branch in the area, including their telephone numbers. It would be very helpful if you could prepare that for when I come on Wednesday?"

"I'll do my best," said Louise. "But everything is in such a muddle."

"You'd better have plenty of black bags ready," Adam said. "I'll see you at ten o'clock on Wednesday morning."

There was a knock at the door and Barry came in holding a piece of paper. He passed it over to Adam and said with a straight face:

"There is a staff meeting tomorrow morning. I trust you will be present?"

"I'll do my best," Adam replied and they both laughed.

"Two coffees please, Sally," Adam called out.

"No," said Barry, quickly. "I can't stop. I have two clients to see this morning. We managers are busy people you know?" and he went out chuckling to himself.

Sally came in with the two coffees and looked around.

"Where's Barry?" she asked.

"He has discovered that office managers are busy people," Adam said with a smile. "So, you will have to drink his coffee."

Sally picked it up and went towards the door but Adam stopped her.

"No," he said. "Manager's coffee must be drunk in a manager's office. That is a rule."

"I've never heard that before," she said as she sat down.

"That's because I have just introduced it," Adam said. "Now you can tell me if Mr Dominic West has shared any more secrets with you."

"They wouldn't be secrets if I told you," she said pertly. "You know that a good secretary can keep information confidential."

"That is true for business," Adam said. "But not for leisure time."

"I don't have to tell you about our private conversations," Sally said. "But I will tell you that he is no longer very happy with the job he does and is considering taking early retirement. He would like to get out of London and buy a home in the country near to a golf course."

"We all have our pipe dream," said Adam. "And sometimes they can come true. Certainly, they did in my case. Twelve years hoping for a second chance. Then I was offered the job here in Oxford and I knew that I would probably see Leah again and we did meet and to cut a long story short, we are back together. I shall always be guilty about what I did but we never stopped loving each other. We are still married and we have worked hard to renew our relationship. Dreams can come true if you believe in them." Adam stopped talking and looked at Sally. "Of course, what I just told you is confidential," he said. "I didn't mean to tell you my past problems but you are so easy to talk to."

Sally paused for a minute.

"It's funny that you should say that. It is exactly what Dominic said to me. Maybe you now understand why I said our conversation was private?"

"Yes, I understand," Adam said. "I shan't ask you again but I am ready to listen if you ever want to tell me anything."

Sally stood up and took the coffee cups off the desk.

"I'd better get back and finish sorting those files," she said as she left.

Adam looked at his watch. It was nearly one o'clock, time for some lunch, he decided but first, he had to phone Leah.

"How is Alice today?" he asked.

"I've taken two days' sick leave so that I can be with her," she answered. "I've made a doctor's appointment later today and I shall make sure she keeps it."

"Did she sleep well?"

"She slept all night and didn't wake until ten o'clock this morning. I've made sure she has had a shower and I intend to take her shopping to buy some new clothes. I've put the jewellery box in a drawer but I think it will need to go into a safe somewhere."

"I have a small safe among my belongings. We can use that one," Adam said. "I am going up to Birmingham on Wednesday, so I'll try and come over for an hour tomorrow evening. I don't want Alice to think that I have disappeared again. I'll ring you this evening to hear what the doctor has to say."

They said goodbye, then he called Sally to tell her he was going out for an hour. He walked up the street to his favourite bistro. Bridget saw him come in and went straight over to him.

"Good afternoon, Mr Richards," she said. "Would you like your favourite order?"

"Yes, please Bridget," he said smiling at her.

She soon brought him a ham roll and a coffee. Adam thanked her and relaxed for the next hour.

As he returned to his office, Sally stopped him.

"There has been a phone call for you from Mr West. I told him you would ring him back."

"I'm sure you know his number," Adam said with a smile. "I'll speak to him as soon as possible."

Five minutes later, his phone rang.

"Mr West wishes to speak with you," she said.

"Thank you, Sally," Adam said very politely. "Good afternoon, Dominic."

"Hello Adam," he replied. "I have some good news for you. I have spoken to the planning department and they are very interested in your ideas. They want to send the team down to do measurements etc followed by a finance team to do costings. Does Wednesday and Thursday suit you?"

"I shan't be here on Wednesday; I'm going to Birmingham. I can't expect Barry to spend time with them. He is finding life as a manager far too hectic at present. I would be available Thursday and Friday if you can possibly re-arrange it?"

"I'll do my best," Dominic said. "I'll leave a message for you with Sally. There is another thing. There is a board meeting on Friday morning when this project will come up for discussion. I don't anticipate any problems and I will come to Oxford on Friday afternoon to discuss the result. I look forward to seeing you," and he put the phone down.

Adam called Sally into his office and told her about the arrangements for later in the week.

"I am going to Birmingham on Wednesday," he said. "I shall bring back as many files as possible, so you had better spend the day transferring the present files to Barry's office. Then we can start the job of contacting all the branches in my area."

"Very well," she said. "I'll get Julie to help me."

She heard the phone ringing in her office and hurried to answer it.

She returned to Adam and said:

"Mr Truscott is on the phone. He wants to speak with you."

"Good," Adam said. "Put him through."

The two men greeted each other.

"I am giving you an update on the progress of your purchase, Mr Richards," said Truscott. "Everything is moving along nicely and it should be ready for completion on the fifth of December."

"Thank you very much," Adam said. "This is good news. There is one more thing which I wonder if you could help me with? I have a friend who might be needing a divorce lawyer in the not too distant future. Does your firm deal with such matters?"

"We have a solicitor who specialises in all kinds of family problems including divorce." Mr Truscott replied.

"Thank you. I will pass on that information."

As he put the phone down, Adam reminded himself that he had to give notice on his rented home. He contacted the lettings' agent and told them that he would be moving at the end of November. It was nearly closing time. He collected his briefcase and said goodbye to Sally.

"Mr West has been on the phone," she said. "He has changed the days as you requested and he will be coming to see you."

"You had better make sure the bed is made up in your spare room," he teased.

"Good night Mr Richards," she said, ignoring his remark.

On his way out, Adam called in at Barry's office.

"How was your first day in your new job?" he asked.

"Hectic! I need an assistant manager as soon as possible."

"You can deal with that after tomorrow," Adam said soothingly. "It will get easier."

He then told Barry about the planners and finance people who were coming at the end of the week.

"I will deal with them," said Adam. "But I will keep you informed about developments. I shall be going to Birmingham on Wednesday;

thank goodness the secretary is still working in the office. I'll see you early in the morning."

When Adam arrived home, he began to think about Leah and Alice. He knew this would mean extra work for Leah, who already had a busy life and he vowed to support her as much as he could. He wondered how they had got on at the doctor's. He sat on his settee and phoned Leah.

"Did you take Alice to the doctor's?"

"Yes," she said. "We saw a lady doctor and she was very good with Alice. She asked her some general questions but nothing too personal. Alice was very weepy and the doctor was most patient. She prescribed some special pills for Alice then she called for an assistant to take Alice to be weighed and have a blood test. When Alice was out of the room, she told me that in her opinion Alice was suffering from stress caused by some trauma and that she was on the verge of a full nervous breakdown. She said that she was hopeful that we had caught it in time and that by taking her out of the stressful environment, there was a good chance that she would recover."

"That is encouraging news," he said, relieved. "But it is going to be a long haul for you especially, as well as for Alice. Did the doctor say anything about counselling?"

"She did mention it is a possibility but she said that it was probable that Alice would give us bits of information which would tell us what had been happening. She wants to see Alice every week to check her progress."

"I've got a really busy week," Adam said. "I shall be away all day Wednesday but I will phone you every day and you can always contact me in an emergency."

"Alice is in the lounge. Would you like to speak with her?"

"Yes, I would," he said and Leah took the phone to her.

"Hello Dad," Alice said. "I'm watching television."

"What are you watching?"

"I don't know. I'm not really interested. It's too noisy."

"Why don't you turn the volume down and just look at the picture?"

"I can't be bothered," Alice muttered. "I'm too tired."

Leah took the phone back from Alice.

"It's nearly bedtime," she said. "We are going shopping tomorrow."

"I'll come over tomorrow after work," he said. "That will give you a break. I love you."

He spent the rest of the evening using the washing machine and tidying up the kitchen. He hoped there was a tumble drier at his new place, as he draped his clothes over the radiators. He switched the television on but there was nothing that interested him, so he switched it off. He had a shower and went to bed. He soon fell asleep and didn't wake until the next morning.

Chapter Nineteen

He was up early and on his way into the office. Many of the staff had already arrived and by nine-fifteen, everyone had assembled. There was a distinct air of excitement and anticipation in the room. Barry called for order and Adam stood at the front and began to tell the staff about the upcoming changes.

"Barry is now the manager of this branch as from yesterday. He is responsible for all the business activities and he will be appointing a new assistant. I am still the general manager and will be available if there are any major problems. But my new role as area manager will keep me very busy and I shall be travelling a lot. The first floor upstairs will be converted into my office and other amenities. The planners will be coming on Thursday to make an action plan for the building work which will take place. It will mean some disruption downstairs too and I hope you will all be patient and understanding while the work is going on. Now, are there any questions?"

One of the male clerks put up his hand.

"You said that a new assistant manager will be needed. Are you going to advertise it or appoint from within the office?"

"We shall be advertising it for one week," Adam answered. "And any member of the present staff is free to apply."

"We are a very busy branch," said a girl. "Will you be taking on more staff?"

"I am hoping we can manage for the next two weeks and by then we should have a better understanding of the kind of staff we need. We shall be doing it as soon as possible. Are there any more questions?"

Nobody spoke so Adam said:

"It is nearly time to open the doors. Thanks to all of you for coming in early. If we can pull together then you will be working in an office which will be the top-rated in the country."

He gestured to Barry to come with him to his office as the customers began to come in. There was a real sense of excitement in the air and everyone was smiling. Barry followed him into the office.

"I'm relieved that we have been able to tell the staff what is happening," Adam said. "I thought they took the news very well. Now we can begin to make some real progress."

"The first thing I want to do is get the advert in for a new assistant manager," Barry said. "But before that, I must speak to my secretary about her promotion. If she accepts then she can start to work more closely with Sally."

"I shall be here all day," said Adam. "I can help you out with any appointments you have if necessary."

Barry thanked him and stood up to leave.

"There's one more thing, Barry. I hope to bring back a large number of files tomorrow, so all the files in here will have to come over to you. Will you have space?"

"I'll do my best but Laura is having to get used to dealing with her new role and she is pretty busy."

"Get one of the junior staff members to help her," said Adam. "Have a word with Sally and see how she organised it."

Adam spent the rest of the morning making sure that the current files were up to date before they were handed over to Barry. He reminded Sally to try and clear her shelves too. He was just about to go for his lunch when Barry came in.

"I've spoken to Laura," he said. "And she has agreed to stay on as my secretary. I've told her that she can liaise with Sally if necessary. The advert has gone to the company magazine and will appear on Friday."

"Good," Adam said." I'm just taking my lunch break and I intend to leave early this afternoon. I've promised Leah to spend some time with Alice. Don't forget that you can now take a lunch break when you want to. A bit of fresh air is always good for you."

After lunch, Adam spoke with Sally.

"I shall be leaving early this afternoon," he said. "I shall be in Birmingham all day tomorrow but I will keep in touch with you."

"Have a good journey," she said. "I wonder what you will find up there?"

"A big mess by all accounts," Adam sighed. "I do hope that Louise

Bell has started to sort it out."

He left the office and drove down to Leah's house. He let himself in with his key and went to find Leah. She was in the kitchen warming up some soup. He put his arms around her and kissed her.

"How are things?" he asked.

"Not that easy. We went to the chemist with the doctor's prescription and got the pills. I had to persuade Alice to take one and I am going to have to monitor it quite closely."

"Did you go shopping?"

"We had a look in one or two shops but Alice wasn't interested. Some of the clothes she has brought with her are really old and dirty. I think I will have to go by myself to buy new things for her. I know she used to have some really nice expensive outfits but there is no way we can go back for them."

"Has she talked to you about the way she feels?" he asked.

"Not really. I think she has had a reaction today, to having actually left the house."

"I'll go and see her," he said and he went into the lounge.

Alice was sitting on the settee just staring into space. He sat down beside her and put his arm around her shoulders.

"Hello Dad," she said in a dull voice.

"Hello, Alice. What are you thinking about?"

Alice looked at him.

"I was thinking about nothing. My brain has gone to sleep."

"Your brain needs a good rest," he said, taking her hand. "You can let other people think for you."

She laid her head on Adam's shoulder.

"I'm glad you are here," she said. "You make me feel safe."

"I won't let anyone hurt you again," he said. "Your mother and I will always look after you and we will do our best to make you happy, but you have got to try hard to get better too. That means listening to people like the doctor and telling us about what happened to you."

"I can't do that," Alice said tearfully. "I don't know what is happening to me."

"Nothing is happening to you now, that can't be put right but it will take time. When something happened to me it took me a long time to recover but I kept trying and now I am in a much happier place in my life."

Leah came to the lounge door.

"I've made some soup or to be more precise I've heated some soup. There is enough for all of us in the dining room."

They sat at the table and Leah gave Alice a small bowl and persuaded her to try it. Alice tried a couple of spoonsful and then put the spoon down. Adam went to say something but Leah gave him a warning look. A few moments' later, Alice picked up the spoon and this time she finished it up.

"I used to enjoy cooking," she said. "I know you aren't very keen on it, Mum. One day I'll cook you both dinner."

"That will be very nice," Adam said. "I usually have to go to Jen's house if I want a good meal."

Alice looked at him aghast.

"I'm sure Mum does her best."

Leah laughed and said firmly:

"Don't believe everything your father says. He can be a terrible tease."

"Of course, I was teasing you," he said.

He collected the empty bowls from the table and kissed Leah on the forehead as he went into the kitchen. Alice stood up and yawned,

"I'm tired," she said. "I think I'll go to bed."

"I'll come up and tuck you in just like I used to when you were little," he said. "I'll even tell you a bedtime story if you would like me too".

"No thanks Dad," Alice said. "I don't believe in happy ever after," and she went upstairs.

Leah gave Adam a glass of water and a pill.

"Make sure she takes this," she said.

He went up to the bedroom and found Alice already in bed. He handed her the pill and she swallowed it with a drink of water.

"Good girl," Adam said and he bent over to kiss her goodnight.

She put her arms around his neck and said:

"I love you Dad. I know you will look after me." Then her eyes began to droop and in two minutes she was fast asleep.

Adam wiped away a tear and went back to the lounge where Leah was waiting with two cups of coffee. She could see that he was a bit upset and she held his hand.

"You have always had a special bond with Alice haven't you, ever since she was a little girl?" she said. "She was always able to twist you around her little finger".

"They say that fathers bond with their daughters and mothers with sons. I think that this is probably true," he said.

"I have a feeling that Alice will find it easier to talk to you than me. It is a different kind of relationship."

"I know what you mean," he said. "And I must be ready to listen when the time comes."

He thought for a moment.

"I gave notice on my rented place today. I have to be out by November 30th so I shall need to stay here for at least a week if that is alright with you?"

"That's fine. "In view of what has happened with Alice, do you think it might be a good idea to come here before your notice expires? I'm sure it will help her if you see her more often."

"That is a possibility," Adam said. "I shall need to think about it and I'll need to decide about the furniture. There are one or two pieces which I am particularly attached to and I need to decide what to do with the surplus. I think I will phone the estate agent and see if we can get into the apartment next weekend. Maybe you could come and look in my house this Saturday or Sunday? It would be a little outing for Alice too."

"I could do it on Saturday afternoon," she said. "I think Peter may be bringing the children down on Sunday. He said that Janet wanted to go Christmas shopping with a friend."

"We'll make it Saturday then. When will you be going shopping for Sunday dinner?"

"I'll have to go on Saturday morning. Alice will be here alone for a couple of hours."

"I could come over earlier on Saturday and I can be with her while you are out?"

"That would be a big help," she said and kissed him.

"We are going to have to snatch precious moments together," Adam said mournfully, as he hugged and kissed her.

"We can survive. The important thing is to sort out Alice's problems."

Adam stood up.

"I shall be away all day tomorrow. Sally knows how to contact me if necessary. I'll phone you in the evening."

On the way home, Adam thought about what Leah suggested. It might be a good idea and take some pressure off her. He would need to organise storage for the furniture he wanted to keep and for all his boxes which shouldn't be too difficult. He decided to get a storage company and when the sale was completed, they could bring it down and put it in the apartment. The only thing to decide then was what to do with the modern furniture. He thought he wouldn't get rid of that. It might prove very useful at a later date.

The next morning, he set off very early for Birmingham. The office was in the middle of the city but fortunately, there was a car park right next to it. He arrived in good time and met Louise Bell at ten o'clock. The office was situated above a shoe shop so she took him upstairs. She unlocked the door and went in. The room was dark, even when she opened the blinds. Adam looked around for the light switch and pressed it. The place was immediately lit by the fluorescent lights but the whole atmosphere was dreary and uninspiring.

"What a depressing place," Adam said.

"Mr Brown was a depressing man," she said.

"Why did you work for him?"

"It suited me. He was out and about quite a lot and it fitted in with looking after the family."

Adam was looking at the shelves which were stacked with files.

"Are these current files?" he asked.

"No, those are on the shelf behind the desk," Louise answered. "Those other files were already there when I came. I've never looked at them."

Adam pulled one off the shelf and blew the dust off it. He opened it and looked at the date. It was more than ten years' old. He looked at several others and they were all a similar date. He then went to the other shelves and did the same. This time the date was current.

"I want to take these up-to-date files back with me. Can you find some boxes to put them in?" he said. "All those out-dated files can be disposed of."

"How am I going to get rid of that lot?" Louise asked. "It is far too many to put in the office waste."

"You can arrange for an industrial company to collect them. They will take them away and shred them. Have you a telephone directory?" Adam said.

She rummaged in the desk drawer and found a directory of local services.

"Phone them now," he said. "And arrange a time that will suit you as soon as possible."

Louise did as she was asked and arranged a collection for two days' time.

Adam was having a good look at the furniture in the room. Most of it was old but the desk seemed to be in good condition. Adam inspected it closely and saw that underneath all the grime and dust it was a real antique.

"I will arrange for the desk to be taken to my office," he said. "But you can get rid of the rest of the furniture. Once the files have been removed, you won't need to lock the office door. I would hope that the place will be empty by this time next week."

"I am hoping to get another job soon," Louise said. "What is my position here?"

"I need you to supervise the clear out of this office. So, you will remain as an employee until a week on Friday. I will inform the financial department and they will be in touch with you early next week."

"I shall be glad to see the back of this place," she said. "It has not been a very pleasant job."

"I understand what you mean," Adam said sympathetically. "But if you can face it for another ten days, I would be most grateful."

"I'll do what you have asked. It is a change to be given precise instructions. Everything has been such a mess but now I know the end is in sight."

He thanked her and she went downstairs to see if the shoe shop had any spare boxes.

Adam looked through the drawers in the desk. There were lots of pens and pencils and other office equipment. Some drawers had loose papers and one drawer had a little black book. Adam picked it up and looked inside it. The pages were covered in names which were mostly of women. I'd better keep this safe he thought and he put it in his pocket.

Louise came back with two large boxes which they filled with files. Adam carried them down to the car which was parked behind the shop. She found another box for the remaining files and put it in the boot of the car. They went back upstairs.

"You can always contact me or my secretary if you have any problems," he said. "All invoices should be sent to me and when the office is empty, you can arrange to have it cleaned professionally. I would like you to phone me at ten o'clock on Monday morning to let me know what progress has been made." He shook hands with her. "Thank you for your co-operation," he said and he left her.

Louise watched him go and thought what a nice man he was, so business-like and decisive. She wouldn't mind working for him. She locked the office door and went off to the Job Centre to look for a new job.

Adam walked out into the busy street. It was nearly one o'clock and he needed a coffee and something to eat but first, he had to speak to Barry. He found a telephone box and called him.

"How's it going?" asked Barry.

"It is a pretty depressing office," Adam answered. "But the secretary there has been helpful and I have sorted out as much as I can at this stage. I've got three boxes of files in the car which I would like to drop off this evening before you close. I shall be leaving here in about an hour and I should be in Oxford by four o'clock. You know how difficult it is to park so can you have one of the men looking out for me, ready to unload quickly?"

"Yes, I can do that. Will you be coming into the office today?"

"No, not today," Adam said. "I'll see you in the morning."

He found a café and enjoyed a quick break. Then he went back to the car and was soon on his way to Oxford. There were no delays on the motorway and he drove straight to the main door of the Branch. As he stopped, one of the male clerks came out and carried the boxes inside.

"Put them in my office please," Adam said.

He decided to go straight home and the first thing he did was phone Leah.

"How is Alice today?"

"About the same," Leah answered. "I'm going to make an appointment at my hairdressers for her. She might feel better when her hair is washed and styled. She needs some decent clothes too and I know she has a wardrobe-full back at her house but how can she get them?"

Adam thought for a minute.

"You told me that Peter was coming down on Sunday. I wonder if he could bring them?"

"We can't ask Peter to go to William and ask for Alice's clothes. I know he would rather not get involved," Leah said urgently.

"I've only just got back from Birmingham. I need a shower and something to eat then I will come over to you. I'll think of something," he said.

After he showered, he drove to his favourite pub and had a good meal. Feeling a lot better, he set off for Leah's house. On the way, he thought about the problem and by the time he arrived, he had worked out a plan.

Alice was sitting in the lounge and he sat down beside her.

"How's my little girl today?" he asked.

"I'm tired," she said. "I just want to go to sleep."

"That's okay," he said. "But make sure you are wide awake on Saturday."

"Why Saturday?" she said in an anxious voice. "What's happening on Saturday?"

"I'm going to take your mother and you for a little ride in the car," Adam said. "I need your Mum's advice on something.

"We shan't be visiting anyone shall we?"

"No, we shall be looking at some of my furniture," he said reassuringly.

Leah came in with a pill and a glass of water.

"Time to go up," she said to Alice. "Remember you are going to have a shower before you go to bed."

"I'll come and tuck you in," said Adam, as Alice left the room.

Leah was about to follow her but Adam stopped her.

"I need to speak to Peter," he said. "Can you give me his number?"

"It's in that address book on the table," she said, as she left the room.

Adam rang Peter and had a long conversation with him. He told him where Alice was and explained the problem of collecting her clothes. They agreed a plan and Adam put the phone down just as Leah came into the lounge.

"Alice is in bed," she said.

"I'll go up and say goodnight," Adam answered.

"You smell nice," he told Alice when he bent over to kiss her.

"I have to use Mum's stuff," she said. "I haven't any of my own."

"I'm sure Mum doesn't mind. When you feel better, you can go to the shop and buy some for yourself. Now sweet dreams and I'll see you to-morrow."

He switched off the light and went back to the lounge where Leah was waiting. He put his arm around her.

"You look tired. Are you sleeping well?"

"I am sleeping okay but it is the emotional side that is so draining. Alice is so depressed about everything that it rubs off on me. She has no interest in anything."

"You need a break from it, even if it is only for an afternoon. I wonder if Jen might help?"

"I'll speak to her about it," she sighed.

"I've been thinking about getting Alice's clothes down here. I've spoken to Peter and he has agreed to collect them but he won't go and ask William," Adam said. "Have you got a telephone number for William?"

"It's here," she said, opening up the address book.

"I am going to phone William and tell him that Peter will collect Alice's clothes and personal belongings on Sunday morning. I shall tell him to have it ready in black bags because Peter doesn't want to go into the house."

"He's not going to like being ordered about," Leah said nervously.

"The alternative is that I go up and collect it and I don't think he is keen on another discussion with me," Adam said firmly and promptly phoned William.

"Hello?" said a disgruntled voice.

"Is that William Rankin?" Adam asked.

"Yes. Who the hell are you?"

"I am Adam Richards, Alice's father."

"What do you want?"

"I'll come straight to the point," Adam said briefly and told William what he wanted him to do.

"You can't order me to do that," William fumed. "I've got too many other more important things to do."

"This is very important for Alice," Adam said firmly. "She needs to have her own belongings including her toiletries."

"If she came back where she belongs there wouldn't be a problem," William said tersely.

"There is no chance of that at present," said Adam. "So, I suggest you co-operate and do as I ask. Her brother Peter will come to your house at ten-thirty on Sunday morning. Kindly make sure that all of Alice's belongings are ready to be collected." He put the phone down. "One more phone call," he said. "And that is all sorted".

He phoned Peter and told him the arrangements had been confirmed, then he returned to Leah.

"I've been thinking about the suggestion you made about me coming to stay here. I think it is a good idea and I'll probably do it in a couple of weeks. You are going to have to find space for Alice's clothes and I really think you should ask Jen to help you. Alice is not going to do much in her present state of mind."

"I'll speak to her tomorrow," she said. "But do you know what I am looking forward to most of all?"

"I've no idea," Adam said with a grin.

"I'm looking forward to sleeping in a double bed with my husband."

Adam put his arms around her and hugged her.

"Hold on to that thought," he said. "You won't have to wait too long," and he kissed her. "I must go, now; busy day ahead" He stood up and looked at Leah. "Do you know?" he said. "William didn't even ask how Alice was."

"Par for the course. I can't see her going back to that house."

"You may well be right," he said and kissed her goodnight.

Chapter Twenty

Adam arrived at work early the next morning. He found three large boxes of files in his office and all of his shelves were empty except for one. He started to empty the boxes and fill the shelves. Fortunately, the files were roughly in alphabetical order and he had nearly finished when Sally walked in.

"Good morning, Mr Richards," she said. "Did you have a good journey yesterday?"

"It was the most depressing place," he replied. "I met the secretary and told her what to do with all of the old files which were covered in dust. I've brought the current files with me but I haven't looked at any of them yet. You must have had a very busy day," he said indicating the empty shelves.

"It certainly was hectic," she said. "All of my files were taken down to Barry's secretary but there was no room for your files to go into Barry's office so I have put them in mine."

"There is one thing which I forgot yesterday. I asked Louise Bell to make a list of the branches which that office was dealing with and I forgot to ask her for it. She didn't mention it either and I wonder if she actually did it. Can you phone and ask her to fax it through?"

"I'll do that this morning," Sally said. "There was a call from the planning department to say they would be coming at eleven o'clock and the finance people will be here to-morrow morning."

"I think I'd better go and speak to Barry," Adam said. "Can you finish stacking these files and get rid of the boxes while I've gone?"

He walked through to Barry's office but Barry wasn't there so he went to speak to Laura, his secretary.

"Good morning, Mr Richards," she said.

Adam didn't answer; he was looking at the state of the office. There were files and paper everywhere, even Laura's desk was stacked with boxes. She noticed the surprised look on his face.

"Mr Wilson was so busy yesterday that he didn't have time to sort out his office. He has several appointments so he needed to keep it tidy."

"Has he any appointments today?" Adam asked.

"Just one at ten-thirty."

"Tell Sally the name and I will take that meeting for him. By the way, where is he?"

"There was a problem with one of the computers. He's gone to sort it out".

Just at that moment, Barry walked in.

"Hello Adam," he said. "I didn't know you were waiting for me. Come into my office."

They went into the room next door and Barry shut the door.

"Yesterday was a nightmare," he said as he sat down. "And today hasn't started too well either."

"Is it the same computer that keeps playing up?" Adam asked.

"Yes, it is. It means that we are one place short on the front desk and that is when the queues get long."

"This has happened several times now. I will contact the technical department and ask for it to be replaced," said Adam. "I could hardly see Laura for files and papers," he went on. "How is that going to be sorted out?"

"The problem is that I have nowhere to put the books and files out of this office. It is not very big and I need to keep it tidy for interviewing clients."

"We shall need to find a space for the new assistant manager," Adam said. "Have we got any empty rooms?"

"The only other room is a storeroom at the end of the corridor. It holds our spare stationery supplies."

"Has it got a window?" Adam asked. "I would never give anyone an office without a window."

"Yes, it has a window but it is not very big."

"It will do as an interim measure," Adam said. "Get one of the male members of staff to help you tidy it up and then move all the files from this office into that room. Then you can tackle what is in Laura's office."

"I have an appointment at ten thirty," Barry said. "I'll start moving after that."

"I've told Laura that I will take your ten-thirty appointment, so you can start straight away. The planners are coming at eleven o'clock and Sally can show them upstairs if I haven't finished. I'll see you after lunch."

Adam went back to his office. He could tell that Barry hadn't come to grips with having a lot more authority than before and he would need some support in building up his confidence. He asked Sally to get him a cup of coffee and when she brought it in, she was also carrying a file.

"This is the file for Barry's client," she said.

"Thank you, Sally. I'm hoping to be free by eleven o'clock but if I'm not, could you take the planners upstairs and stay with them until I have finished?"

He glanced at the file and was pleased to see that it was someone he had already dealt with. This should be quite straightforward he thought as he drank his coffee. The client arrived punctually and the business was done quickly.

Adam called Sally and asked her to put him through to the technical department. He had a long conversation with them and they agreed to replace the computer. He then went to find Sally but she was not in her office. He went into the main office and spoke to the receptionist. She told him that Sally had met the two visitors and had taken them upstairs. Adam went up to the first floor and the men introduced themselves.

Adam explained to them the plan which he had in mind. They discussed it thoroughly then Adam suggested that they went back down to his office. He asked Sally to get some coffee and to ask Barry to come along. They sat there enjoying the coffee and Mr Forbes, the chief planner, said:

"It seems to me that you have both put a lot of thought into this enterprise and it will certainly be a unique development. I see no reason why what you have in mind cannot be achieved. Of course, the ultimate decision will be with the Board of Governors but I will definitely recommend your plans to them. I understand that the finance people are coming tomorrow?"

"Yes, they will be here in the morning. Thank you for your support.

I hope they will be generous," Adam said.

They all shook hands and the men left. Adam looked at Barry and grinned.

"That's the first hurdle jumped," he said. "Keep your fingers crossed for tomorrow."

He told Barry that a new computer would be coming early next week and asked him how he was getting on with sorting Laura's office.

"We have moved my files into the storeroom," Barry said. "Now Laura and I can start to clear her office."

"That's good. I want to have a look at the files I brought down yesterday. I shan't be late leaving. I try to see Alice every day if I can, even if it is only for a few minutes. I think Leah is beginning to feel the pressure."

"Has she talked to Jen about it?" Barry asked. "She might be able to help Leah."

"I suggested that to her last evening and she promised that she would speak to Jen today," Adam said. "I've given notice on my rented house and I will move in with Leah until my purchase is completed in early December. I'm hoping that Alice will soon be able to give us some clues about what has been happening to her."

After Barry had left, Adam took down one of the files. When he opened it, he found the name of the branch on the first page together with the telephone number. He turned over the page and was surprised to find very little relevant information and no record of any visits made by James Brown. He checked several more files and they were in the same state. He called Sally in and showed her what he had found.

"We shall need to compile new files for each branch," he said. "These are quite useless."

"That is a big undertaking," Sally said. "It is going to take some time."

"You are going to need some help. Have you spoken to Julie yet?"

"I haven't said anything to her until I knew exactly what was happening. I will speak to her to-day."

"Did you manage to get through to Louise Bell about the list of names she promised me?"

"I've tried several times but there is no reply."

"Don't waste any more time on it," he said. "We shall have to do it ourselves. I just hope that she does the other things I asked her to do. It looks as if I may have to take another trip up there next week to check on it."

"What would you like me to do first?" Sally asked.

"You need to look inside every file and make a note of the name and address of the branch plus its telephone number. Then we shall have to look closely at each individual file and decide which papers to keep and which ones to throw. Julie will be kept busy using the shredder. You can use my office when I am not here."

"I'll start on the list today. It will be ready by Monday at the latest."

"That's fine," he said. "We've got the finance people tomorrow morning and Dominic West in the afternoon. We should be able to start getting more organised next week."

Adam spent the next two hours looking at the files and then he told Sally that he was leaving the office. On his way out, he went to see how Barry was getting on with sorting out his muddles. He was pleased to see that Laura's office was relatively tidy and he went next door to find Barry. He was just putting the last pile of books on a shelf.

"That looks much better, Barry," said Adam. "It has been quite a task hasn't it?"

"It was hard work," he said. "I shall be glad to finish today."

"The advert should come out tomorrow. I wonder what the response will be. Did you ask the applicants to send a C.V.?"

"Yes, I included that and the closing date is next Friday."

"It will be interesting to see what talent is out there," Adam said. "We must remember about equal opportunities. I'll see you in the morning."

He went straight home and phoned Leah but there was no answer. So, he made himself a cup of tea and looked at his post. Most of it was junk mail but there was one letter from the letting agency acknowledging the notice he had given them.

He sat on the settee and thought about moving house. He felt relieved to be staying with Leah for an extra week or two. Now, it was just a matter of deciding which furniture to take. He remembered Leah's comment about Alice not going back and it occurred to him that if that was the case, Alice would eventually need a house of her own. He could see it all ending in divorce and a messy one. William was a slippery character and would fight all the way. He decided it might be a good idea to put all his excess furniture in storage for a while. All this was going to need some very careful planning and he made up his mind to take two days' leave when the time came.

He went into the kitchen and cooked himself scrambled eggs on toast and made another cup of tea. Then he returned to the lounge and tried again to phone Leah. This time she answered.

"I rang about an hour ago but got no reply," he said.

"We went to the hairdressers. Alice had her hair washed and cut. It looks very nice but it was quite an ordeal for her."

"What do you mean? What happened?"

"I warned my hairdresser about Alice's state of health and she was very patient with her. But when she picked up the scissors, Alice panicked and it took ten minutes to calm her down."

"Are you saying that the sight of scissors caused Alice to be so frightened?"

"That's what it looks like," Leah answered. "She actually came out in a cold sweat."

"You must mention that to the doctor. I've just finished my tea and I'll come over. I'll be with you in half an hour."

When he arrived at Leah's house, he found Leah and Alice sitting on the settee. Leah stood up to go into the kitchen and Adam took her place. He put an arm around Alice.

"I like your new hairstyle."

"Thanks, Dad," she answered. "Mum took me to the hairdressers".

"Do you like your new look?"

"I like it now," she said. "But I didn't like having it cut."

"Mum said the hairdresser was very gentle," Adam said. "What didn't you like about it?"

"I don't like anyone using scissors near me," Alice said abruptly.

Leah came in with the cups of tea and a tin of biscuits.

"Are you going to have a biscuit this evening?" Adam asked her.

"I'm not hungry," Alice said. "It is not long since we had our tea."

"What did you have for tea?"

"Auntie Jen brought a cottage pie," Alice replied. "I had some of that. It was nice to see her."

"It's getting late and you have had a busy day," Leah told Alice. "Time for bed I think."

"I'm ready for sleep. Although I don't feel as tired as I have been."

"That's good news," Adam said. "Up you go and I'll come and say goodnight."

Alice went up to bed and they heard her go into the bathroom to clean her teeth. Five minutes later Adam went up to tuck her in.

"I think you have been a very brave girl today and I am really proud of you," he said encouragingly.

"Thanks, Dad," Alice said as she put her arms around his neck. "I could only do it because Mum was there to help me."

"That's what we want to do," Adam said. "We want to help you feel better." He gave her the pill and a drink of water and kissed her goodnight. "Sleep well," he said as he switched off the light.

Downstairs, Leah was waiting in the lounge. He sat down by her and kissed her.

"I thought Alice seemed a little better," he said. "She was certainly more talkative."

"She relaxed when we got home," Leah said. "But I've never seen her in the state she was in at the hairdresser's."

"It's very strange that scissors can cause such a reaction. There must be some underlying connection that we don't know about yet."

"I spoke to Jen today and told her the whole story and she has offered to do anything to help. She suggested that Alice should go round there one afternoon and do some cooking with her. I know she will love that."

"Leah, do you think we should try and contact some of her old friends who still live here? There must be one or two who would come and talk to her."

"That's a good idea," she said. "I'll try and find out from her which ones she remembers. William managed to alienate all her friends as well as her family."

Adam then told Leah the thoughts he had about Alice's future and the possibility of a divorce.

"It will be a long hard road," he said. "But I will find her the best possible lawyer. I don't trust William and we shall have to go through everything with a fine-tooth comb."

"We are not at that stage yet," she said, firmly. "And in any case, the desire for a divorce must come from Alice, not from us. I wouldn't even mention the word to her at this stage."

"I only thought about it in relation to the necessity for her to have her own house. I decided to put my unwanted furniture in storage because it may be useful at some later date. I shall probably put some of the ultra-modern items in storage as well. They can always be sold later if necessary."

"You like to plan way ahead don't you?" she said admiringly.

"Planning ahead is a way of organisation which avoids problems and means you can go on and think about other things at the same time," he said. "I'll come and stay for two nights at the weekend."

"That will be nice," Leah said dreamily. "Maybe it's my turn to give you a little surprise."

Adam gave her a look and smiled.

"Can't wait," he said as he kissed her goodbye.

Chapter Twenty-One

The next morning the finance team arrived promptly and Adam had a lengthy discussion with them.

"The planners were very impressed with your ideas," the chief spokesperson said. "And I must say that your plans are very interesting. I see no reason why they should not go ahead once the Board has ratified them."

"That is good news," he said. "We are certainly tight on space at present and we look forward to getting ourselves properly organised."

He escorted the visitors to the front entrance and shook hands with each of them. When he returned to his office, he called Sally in.

"That was a very good discussion," he said. "And I hope it won't be too long before we get some action."

"There has been a phone call from Mr West," said Sally. "He will be here at three o'clock this afternoon."

"Did he say anything else?" Adam asked with an innocent expression.

Sally gave him a sly look.

"He said he would like to take me out for dinner this evening. That is all," she said.

"No fish and chips tonight then?"

"Who knows?" she said. "I might choose that as my main course."

Adam laughed.

"Enjoy your meal," he said.

Sally returned to her office and Adam went to find Barry. He was not in his office and Adam asked Laura where he was.

"He has gone out to get a sandwich," she answered. "It is his lunch break."

Adam decided to take a tour of the main area. It had been a while since he spoke to the staff there. He was pleased to find it running smoothly and the staff seemed to be quite happy. He returned to his own office and on the way, he spoke to Sally.

"How are you getting on with that list?" he asked.

"I'm more than halfway through," she answered. "Do you realise there are fifty-one branches in your area?"

"That is more than I thought. It is certainly going to be a full-time job. Perhaps a major re-organisation will be necessary?"

He spent the next couple of hours leafing through some of the files then he rang for Sally.

"You'd better make sure the coffee machine is working and the biscuit tin is full," he said with a grin. "Our visitor will be arriving soon and he will expect to be met by you."

Sally just gave him a look and went off to follow his instructions. At three o'clock exactly there was a knock on his door.

"Mr West is here to see you," said Sally.

"Thank you, Sally. I am sure Mr West is looking forward to a cup of coffee with milk and one sugar," Adam said with a straight face as he shook hands with Dominic.

She went away and the two men smiled at each other. Dominic looked a little confused.

"It's alright," said Adam. "Sally knows I am only teasing her."

She soon came back with the coffee and poured out two cups. She pushed the sugar bowl towards Dominic but she didn't say a word.

"Your boss is in a very playful mood today," Dominic said. "I'm sure it will pass."

"It can't pass quickly enough for me," Sally said drily and she left the room.

"She'll get over it," Dominic said. "I'm taking her out for a meal this evening."

"I haven't taken Leah out for some time," Adam said thoughtfully. "I must do something about that but it may be difficult at present."

"You'll have to make time," Dominic said.

"There is an added complication for now."

He gave Dominic a brief outline of Alice's problems. He was very sympathetic.

"If you need a good lawyer, I could give you the name of mine. He is doing a great job sorting out my affairs and they should be settled by the end of the month."

"Thanks," Adam said. "I'll bear that in mind."

"Now, down to business," Dominic said. "The planners let me have an interim report for this morning's Board meeting. Their recommendation was that it should all go ahead and the Board unanimously endorsed it, subject to the report from the finance department. So, the detailed plans should be done by next week and then it is just a question of choosing a contractor."

"That is all good news," Adam said in a delighted voice. "We urgently need that extra space."

"How did you get on in Birmingham?"

"It was a pretty dreary office and the secretary was not over efficient but I sorted it out as much as possible. There were shelves with ancient files which will all be thrown out and shredded. The furniture was mostly broken except for the desk which I intend to keep. The rest can go to the tip."

"I assume you brought the current files back with you?"

"Yes, they are the ones on these shelves," Adam said and he reached up and took one down. He passed it to Dominic who quickly looked through it.

"There is very little useful information in here," Dominic said. "Are they all like this?"

"Yes, they are. We are going to have to check each one and then make new files."

"That is a lot of extra work, Adam. How are you going to fit it in?"

"Sally is going to have an assistant to help with the day-to-day running of the office so that she and I can concentrate on sorting this lot out. There is something I need to pass on to you," he added as he reached into his pocket and took out the little black book.

"What is it?" Dominic asked as he took it from Adam.

"I found it in one of the drawers in James Brown's desk. I didn't think it should be left lying around."

Dominic was looking closely at the pages, then he looked at Adam.

"This is full of women's names and ages. Some of them are teenage girls," he said in a shocked voice. "This needs to be kept in a safe place, it is truly damning evidence if ever we need it." He put it in his briefcase. "It would appear that James Brown was more dangerous than we imagined. Perhaps we should alert the Police," he said thoughtfully.

There was a knock at the door and Sally came in to collect the dirty cups.

"We have finished our business," Adam said to her. "Why don't you go home early today? I'm sure Dominic will give you a lift."

Sally looked at Dominic.

"That's fine," he said. "I'm ready when you are."

"I'll just go and wash up these cups. Then I will be ready."

When she left the room, Adam said:

"Sally is a lovely person with a very kind heart. You will look after her, won't you?"

"I am very fond of Sally," Dominic answered. "I promise you I would never do anything to hurt her, in fact, I am more likely to spoil her but not until after my divorce is settled," he said quickly.

A few minutes' later Sally returned and she and Dominic went off together. Well, that's my good deed for the day, he thought. There may even be a happy ending ahead. He picked up his briefcase and went to tell Barry that he was just leaving. He told him what Dominic had said.

"He doesn't waste time, does he?" said Barry.

"No, he doesn't," said Adam and thought about Sally. "I don't believe in wasting time either. If something needs to be done then get on and do it."

"I don't function like that," Barry said. "I'm a bit more circumspect about things. By the way, we have already received ten applications for the job we advertised. I shouldn't be surprised if that trebles by

Monday."

"We must be sure to pick the right one," Adam said. "That should keep you busy next week."

"I'm hoping you will have some input. I could do with some guidance."

"Of course, I will do what I can to help, but the final decision is yours," Adam said firmly. "I'll see you on Monday."

He left the office and drove home. He found a ready-made lasagne in the fridge and he put it in the microwave. He ate it in the lounge as he watched the news on the television. He felt quite out of touch with what was happening in the world, he had been so busy with everything in his life.

When the news had finished, he switched the television off and went upstairs to have a shower. Then he packed his overnight bag with some clean clothes and he was soon ready to leave the house. Fifteen minutes later he arrived at Leah's and let himself in with his key. Leah was talking to someone on the phone and he went straight into the lounge. Alice was sitting on the settee looking through a magazine. He kissed her.

"Are you looking for anything in particular?" he asked.

"Not really," she said. "It is ages since I even picked up a magazine."

Leah came into the room and gave Adam a kiss.

"I heard you come in," she said. "But I was on the phone." She turned to Alice and said: "I was talking to your old school friend, Penny. Do you remember her?"

"Of course, I do," Alice answered. "I haven't seen her for years."

"She rang up to find your address," Leah continued. "She is organising a reunion of your year and wanted to know how to contact you."

Alice looked terrified.

"I can't go to a reunion; William might be there."

"Don't worry," said Leah in a soothing voice. "I told her you were staying here and explained the reason. She said that she would love to come and see you when you felt well enough."

"I don't want to see anyone," Alice said. "They might tell William where I am," and she began to cry.

Adam put his arms around her and held her until her sobs subsided. Then he looked straight at her.

"William knows where you are but he would not dare come near you. If he did then I would take him to court and he would lose what little reputation he has. But you must tell us why you are so afraid of him. Has he ever threatened you with violence?"

Alice did not answer but Adam knew that he had touched a nerve. She went very pale and her eyes were as big as saucers. She began to shake and beads of sweat appeared on her forehead. Leah quickly fetched a glass of water and gave Alice a drink.

"That's enough," she said urgently to Adam. "No more questions."

But Adam shook his head.

"We must find out the truth," he said. "It is imperative that we know."

Alice was beginning to calm down but Leah was still very anxious.

"Are you sure you are doing the right thing, Adam?"

"Yes, I am sure," he said. "Alice, look at me."

She slowly raised her eyes.

"I know this is going to be painful for you but I want you to be very brave. When you have told us, then you won't have such a terrible secret that you have been hiding. All I ask is that you answer my questions truthfully."

Alice was staring at him as if she was looking right through him, but Adam continued.

"Has William ever threatened you?" he asked.

He waited for her answer and eventually she nodded her head.

"Has he ever threatened to kill you?" Adam said.

She shook her head. He thought for a moment then he remembered the incident with the scissors.

"Has he ever threatened you with a knife?"

She shook her head.

"Was it with scissors?"

Her eyes opened wider and her lips began to quiver.

"Was it scissors?" Adam asked again.

She slowly nodded her head.

"Can you tell me what he said?" Adam asked her gently.

She did not reply and Leah stepped forward to intervene but Adam put his hand up to stop her. He put his hands on Alice's shoulders.

"Please Alice. Tell me what he said?"

She looked at her father and spoke haltingly.

"He said that if I ever left him, he would…" and she stopped speaking but she ran her forefinger down the length of her cheek.

Adam and Leah were horrified.

"He said that he would disfigure you with scissors?" Adam said incredulously.

Alice nodded her head and lay back with her eyes closed.

"She's exhausted," said Leah.

Adam was still stunned by what he had heard. Leah left him holding Alice and went to the kitchen. She made three cups of coffee and took them into the lounge. Adam and Alice had not moved but Alice opened her eyes.

"I've made some coffee," Leah said. "I think we can all do with a drink."

Adam and Alice sat up and they drank their coffee in silence. Alice was the first to speak.

"I feel like a weight has been lifted off my shoulders," she said. "I feel as light as a feather."

"It is hard to talk about something which has been worrying you for a long time," Adam said. "The longer you hold on to it, the bigger it becomes. I know you will be relieved that you were able to share it with us. Now we can do something about it."

"But there is nothing you can do," Alice said, her voice filled with anxiety.

"Wherever there is a problem, there is a solution," Adam said wisely. "If you are patient enough, problems will often solve themselves. But there is one important thing that you must understand right now. There is absolutely no chance of William touching you. Underneath all that big talk, he is actually a coward and the thing he values most is his supposedly good name. He would do anything to avoid tarnishing that."

"I've never thought of it that way," Alice said. "When you live with it day after day you lose sight of any alternative."

"I really think it is time for you to rest," Leah said.

"I shall sleep more comfortably tonight," Alice said.

She went upstairs and Adam followed her to say goodnight.

"I'll see you in the morning," he said.

"Are you are staying here tonight?" Alice asked.

"Yes, I am."

"That's a first," she said, sleepily.

"Not quite," Adam smiled at her but she was fast asleep.

Later that evening, when they were in bed, Leah said:

"I can't get it out of my mind what Alice told us. No wonder she has become a nervous wreck."

"It is unbelievable that anyone could be so callous and selfish," Adam said. "I know it looked as if I was being hard on Alice but I just sensed that the time was right to try to get her to talk."

"You were right as usual," she said. "Let's hope that it is a new beginning for her."

"I'm sure she will find it easier to be honest with us now that she has shared what was worrying her most"

Leah turned to face him.

"I could never have done what you did this evening. I told you that Alice was more likely to respond to you," she said gratefully. "I'm so glad that you were here to help her."

He put his arms around her.

"I am here for you as well," he said sincerely. "I promise you that I will always be here for you. I am a very lucky man to be with the person I love most in the world."

Leah kissed him.

"That makes two of us," she said and they lay in complete harmony.

Chapter Twenty-Two

Sally and Dominic were also having a happy time. When they left the office, they had walked up the street towards the car park. On the way, they passed a jeweller's shop and Dominic stopped and said to Sally:

"I want to buy you something to remember me by."

"You're not going away are you?" she asked in a worried voice.

"No," he smiled. "I'm not going away but I'm not always with you and I want you to have something I've given you so that you cannot forget me."

"I won't forget you," Sally said. "I don't need anything to remind me of you," but Dominic had taken her arm and guided her into the shop.

He looked around the display cabinets and finally decided on the one which contained a selection of gold bracelets. He took Sally over to it and asked her which one she liked best. He was so insistent that she knew it would be useless to argue with him. She chose a simple gold bangle with a twist in the middle which was almost the shape of a heart. Dominic slipped it on her wrist and looked at it admiringly.

"It suits you perfectly," he said happily as he gave it to the assistant to be wrapped up.

He paid for it and gave Sally the bag to hold. They were soon driving out of Oxford. Sally sat in the passenger seat holding the bag and Dominic looked at her and smiled.

"It's a good job I remember the way to your house," he said. "You haven't said a word."

"I'm sorry," she said. "I haven't even said thank you. I've never had anyone buy me such a lovely present and I was just lost for words."

"Wait until we get to your house then you can thank me properly."

When they arrived, Dominic parked the car and Sally unlocked the front door. She switched on the lights and went into the lounge and lit up the electric fire. Dominic followed her and on the way, he dropped his overnight bag in the hall. The room felt warm and cosy as they sat down on the settee. Sally placed the bag containing the bangle on the coffee table. Dominic picked it up and took the bangle out of its box. He held Sally's hand and slipped it over her wrist. She looked at it, then looked at Dominic. He stood up and pulled her to her feet. He put his hands on her shoulders and drew her close to him.

"I want to kiss you," he said softly.

She put her hands around the back of his neck.

"What's stopping you?"

He held her tight and as his lips touched hers a great swell of emotion engulfed them. They stood there for several minutes as if in a dream until Sally said:

"I need to sit down. My legs are like jelly."

"Don't worry," Dominic smiled. "I'll hold you up."

They both sat down and Dominic held Sally's hand, stroking her fingers.

"The next thing I slip on your hand will be much smaller but it will mean everything to me."

Sally looked at him incredulously.

"What are you saying" she gasped.

"I'm saying that I love you and want to marry you," he answered.

Sally didn't answer immediately, in fact, it was several minutes before she spoke. Dominic was beginning to feel concerned.

"You've gone very quiet. Are you alright?"

"Yes, I'm alright," Sally replied. "I was just trying to come to terms with what you said."

He looked at her in surprise.

"What do you mean, coming to terms with?"

"I'm trying to understand what you said to me," Sally said. "Everything is happening too fast. I need to step back a little."

"I really meant what I said."

"I know you did," Sally said. "I believe you when you say that is what you want but you haven't asked if it is what I want."

He stared at her, stunned at her words.

"Are you rejecting my proposal?" he stammered.

She looked straight at him.

"Dominic, I am not rejecting you or what you said but it was not a proposal."

"But I told you I wanted to marry you and that I love you," there was a hint of impatience in his voice. "Surely you understand what I'm saying?"

"I know exactly what you are saying and I understand every word of it," Sally assured him. "You have made it very clear what you want. You have made a statement, not a proposal."

"You are just playing around with the meaning of words. I don't understand," Dominic was now getting quite agitated.

"I assure you I am not playing around. I am very serious. A proposal is made from one person to another and it involves a considered response from the second person. It is asking a question and expecting an answer not providing one's own answer."

Dominic was silent and there was a frown on his face. He was not used to having his actions questioned like this.

"Why are you making such a fuss about it?" he said angrily. "Why have you turned my words against me?"

Sally was surprised at how angry he was and she wasn't sure what to do next. They sat in silence for a few minutes but at last, Sally spoke.

"Dominic," she said. "I didn't mean to make you so angry. I love you too much to want to hurt you."

"You have just said that you love me but you won't marry me. I don't understand."

"You haven't asked me to marry you," Sally said quietly. "You have just said that you want to marry me."

Sally watched his face as her words sank into his brain. It was a few minutes before he spoke and she waited patiently.

"I'm sorry," he said and his voice shook with emotion. "I'm so sorry."

He put his arms around her as the tears started to flow. His head rested on her shoulder until he stopped crying. She stroked his face and kissed him on his forehead.

"It's alright," she said as if comforting a child. "Don't worry. Everything will be alright."

"I have to make it alright," his voice trembled and he knelt down in front of Sally.

He held both her hands and looked at her with his tear-stained face, then he said in a clear, decisive voice:

"Sally, I love you with all my heart. Will you do me the honour of becoming my wife?"

She looked at him with tears in her eyes.

"Yes, Dominic. I will."

They both stood up and fell into each other's arms. Eventually, Sally said:

"I think a celebratory cup of tea is called for," and she went into the kitchen.

Dominic went to wash his face and compose his thoughts. She brought the tea into the lounge and they sat together on the settee.

"Are you okay?" she asked anxiously.

"I think so. You have nearly turned my life upside down and I must get used to it."

"Have I upset you?" she asked, puzzled. "I didn't mean to."

"You have upset me well and truly," he said with mock severity. "I shall never be the same again."

"Oh dear," she said quickly. "I'm really sorry," and she gave him a scared look.

But he held her hand and said:

"My whole life seemed to flash before my eyes when you were talking. At first, everything seemed to be the wrong way round and then suddenly it made sense." Dominic paused before continuing. "I saw myself as a businessman used to ordering people about and that is how I was brought up. The whole atmosphere at home was business orientated and I was expected to carry on the tradition. I've already told you how unsettled I feel in my work but I couldn't understand why I felt that way. It has even influenced the way I thought about you. Then when you were talking this evening it all suddenly fell into place. I was speaking to you as I would to an employee or business associate. I wasn't recognising that you had feelings too and I knew that what you were saying was so true. I can't believe how selfish I was, my only excuse is that it has been bred in me. But now I understand I can do something to change it if you will be there to help me?"

"I'll be there for you, for as long as you want me."

"That's forever then," he said. "I need you to help me to become a proper human being, not a business robot."

Sally smiled at him.

"I think you are already a proper human being. You just need more practice at it."

Dominic kissed her and said:

"This proper human being is hungry. We were going out for a meal but we will do that tomorrow."

"I could do some beans on toast," Sally said. "I need to go shopping in the morning."

"Beans on toast will be a treat," he said. "I haven't had that since my student days."

Later that evening Dominic said:

"My divorce will be finalised in two weeks then I shall be selling my house and looking for a new home in the country. I would like you to choose it with me."

"I'm sure that can be arranged," she said with a smile. "There is only one thing I would hope."

"Your wish is my command," Dominic said gallantly.

"I hope that it will be in commuting distance to Oxford," she said.

"Why do you want that?" Dominic said in a surprised tone. "You won't need to work. You can live a life of luxury."

"I don't want a life of luxury," she said firmly. "I want to stay in my job. I don't want to let Mr Richards down especially now with all the exciting developments taking place."

"Is there anything else you are hoping for?" he asked.

Sally thought for a minute.

"I hope that you won't completely retire because you will soon get bored. I hope that there is a golf course nearby so that you can get some exercise."

"Anything else?" Dominic spluttered as he burst out laughing.

"I don't think so," Sally said pretending to be serious. "Although there may be one other thing."

"What's that?" he asked, wondering what was coming next.

"I hope that you will leave your business side at work and bring your proper human being side home."

"It looks as if I am going to have to get used to taking orders," he said with a grin. "That will bring some spice into our relationship."

Sally collected the dirty plates and took them into the kitchen.

"Do you want another drink?" she asked.

"No thanks," he replied. "But there is something I want."

Sally stood in the doorway.

"What's that?" she asked.

"I want to share your bed tonight," he said. "On a perfectly friendly basis," he hastened to add.

She hesitated and Dominic went to her.

"I give you my word," he said. "I just want to be near you. When I am a free man then I will show you how much I love you."

Sally looked at him and she knew she could trust him.

"Alright," she said and they went up the stairs together.

Chapter Twenty-Three

On Saturday morning, Adam and Leah were woken by a voice saying:

"I've brought you a cup of tea."

Alice was standing at the end of the bed with three cups on a tray. Adam and Leah sat up as Alice put a cup on each side of the bed.

"This is a nice surprise," Adam said.

Alice took her cup to the doorway then she turned.

"I just wanted to make sure you were in bed together. I'm going back to sleep," and she left the room.

Adam and Leah looked at each other and smiled.

"Well, I never," Leah said. "I wouldn't have believed it."

"Perhaps she has turned the corner," Adam said thoughtfully. "But we mustn't expect too much too soon."

They lay in bed for a while until Leah said:

"I must get up. I need to go shopping."

They both got dressed and went downstairs. Leah was soon ready to go out and she reminded Adam that he needed to move his car from the front of the garage. When he came back in, he said:

"It's a bit nippy this morning. I think there must have been a frost last night."

"I shouldn't be too long," she said. "I know exactly what I need to get."

"Can you bring me a newspaper?" Adam called to her as she left.

He went back upstairs and tidied the bed. He cleaned his teeth and had a good wash. Then he peeped into Alice's bedroom. She was fast asleep. He collected the dirty cup and went downstairs. He did the washing up and cleared the kitchen table. Figuring that was his chores done for the day, he went into the lounge.

It was after ten o'clock and he was half asleep when Alice came in.

"Where's mum?" she asked.

"She's gone shopping," Adam replied.

"I must go shopping with her soon," Alice said. "I need to buy some decent clothes."

"Peter is coming to lunch tomorrow and he is bringing all your clothes with him."

Alice looked at him in amazement.

"But how is he going to get them?" she asked. "I know Peter won't go and speak to William."

"It has been arranged," he said. "Peter won't need to go into the house. William has been told to have it ready in bags for Peter to collect."

"William doesn't like to be told what to do," she said anxiously.

"I think William knows that it is in his best interest to do as he is told," Adam said. "He is fully aware of the consequences if he refuses." Adam stood up. "Now it is my turn to make you a cup of tea and get you some breakfast," he said.

He made tea for both of them and persuaded Alice to have a small bowl of cornflakes. Then they went back to the lounge.

"You said last night that William was a coward. I don't understand why you said that, Dad."

"People who bully others are usually cowards," he said. "They hide their insecurities behind a mask of assertiveness and it feeds their own inadequacy."

"But William has no reason to be insecure or inadequate," she said. "He has a good job which pays well and he has a big house. The only thing he hasn't got is any friends to share it with."

"That is the point," Adam said. "He thinks that by having all the material things it gives everyone the impression that he is a successful man. But inside him, he is always scared that someone or something will see through him and so he controls them with threats and unpleasantness."

"But why hasn't he got any friends?" she asked. "I used to have friends but they gradually stopped coming. William was so rude to them."

"It was a deliberate act to isolate you so that you would not talk to anyone about what was happening at home. He even tried to cut you off from your own family."

"He doesn't sound a very nice man when you describe him like that," Alice said. "But we did have some good times in the past."

They heard the back door open.

"Mum's back," said Adam. "I'll go and help her unload the car."

"I'm ready for a coffee," said Leah as they carried the groceries in.

"I'll make it," said Adam. "You go and sit down. Alice is in the lounge."

Adam put most of the groceries away while he was waiting for the kettle to boil. Then he made three coffees and carried them into the lounge, together with the biscuit tin.

"You've bought enough food to feed an army," he said to Leah.

"It will do us for the week," she said.

"I must help you out with the finances," he said, handing her the coffee.

"What have you been doing this morning, Alice?" asked Leah.

"I had some breakfast and Dad and I have been talking."

Leah looked at Adam and raised her eyebrows.

"We had a good chat didn't we Alice?" Adam said.

"It was interesting. Dad explained some things to me," she said and she stood up and left them.

"Was she alright?" she asked anxiously. "Did she talk to you or just listen?"

"I explained to her how bullies function and how they are permanently scared of being found out and she asked me several questions concerning William's behaviour."

"Do you think she understood what you were saying?"

"Yes, I think she did but she needs time to work it out for herself," he said then paused for a moment. "If we go to my place to look at the furniture at twelve o'clock, I could then take you both out to lunch."

"I'm not sure if Alice will do that," Leah said. "We'll have to ask her."

She had not noticed that Alice had come through the door.

"What do you have to ask me?"

"Dad would like to take us out for lunch," said Leah. "How do you feel about that?"

Alice considered this offer and finally said:

"I think I would like that providing it is not too noisy."

"It is not a noisy place and there are plenty of quiet corners," said Adam. "I know the barman well and he will look after us."

Later that morning, Adam drove them to his house. They went inside and had a good look at the furniture Adam had already decided he wanted to keep the settee but most of the rest could now go into storage.

"I may want my own bed," Adam said. "It depends on how comfortable the new one is."

They returned to the car and Adam took them two miles up the road to his favourite pub.

"Hello Adam," Bob the barman said. "We haven't had the pleasure of your company lately."

"I've been busy," Adam replied. "But I've brought two extra people to make up for it. This is my wife and daughter."

"Pleased to meet you," Bob said. "What can I get you to drink?"

"First of all, we need to find a quiet corner then I'll come back and order," Adam said.

"Try over there to the right," Bob suggested. "I'll send one of the girls over to take your order."

They found a table and sat down. There were not too many people in the pub and the music was playing softly in the background.

"Are you okay?" Leah asked Alice.

She nodded her head. The waitress brought the menu and they ordered their drinks. Alice looked at the list of food and said:

"I'm not very hungry. This is all too much for me."

"You don't have to have anything you don't want," Adam said soothingly. "You can just have a packet of crisps or a few chips if you like. You won't mind if your Mum and I choose a meal, will you?"

"Go ahead," Alice said. "I shan't mind."

The waitress came back.

"Are you ready to order?"

Leah chose cod and chips and Adam chose steak and kidney pie and chips. He looked enquiringly at Alice.

"Is there anything you would like? You can share my chips if you like."

"I'll do that," she said.

Leah was looking around the pub and she noticed a couple standing at the bar. The man was nodding his head in Adam's direction and they started to walk over.

"I think someone is coming to speak to you," she said in an urgent voice.

He turned to look and as he did so a familiar voice said:

"I thought it was you."

"Dominic," Adam said in amazement. "And Sally. What a surprise." He turned to Leah. "This is Sally my secretary and Mr West who I told you about."

Sally and Leah smiled at each other.

"This is our daughter Alice," said Leah. "She is staying with us for a while."

Dominic stepped forward and kissed Leah's hand.

"I am so pleased to meet you, Leah, I'm Dominic West and I hope that your husband has not been too hard on me." Then he turned to Alice. "How nice to meet you too Alice." And he kissed her hand. Alice smiled shyly at him.

"This is my local pub," Adam said. "What brings you here?"

"Sally and I are out for lunch," Dominic answered. "She had heard that they have a good restaurant here so we thought we would try it. The table is booked for one o'clock so we were having a drink first."

Sally had seated herself between Leah and Alice and all three were chatting. Dominic looked at them.

"I get a bit jumpy when women get together like that," he said and Adam laughed.

"You'll have to get used to it," he said. "It happens all the time."

"There are a lot of things I shall have to get used to if I am to become a proper human being," he said mournfully.

"What do you mean by a proper human being?" Adam asked incredulously.

"It's just a joke between Sally and me but it nearly scuppered me last evening. Sally knows her own mind and is not afraid to disagree with me. I'm not used to that. I'm used to giving the orders not taking them."

"I had to be patient when Leah and I met again. I also had to work hard at it and remember that her feelings may not coincide with mine," said Adam.

"I've got a lot of lessons to learn but it will be worth it," Dominic said gazing at Sally.

The waitress came to the table carrying the dinners.

"Time for us to go," Dominic said. "Our table should be ready. I hope we shall meet again soon," he said to Leah and Alice.

After they had left, Leah said to Adam:

"He has quite a personality. Sally will have her hands full with him."

Adam smiled. "He will learn his lessons," he said wisely.

They enjoyed their meal and Alice had a few chips. Leah could see that she was getting restless.

"It's time to go home," she said to Adam as she led Alice out to the car.

Adam paid the bill and joined them in the car but he just sat there thinking.

"What's the matter?" Leah asked.

"I was wondering if it might be nice to ask Sally and Dominic to spend some of the evening with us?" he said.

"I don't mind," Leah replied. "I enjoyed talking to Sally"

"I'll go and see if I can find them," Adam said and he went off towards the restaurant.

It was not a busy place and he soon spotted them. He gave them the invitation.

"I'd like to talk to Leah," said Sally. "We got on very well."

"This afternoon we are driving around Oxfordshire looking at the countryside," Dominic said. "What time would you like us to come?"

"It gets dark quite early," said Adam. "You won't see much of the countryside after four o'clock."

"I'd like to go home first," Sally said. "Would seven o'clock be convenient?"

"The Lady has spoken," Dominic said drily.

"Seven o'clock will be fine," Adam said and he gave Dominic the address and how to find it.

Adam returned to the car and grinned at Leah.

"Sally suggested seven o'clock and Dominic agreed," he said.

"I hope you won't mind if I don't join you," Alice said. "I am feeling rather tired."

"Why don't you take my radio into your room then you can be in bed and listen to whatever you fancy?" said Leah.

"Thanks, Mum," Alice said. "I think I'll do that."

On the way home, Adam stopped at the shop to buy some nibbles, a bottle of wine and some cans of lager. He parked the car and they went in through the back door. It was already getting dark and Leah closed the curtains. She switched on the lights outside the front door and they all went into the lounge. Adam put his arm around Alice.

"How do you feel Alice? Did you enjoy your little outing?"

"It was nice to go out," she answered. "I can't remember the last time I went out for a meal."

"What have you been eating at home?" he asked.

"Sometimes I had a bowl of cornflakes or when William cooked a meal for himself and the children, I had a bit of that," she answered.

"Wasn't he worried that you weren't eating properly?"

"He never said anything about it. He hardly ever spoke to me about anything," she said tearfully.

Adam put his arms right around her.

"Don't cry," he said in a quiet voice. "The nightmare is over."

"It's not over," Alice sobbed. "I shall have to go back there at some time. I can't stay here forever. I won't have a home."

Adam stroked her head to calm her down and when she stopped sobbing, he said:

"You can stay here as long as you like. This is your home. You won't ever need to go back to that house if you don't want to."

"But William won't let me go. He will come after me," she cried.

"William may not want you to go back," Adam said quietly.

Alice pulled away from Adam and looked at him in horror.

"What do you mean?" she stammered.

"You may have to live your life without William," Adam repeated. "Would that upset you?"

Alice looked at Adam then she looked at her mother.

"Mum, what does he mean?"

Leah thought carefully before she answered Alice.

"He means that at some time in the future you will have to decide how you want to live your life. Do you want to go back and live in fear, or do you want to be free and live in hope?" she said clearly.

"Do you mean leave William for good?" Alice stammered. "But I shall be left with no money and nowhere to go and what about the children?" her voice became more and more anxious.

"You are forgetting something very important," Adam told her. "You are still William's wife and you are entitled to half of the value of all his assets. You would certainly not be penniless; in fact, you would probably have enough money to buy your own little house."

Alice looked at her father but she didn't say a word. She was thinking about what Adam had said and finally, she blurted out:

"But William has always said I would have nothing if I left him."

"William is lying in order to take advantage of you," Adam explained. "It is his way of controlling your life."

"But I believed what he said. He kept on saying it."

"That is the way he lives his life, through fear in himself and making others fearful by threatening them," Adam replied. "There is only one decision which you need to make and that is do you still love him? Everything else will fall into place depending on what you decide."

"But how can I leave him? How can I do it?" Alice cried.

"You can divorce him on the grounds of adultery," Adam said bluntly.

Alice rushed out of the room and went upstairs to her bedroom. She flung herself on the bed and cried and cried until she was totally worn out, then she went to sleep. Leah wanted to go up after her but Adam stopped her.

"She has had a shock," he said. "Give her time to get over it."

But Leah insisted on going up to see her. She found Alice fast asleep on the bed and gently covered her with the duvet. Then she went down to the kitchen and put the nibbles into two dishes which she then took into the lounge. Adam was still sitting there with his eyes closed.

"Are you asleep?" she asked.

"No, I'm just thinking. Alice has a big decision to make. I know it is difficult for her to think for herself after all the brain-washing she has been subjected to but the decision has to be hers."

"We must give her time, Adam. But at least she now knows that there are alternatives."

She sat down by Adam and rested her head on his shoulder. He put his arm around her and they were happy in each other's company. They were both half asleep when they heard Alice come down the stairs and into the lounge. Her face was tear-stained and she was quite pale.

"Can I make a cup of tea, Mum?" she asked.

"Of course, you can," Leah said and immediately stood up and went into the kitchen with her.

"How are you feeling?" Leah asked.

"I'm trying to understand what is happening to me but I am so confused," Alice said in a worried voice.

"Don't try too hard," Leah said. "Sometimes things have a way of working themselves out if we are patient."

"I wonder if I shall ever stop being frightened of William?" Alice said slowly. "I don't know what to believe any more."

"Give yourself time, Alice. At the moment your thoughts are like a big, tangled ball of string. Once you find the right end it will unravel itself."

"Your friends will be here soon," Alice said. "I think I'll take my tea back upstairs."

"I'll come up soon and give you my radio," said Leah.

She took the other two cups into the lounge and sat down by Adam.

"Alice is struggling with everything at present; I don't want her to get too upset," she said.

"It will be interesting to see her reaction when Peter brings her clothes tomorrow," said Adam. "I know it is hard for her but she has been living a strange existence and we have to explain to her what normal life is like."

"I'll just go up and make sure she is comfortable," Leah said. "Our visitors will arrive soon."

She took the radio from her bedroom into Alice's room and plugged it into the socket. She could hear Alice in the bathroom and she waited for her to come out.

"I'll come up later with your pill," Leah said. "Now cuddle down and don't worry."

At that moment she heard the front doorbell and Adam going to answer it. She waited a minute or two on the landing to compose herself and then she went to the lounge. They greeted each other with handshakes and kisses. Adam poured the wine and soon the conversation was flowing.

"How much of the countryside did you manage to see?" Adam asked.

"Not a lot," replied Dominic. "It soon got dark."

"Were you looking for anywhere in particular?" Adam said in his most innocent voice.

Sally looked at Adam. She had heard that voice before and knew that he was being inquisitive.

"Nothing in particular," she answered quickly. "We were just out for a drive."

Adam smiled at her. He had forgotten that she knew him better than Dominic did. The conversation continued in general terms until Adam said:

"I'll take these glasses out. I'll come back for the empty bottle."

"Let me help you," Dominic said and followed him into the kitchen.

"Where is Alice this evening?" he asked.

Adam gave him a brief outline of what had occurred and Dominic was full of sympathy.

"It must be a great worry for you and Leah?" he said. "How do you manage to cope with it all and remain cheerful?"

"When I did my degree in business studies, I also did a course on psychology," Adam told him. "It taught me how to differentiate between work-related problems and those in one's personal life."

"You've cracked it," Dominic said admiringly. "You have become a proper human being."

"I don't know where Sally got that phrase from," Adam said. "It certainly wasn't from me."

"Another of those mysteries about women and their intuition," Dominic sighed. "Women are such complex creatures. I'd rather deal with a man any day."

Adam laughed.

"You don't come across many women in your business world," he said. "Except of course secretaries," he added with a hint of sarcasm.

"Don't worry," Dominic said crisply. "I've already been told that we must live within commuting distance of Oxford and that she has no intention of giving up her job."

Adam was astounded at what he had just heard.

"You haven't wasted any time," he gasped. "Have you already proposed to her?"

"Yes, I have," Dominic sighed. "And I very nearly made a mess of that."

Adam was still looking at him in wonder.

"What on earth did you say to her?" he asked.

"I told her I loved her and wanted to marry her."

"You say that you told her, you didn't actually ask her?"

"That was my big mistake," Dominic said sadly, "but it all came right in the end."

"So, what did she say when you finally asked her?" Adam asked impatiently.

"She said yes, of course," Dominic replied. "It was nice making up and it was then she said that she hoped I would leave my business persona at work and become a proper human being at home. Do you think we have a hope of making it work?" he asked in a worried tone.

"I think it will work wonderfully well! You will have plenty of opportunities to have the pleasure of making up."

"It was nice last night to have company in bed again," Dominic said dreamily.

Adam looked at him in amazement.

"You didn't?" he spluttered.

"No, I didn't," Dominic said indignantly. "It was all quite innocent."

Leah and Sally came into the kitchen.

"There's a lot of hilarity in here," Leah said. "But I don't see any sign of coffee."

She sent the two men to the lounge. Sally gave Dominic a suspicious look as he passed her and kissed her on the neck.

"Those two have been having a discussion about someone," Sally said. "I don't trust them when they go into a huddle."

Leah laughed.

"You'll get used to it," she said. "I know Adam can be a dreadful tease; it's all harmless fun. But I do find it difficult when he keeps springing surprises on me."

Sally pointed to the bracelet on her wrist.

"This was a complete surprise," she said. "We were walking up the street and he hustled me into this jeweller's shop and said he wanted to buy me something to remember him by and told me to choose the one I liked and that was that."

Leah looked closely at the bracelet.

"It is a beautiful piece of jewellery," she said, admiring it.

"I know it is but I'm not used to being given expensive presents. I hope he won't keep doing it."

"I think you will have to get used to it," Leah said wisely. "It is his way of showing how much he loves you."

"I genuinely do love him but I have so much to learn about him. His background is very different from mine."

"You seem to me to be a well-grounded person and I'm sure you will be able to react properly in any situation. I think you can make a success of it and have a good life together," said Leah.

Sally smiled at her and helped to carry the coffee into the lounge.

"I have plenty of practice at this," she said as she put the cups on the coffee table. "Milk and one sugar I presume?" as she gave Dominic his cup.

Adam burst out laughing.

"I'll never forget that," he said.

It was getting late and Sally and Dominic prepared to leave.

"I hope your mother doesn't decide to come and stay tonight," Adam said seriously.

Sally gave him the dirtiest look she could manage while Dominic started to chuckle nearby. Leah quickly stepped in.

"Sally's sleeping arrangements are none of your business," she said to Adam. "Don't be so annoying."

They said their goodbyes and Leah locked the door. Adam had returned to the lounge and was clearing the dirty cups.

"I was only teasing her," he said sulkily.

"You don't realise that what you call teasing can sometimes cause offence and it can be hurtful."

"Sally knows I wouldn't deliberately hurt her."

"Sometimes the person you think you are teasing has not had a good day or maybe they are not feeling well. It may be that they don't know you well enough and can take what you say at face value," she said.

Adam put the cups back on the coffee table and sat down.

"I hope I didn't offend Sally," he said with a voice full of remorse. "I'll apologise to her on Monday."

Leah sat down beside him.

"You are right, of course," he said. "It was a thoughtless thing to say."

"It was a very interesting evening," she said thoughtfully. "Did you notice Sally's bracelet? It was pure gold," and she told Adam the story about it.

"Dominic seems to be a very impulsive person where Sally is concerned and yet he is a very acute businessman," he said. "I think his background and upbringing have a big influence on his attitude to women."

He told her about the 'proper human being' episode and she laughed.

"It sounds as if Sally has got the measure of him already," she said. "Good luck to her."

"I don't think she needs the good luck," Adam said strongly. "It is Dominic who will need that."

Leah stood up and sighed.

"You men stick together don't you?"

Adam put his arms around her.

"We have to put up some resistance to you coven of mischief makers," he said as he kissed her.

"I'm ready for bed," she said. "I'll go up and check that Alice is alright. You can clear the cups and put the lights out and make sure you lock the back door," she said as she went out.

By the time Adam went upstairs, Leah was already in bed.

"Is Alice okay?" he asked her.

"Yes, she's fast asleep."

"I wonder," Adam said as he got in beside her.

"What do you mean?"

"I wonder who gets into bed first, Sally or Dominic?"

"It doesn't matter, does it? They are in separate rooms."

"They only need one room and one bed," he said.

Leah sat up and looked at him.

"How do you know that?"

"A little bird told me," he said and pulled the duvet over both of them.

Chapter Twenty-Four

On Sunday morning Peter got up and made sure that his car was empty. He was not looking forward to seeing William and he hoped that it would all be ready as promised. At ten-thirty, he pulled up on the drive outside the front door. There were no other cars parked anywhere but the door was open. He rang the bell and waited. It was answered by Jessica.

"Hello Jessica," he said. "Is your father here?"

"Hello, Uncle Peter. Dad has gone shopping."

"Are you here by yourself?" Peter asked.

"No, Jonathan is upstairs playing on his computer."

"Did Dad leave a message for me?"

"Yes," she said. "You have to collect all these bags of Mum's clothes. Does that mean that she won't be coming home?" and there were tears in her eyes.

"I don't know. I was told to collect the clothes and take them to Granny Leah's house."

"Will you see Mum?" Jessica asked tearfully.

"I expect so. I know she is staying there."

"Will you tell her I love her and I miss her?" Jessica said through her tears.

"Yes, I'll tell her that," Peter said gently. "And what about Jonathan?"

"He doesn't talk about her, just like Dad, but I think he misses her."

"I'll try to get all these bags in the car," Peter said. "Will you take empty bags and go up to Mum's room? Make sure that all the drawers are empty and the wardrobes. I'll wait here until you come down."

He started to pack the bags into his car but it was a tight squeeze to get them all in. Jessica came back with a bag half full and he just managed to get it into the boot.

"You won't forget to tell Mum, will you?"

"I won't forget," he said and his heart went out to the unhappy little girl.

He went back home to collect Benjie and Lucy. They had to sit on top of the bags on the back seat with their feet resting on other bags on the floor of the car. Peter managed to get their seat belts on and they thought it was great fun.

He arrived at Leah's house and undid their seat belts. They went running up the path and started to knock on the door. Adam heard them and went to open the door. They rushed in and Lucy jumped up into Adam's arms. Benjie was shouting:

"Granny Leah, Granny Leah, where are you?"

Leah came out of the kitchen and kissed them both. Adam put Lucy down and the children went into the lounge. Peter came up the path and greeted his father.

"I've got a car full of black bags," he said.

"I'll help you unload it in a minute," Adam said. "I think you ought to say hello to Alice first."

They went into the lounge where Alice was sitting. Peter went up to her and kissed her.

"Hello, Alice. It's been a long time."

"Yes, I know," she replied. "You have two lovely children."

Benjie was standing by his father and he looked up at him.

"This is your Auntie Alice," Peter said. "Go and introduce yourself."

Benjie went up to Alice and said:

"I'm Benjie Adam Richards and I'm nearly six years old."

"I'm very pleased to meet you, Benjamin and who is this?" she nodded towards Lucy who was standing by Adam.

"Everyone calls me Benjie," he explained to Alice. "This is my sister Lucy; she is only three and a bit."

"Hello, Lucy. My name is Alice."

"This is my Grandad Adam," said Lucy. "Do you know him?"

"Yes, I know him," Alice said with a smile.

Leah had been watching all this from the dining-room door.

"I must go and check the dinner," she said.

Benjie followed her into the kitchen.

"What are we having for dinner?" he asked.

"Sausages, mashed potatoes and peas," she answered.

"I love sausages but I can't keep the peas on my fork," he said and he ran off shouting: "I love sausages!"

Lucy had moved into the conservatory and Benjie joined her.

Adam and Peter started to unload the car.

"Where shall we put these bags, Leah?" asked Adam.

"You had better put them in the big bedroom for now."

They carried all the bags upstairs and Alice watched them through the window. When the car was empty, Adam and Peter collapsed on the settee.

"I could do with a beer," Adam gasped. "How about you Peter?"

"Yes please," he said. "I don't know why women need so many clothes."

"I'll get them for you," Alice said.

She went to the fridge and took out two cans of beer. She gave them to Adam and Peter.

"Thank you for doing that for me," she said. "I'll go and see if I can help Mum in the kitchen."

Peter looked at his father.

"How is she?" he asked. "I feel guilty that I didn't go around to see her but William was so unpleasant and intimidating."

"She is much better than when we first brought her down but she is faced with some pretty big decisions about the future."

Peter told him what Jessica had said to him and Adam looked sad.

"The children have been deliberately taught to disrespect their mother and as long as they are under their father's influence that will continue."

"He is a devious person," Peter said. "If Alice is thinking of divorcing him, she will need a good lawyer. I know from experience how underhand he can be."

"I have a friend who lives in London and he is just going through a divorce. He has recommended his lawyer and I might take him up on it. Don't worry, I'll make sure that Alice gets her fair share of everything. He won't get away with anything."

"I don't remember you being as confident and forthright as you are now."

"Life has taught me many lessons," Adam said. "And I have learned from them. I am not really a different person. I am still the same in my heart. I have had to cope with guilty feelings too but I have always loved Leah and now I have the opportunity to love my children too. I intend to make the most of it."

"Dinner's ready," Leah called.

Peter went to get the children to wash their hands. When they were sitting at the table Benjie suddenly announced:

"I need a wee."

"Why didn't you go before you washed your hands?" Peter asked him in an exasperated voice.

"I didn't want to go then," Benjie said.

"Come on then," Peter said. "I'll come with you."

"I can manage," Benjie insisted.

"No, you can't," Peter said. "You know you don't aim straight." And they left the table.

"I don't wear nappies now," Lucy piped up. "I have special knickers." She looked at Alice and said: "Do you have special knickers? I have a teddy on mine."

"I don't have any with a teddy bear on," Alice answered solemnly. "I do have a little pink flower on them."

"I'll have pink knickers when I grow up," Lucy decided and she started to eat her dinner.

Peter and Benjie returned to the table as Lucy made her last observation.

"I'm sorry to lower the tone of the conversation," he said. "They have this obsession with hygiene at present. It drives Janet mad."

"It's alright," said Leah. "It was actually quite funny."

They all enjoyed their dinner and the apple tart and custard which followed it.

"I think I'll take the children for a walk, get rid of some of their energy," Peter said.

"I'll come with you," said Adam. "I'll just help Mum with the table first."

"I'll help Mum," Alice offered and she stood up.

"Can we go to the stream?" Benjie asked. "I want to catch some fishes."

"There won't be any fish in the stream," Peter said, "but if we walk through the woods, we might see a squirrel."

"I like kwirrels," Lucy said as she struggled into her coat. "I want a kwirrel for Christmas."

"You can't have a squirrel for Christmas," Benjie told her. "You could have a dog or a pet mouse."

"I don't want a mouse," Lucy shuddered, "but I'll have a dog."

"I don't think you will," Peter said. "Mummy doesn't like cats or dogs because they leave hairs on the furniture."

Lucy was going to argue but by this time they were ready to go. They walked up the road and round the corner and there was a stream right in front of them. Benjie ran right to the edge of the water. He found a stick and started to prod the water with it.

"For goodness sake don't fall in," Peter shouted at him.

"I won't fall in," Benjie shouted as his foot slipped on the bank and Peter put out a hand to hold him.

"Come away," he said. "We shall all be in trouble if you get wet."

He pulled Benjie back onto dry ground and they went through the wood. The children had great fun shuffling through the dry leaves and exploring all the little pathways.

Adam looked at Peter and said:

"This reminds me of when you four were growing up. You had the freedom to explore in the woods and to climb the trees. You all enjoyed the outdoor life."

"Yes, we had an ideal childhood," Peter said. "I don't remember any family rows or unpleasantness. We were very happy and secure."

They walked on in silence until Adam said:

"I never really felt comfortable with my job in the garden centre and I know it was hard for your mother to have to live in those isolated places. When I got the job up here it was not easy for her to move away from what little family she had but she never complained. But I never really settled and then I made the biggest mistake of my life. I was so besotted that I never thought of the impact it would have on all of you. Believe me, I know what it is like to hit rock bottom and I know how hard it is to drag yourself up again."

"But how did you start again in a completely different career?"

"I was working as an assistant manager in a supermarket," Adam said. "It was a dead-end job but the manager was off sick for a couple of weeks and I was asked to take over. When he returned, he called me into his office and I thought he was going to fire me but instead, he suggested that I did a course on business studies at the local college. He even came with me when I signed up for it. I actually found it very interesting and I finished up top of the group. My tutor said I should do the full degree course at university, so I enrolled for two years. I worked very hard and came out with a first in business and finance. It was then that I applied for the assistant managers post in the local building society and was lucky enough to get it. When the manager retired, I took his place and after three years I moved to Oxford. I expect to stay here now."

Peter had been listening to his Father's story.

"How can you be sure that you won't be transferred elsewhere?" he asked.

"I've just been made area manager and my office will be in Oxford."

They were nearly at the end of the path and Peter called the children. They came running up and their shoes were covered in mud.

"I'll have to clean those shoes before we go home," Peter said in a resigned voice. "Make sure you take them off before you go into Granny Leah's house."

"I'm tired," Lucy said. "Will you carry me, Daddy?"

"It's not far to Granny Leah's house. You can hold my hand," Adam said.

Five minutes later they were back home. They sat in the lounge and Lucy curled up against Adam and went to sleep.

"Have you made a list for Father Christmas, Benjie?" Leah asked.

"Not yet," he said, "but I know what to ask for."

"Let's go into the dining room and I'll find you a pencil and paper and you can start it now," Leah said and they went to sit at the table.

Peter looked at Alice and remembered his promise to Jessica.

"Alice," he said. "When I went to your house this morning, I saw Jessica. It was she who answered the door. She said that William had gone shopping."

"Did she say anything else to you?"

"Yes, she wanted me to tell you that she loves you and misses you very much."

Alice's eyes filled with tears.

"She has never before told me that she loves me. Did you see Jonathan?"

"No, he was upstairs playing on his computer. He didn't come down."

"I know I wasn't a very good mother," Alice said quietly, "but I do miss them."

"When you feel strong enough, we will ask them to come here," said Adam. "You will see them again."

Alice was about to ask Adam more questions but she stopped herself. She knew how much he had already done to help her and she felt confident that he would keep his word. Instead, she said:

"Thank you, Peter, for helping me. I really appreciate it."

"I think it is time for us to go," Peter said as he stood up. "I'll just go and try and clean their shoes."

Leah followed him into the kitchen and they managed to get most of the mud off with kitchen towel. Lucy was still asleep so Adam carried her out to the car and Peter carried Benjie.

"Thanks for dinner Mum," Peter said as he kissed her goodbye. Then he kissed Alice and said: "I'm glad you are safe here. I know Mum and Dad will look after you." He said goodbye to his father.

"Thanks for helping Alice," said Adam.

"It's the least I can do," Peter answered. "She is my sister."

He drove off and the two children slept all the way home. Adan and Leah went back into the lounge. Alice was sitting there very quietly.

"Are you alright?" Leah asked anxiously.

"Yes, I think so," Alice replied. "I was thinking about Jessica. She sounds an unhappy child."

"Unfortunately, children do suffer in these sorts of situations, but the time will come when you will see her," Adam said.

"I shan't see her while she is living with William. I wish she could live with me," Alice said tearfully. She stood up. "I'm tired," she said. "I'm going to bed," and she left the room.

Adam and Leah looked at each other.

"The only way Jessica can live with Alice is if she has her own house," Adam said slowly. "I think she is beginning to think ahead."

"It is a start," she said. "But it's going to cause her a lot of heartache."

"I had a long chat with Peter today when we were out on our walk. I think he was surprised at the importance of the job I do," Adam said.

"I wish he would get a permanent job instead of relying on contracts. He gets really stressed when he has to look for his next contract," she said in a worried voice.

"I'll talk to him about it next time he comes."

"Are you staying tonight?"

"I think I will," he replied. "That is if we can both get into the bedroom."

"What do you mean?"

"The room is full of black bags!"

Chapter Twenty-Five

Adam was up early the next morning and returned to his house before going to work. Sally was already there and he called her into his office. She stood waiting for his instructions but he said:

"Please, sit down Sally."

She sat down and looked at him expectantly, wondering what was coming. He looked a little nervous.

"I owe you an apology," he said. "What I said to you on Saturday evening was quite out of order. It was very rude of me and I'm sorry."

"Apology accepted," she said, smiling at him. "Although it did cause a bit of friction."

"I do hope that didn't last for too long?" he asked, anxiously.

"Oh no," Sally answered. "It soon passed after I explained my point of view to Dominic."

"We had a chat in the kitchen," he said. "I think he is sailing in uncharted waters. Most of his business friends are men and he is less confident when dealing with women."

"Don't worry, I can read him like a book even when he thinks he is assertive. I genuinely do love him despite his foibles and I'll make sure that he becomes that proper human being."

Adam laughed.

"I believe you will," he said. "I think we will become good friends but we must be careful not to let that intrude into our daily business. After all, he is the top man, the Managing Director."

"I know what you mean; he will still be Mr West if I am speaking to his secretary."

"Good," Adam said. "Now as my secretary, we'd better get down to business. Firstly, I asked Louise Bell to phone me at ten o'clock this morning. If she hasn't phoned by ten-thirty then you must try to phone her. Have you completed the list of branches?"

"Nearly; I have about six more files to do."

"When you have finished bring it in then there will be a lot of phone calls to make," he said. "I'm hoping to start looking at the individual files today."

There was a knock at the door and Barry walked in. He was holding a pile of papers in his hand. Sally left the office.

"Here are the answers to our advert," he said. "All thirty-five of them."

"Have you looked through them?" Adam asked.

"Not yet. The fax machine has been working overtime this morning."

"What are you going to do next?" Adam asked with interest.

"The closing date was actually last Friday. I'm going to turn off the fax machine, then I'll have an initial look through them and discard any unsuitable ones."

"I think you should acknowledge those with a letter saying thank you for applying but unfortunately they have been unsuccessful. That is good business practice."

Sally's voice came through the intercom:

"I have Louise Bell on the phone for you."

"Put her through," Adam said as Barry left the room. He asked how she was getting on with clearing the office.

"The recycling people have collected the old files," she said. "And I have got rid of most of the furniture but your desk is still here and I have arranged for the place to be cleaned."

"Thank you," Adam said. "You have done well. Can you give me the name and telephone number of the removal firm who would bring the desk to Oxford?"

"I'll look in the directory," she said and Adam heard her open the desk drawer. She came back to the phone and read the details of two firms for him.

"I'll ring them now," he said, "and I'll get straight back to you."

The first company he phoned agreed to do it the next day and Adam phoned back to Mrs Bell, told her the arrangement and said that they would collect it at ten o'clock the next morning.

"I would be grateful if you could be there when the men arrive," he said. "Once the desk has gone then you can get a cleaning company in before the end of the week. Don't forget to tell them to send all invoices to me," and he gave her the Oxford address. "Can you manage to do what I have asked?"

"Yes, I'll do it," she answered.

"Thank you," Adam said. "I shan't need to visit you again and I will let the finance department know that you will be leaving on Friday. I'd like you to phone me on Friday morning to confirm that everything has been done," and he put the phone down.

He called Sally to get the finance department for him and he explained the situation to them. They promised to deal with it and Adam felt relieved that he wouldn't have to go up to Birmingham again. Almost immediately his phone rang again.

"I have Mr West on the phone," Sally said in her formal voice. "He wishes to speak to you. I'll put him through."

Adam could hear Dominic chuckling to himself but he was determined to be business-like.

"Good morning, Dominic," he said. "How are you this morning?"

"Hello Adam," he said. "There is nothing like a relaxing weekend to raise the spirits, although my spirits took a bit of a battering after we left you on Saturday evening."

"I'm sorry about that," Adam said. "I have apologised to Sally."

"I don't mind the battering; it's the making up that I enjoy most. Now down to business. I've arranged for the architects to draw up the plans this week. They will be with you on Wednesday. I want the details ready for the Board Meeting on Friday morning. I can give you the final go-ahead when I come down on Friday afternoon. Give my love to Sally," he added.

"You can do that for yourself," Adam said sweetly. "I'll put you back through to her."

Fifteen minutes later, Sally came in with the completed list. Adam smiled at her.

"I assume you got the message from our M.D.?" he said.

"Yes, thank you but I told him I was a busy woman and he just laughed at me," she said crossly. "I've brought you all the information you need."

"Now the hard work really starts," Adam said seriously. "I'd like to speak to each manager but I think that is going to take a long time. Would it be possible to send a fax message with my details and how they can contact me?"

"I can do that to the bigger offices," Sally answered, "but some smaller branches don't have that facility."

"You'd better make a couple of photocopies of the list. Let me know which ones I shall have to contact by phone."

Sally went off to the photocopier but as she went past her office, she heard her phone ringing. It was Mr Flack the estate agent and she transferred the call to Adam.

"Good morning, Mr Flack," Adam said. "What can I do for you?"

"Good morning Mr Richards. I thought I had better update you on the progress of your purchase."

"I understand from my solicitor that it should be completed by the second week in December?"

"Quite so, quite so," Mr Flack said hurriedly. "I just wondered if there is anything else, we can help you with?"

"There is one thing," Adam replied. "I need to have a good look at the furniture. I'd like to do that at two o'clock on Saturday."

"That can be arranged."

Adam thanked him and put the phone down. Sally returned with the photocopied lists and they spent the next hour sorting them out. Eventually, Adam stood up.

"I need to stretch my legs and have a coffee," he said. "Let's have a break."

"I'll go and get your coffee," Sally said as she stood up.

"You get one for yourself. I'll go and see how Barry is coping with the job applicants."

He walked out into the main office which was very busy and looked around for Barry but he was nowhere to be seen. Then he noticed an engineer at one of the tills and went over to speak to him.

"Have you brought us a new computer?" he asked.

The engineer was just lifting the machine into place.

"Yes," he said. "The old one was really clapped out."

"We shall soon be having a complete update of all the equipment," Adam said.

"Modern technology has moved on from the machine which you have here," said the engineer. "It is much more reliable and faster."

Adam thanked him and went to find Barry. He called in at the staff room and made two cups of coffee and took them to Barry's office. Laura was sitting at her desk looking a bit flustered.

"Is there a problem?" Adam asked.

"It's all these job applications," she replied. "Every time we start looking at them the phone rings or Mr Wilson has an appointment. I think he has just finished with one. He is free now until two o'clock."

"I'll take him his coffee and have a chat," Adam said.

He knocked on Barry's door and went in.

"I've brought you a coffee. You look as if you need it."

"Thank you," Barry said. "It has been a frustrating morning."

"Laura said that you haven't been able to look at the applications. Perhaps I can help?"

"I would be grateful for any help at the moment," Barry sighed.

There was a knock on the door and Laura came in.

"I'm sorry to interrupt," she said. "The engineer has finished and he needs a signature. He also wants to explain the new computer to you."

"I'll have to go," Barry said. "I'll see you later Adam." And he went off to the main office.

Adam turned to Laura.

"Put all those papers in a folder," he said. "I will have a quick look through them."

Laura gathered them up and gave the folder to Adam.

"Tell Mr Wilson to come to my office this afternoon," he said and left.

He called Sally as he passed and she followed him into his office.

"A slight change of plan," he said. "Barry is drowning under this flood of applications. You can help me to sort them out."

"What skills are you looking for?" she asked.

"Most importantly we want someone who will fit into the way we work. No arrogant or pushy people but not too reticent either. Good technical skills, particularly since we shall be having the latest technology."

"Male or female?"

"We must remember about equal opportunities but personally I would prefer a man," Adam stated firmly.

He took the papers out of the folder and gave half of them to Sally. For the next half hour, they worked in silence until they each had two smaller piles in front of them.

"Now we will swap over," Adam said. "And see if we agree."

Half an hour later, they finished checking and found that they had agreed with each other's selection. There were seven possible candidates and the rest were rejected.

"Was there any one C.V. which caught your eye?" Adam asked.

"There was one," she answered and leafed through the papers until she found it. "It is from William Birch. There was something friendly about the way he described himself and he seems to be quite a computer buff."

"I see what you mean," he said, looking at the application. "And he works up north in my previous area. I could find out more about him from my old area manager." He put the papers back in the folder. "That was a good hour's work, Sally," he said gratefully. "It's up to Barry now to make the decision. I'm going out for a sandwich but I won't be long."

He was glad of some fresh air as he made his way to his favourite bistro. Bridget, the waitress, brought him a ham roll and a coffee and he sat there thinking about Barry. The quicker they could get him an assistant the better. He made his way back to the office and as he passed Sally he said:

"Have there been any phone calls?"

"Not for you," Sally answered and blushed a little.

"Ask Barry to come to my office when he is free? I want him to get on with finding an assistant."

It was forty minutes later when Barry arrived.

"I had a two o'clock appointment," he said, "and it went on longer than I expected."

"Did Laura tell you that I have all the applications in the folder?"

"Yes, she did," Barry replied. "I assumed that you were going to look at them."

"Sally and I have been through them all and we rejected many of them but there were seven possibles for you to look at."

Barry looked at Adam in amazement.

"How on earth did you manage that in such a short time?" he said.

"We looked for specific qualities," Adam said and he went on to explain to Barry what those qualities were.

Barry listened to every word he said.

"Thank you for your words of wisdom. I have so much to learn but I couldn't have a better teacher."

"The seven applications are on top of the others but I think the very top one is the most interesting," said Adam.

Barry opened the folder and took out the top copy. He sat there reading it for a few minutes then he looked up at Adam.

"Do you know who this is from?"

"All I know is that his name is William Birch."

"This is unbelievable," Barry said. "It is my old friend Bill."

"You mean the one who told you I was destined for greater things?"

Adam said with a smile.

"Yes, that's the one. I'll take this folder home tonight and read through the ones which you recommended and get Laura to send letters to all the others tomorrow." He stood up and walked to the door. 'Well, well fancy that,' he muttered to himself as he went out.

Adam sat in his chair and laughed. Sally came in and he told her what had just happened with Barry.

"What a coincidence," she said, "but it will be easier for Barry to work with someone he knows."

"Tomorrow I will phone my previous area manager and find out a bit about William Birch. It will be like old times to chat with him. He was a good friend to me," Adam said. "I think I'll take some of these files home with me. At least that will be a start." He took half a dozen files from the shelf and put them in his briefcase. "First thing tomorrow I want to speak to Mr Carr, my old area manager. It will be interesting to hear what he thinks of William Birch. It's been a busy day. I shan't be sorry to get home."

He said goodbye to Sally and left the office. He drove straight home and immediately phoned Leah.

"How is Alice today?" he asked.

"I went to school this morning and left her on her own for a couple of hours. When I came home, I found that she had started to sort out her clothes. The effort made her quite tired and she needed a rest this afternoon."

"It's good that she is beginning to think for herself and make decisions," he said. "I don't think it will be long before she makes the most important decision of all."

"We must be patient," she said, "but I think it was Jessica's message which affected her most."

"We must try and get Jessica down to see her mother," Adam said. "I'll think about it."

"Are you coming over this evening?"

"No, not this evening. I've had a busy day and I've brought some work home with me. When Alice is ready for bed get her to ring me and I'll say goodnight to her then."

"I shall sleep in my own room tonight," Leah said. "The double bed is covered with clothes. I shall miss you."

"I shall miss you too. Make sure the bed is cleared as soon as possible."

He ended the call and made a cup of tea. He looked in his fridge for something to eat and ended up making cheese on toast. He watched the six o'clock news and then took the files out of his briefcase and started to study them. He soon realised they contained very little information other than the name and telephone number of the Branch. Mr James Brown covered his tracks well, he thought, realising that the man had left no record of his activities. They would have to start from scratch and that meant a lot of extra work for him and Sally. He would have to make sure she had a proper assistant. He went to the fridge and took out a cold beer but before he could open it, his phone rang.

"Hello Dad," Alice said. "I missed seeing you this evening."

"I'm sorry I couldn't come over," he said sincerely. "I had a very busy day at work and I had to bring some of it home with me."

"I've had a busy day too," she said. "I've started to sort out all those bags of clothes. I didn't realise that I had so many. Some of them will be going to the charity shop."

"I'm glad you've been busy," he said encouragingly. "It helps the time to go more quickly."

"I've been thinking too and I want to talk to you and Mum. When will you be coming home?"

"I'll come tomorrow evening," he said. "Is that okay?"

"Yes, I'll see you then. I'm going to bed now. Do you want to speak to Mum?"

"Yes, I'll have a quick word. Sleep well," he said as Leah's voice came over the phone.

"I heard all that," she said. "It was unexpected."

"I'll make sure I come tomorrow. I wonder what she has been thinking about?"

"We must wait and see," she said, wisely. "I'll see you then."

Adam opened his beer and sat on the settee. He thought about what

Alice had said to him and wondered if she was getting closer to that big decision. He finished his beer and went upstairs.

The next morning, he was late getting to work. There had been an accident on the A34 which was causing long delays on all the approach roads. When he finally arrived, Sally was waiting for him. She followed him into his office.

"There have been several phone calls," she said. "The architects are coming this afternoon instead of tomorrow. Apparently, Dominic wants the plans for Friday's Board Meeting so they had to bring their visit forward. There was a call from a removal firm in Birmingham saying that they expect to be here with a desk at two o'clock and Barry has been looking for you."

"It's going to be one of those days," he sighed. "I can feel it in my bones."

"First things first," Sally said calmly. "Where do you want them to put the desk?"

"Ask them to take it upstairs and stand it in a corner. I might well be up there with the architects when it arrives."

He opened his briefcase and took out the files together with the notes he had made. He passed them over to Sally.

"I had a good look at these last night. I'd like you to look through them this morning and tell me what you think?"

"Shall I tell Barry you are here now?" she asked.

"I want to speak to my previous area manager first," Adam said. "See if you can get him on the phone. His name is Mr Carr."

Sally returned to her office carrying the files. She placed them in her desk and found Mr Carr's number. She phoned his secretary and told her the reason for the call.

"I know he will want to talk to Mr Richards," she said. "They always got on very well."

Sally put the call through to Adam and the two men had a long conversation. Adam was impressed by what he heard about William Birch.

"I always said you were destined for greater things," Mr Carr said, "and I was right. Good luck to you."

Adam put the phone down and sat back in his chair. He had enjoyed chatting to his old mentor but it had also stirred up painful memories. He was determined to pull himself together. The past was history; he needed to concentrate on the present. He called Sally and asked her to get him a coffee.

"You can tell Barry that I am here now," he said.

Five minutes later, there was a knock on the door and Barry walked in, carrying two cups of coffee and a folder.

"I saved Sally a journey," he said as he put the cups on the desk.

Adam inspected the folder which Barry had under his arm.

"That looks a lot thinner than it did yesterday."

"I have given all the rejects to Laura," Barry said. "And she is sending a letter to each of them. I looked through the possibilities last night and I really think Bill is the best."

"Why did you think that?"

"There are several reasons. He has already had some experience as an assistant manager in a small branch but he obviously feels that if he wants to further his career, he needs to be in a more forward-looking and bigger branch."

"Anything else?" Adam asked with interest.

"He knows a lot about computers and could take a responsible role in our new systems. He has the sort of personality which would fit in with us here."

"What kind of personality is that?"

"He is intelligent and hard-working and a very likeable chap; good in a crisis and never gets ruffled."

"What sort of crisis do you have in mind?"

"Supposing all the computers went off at the same time? Or if we had a robbery. He plays rugby and is very strong."

"What are you going to do next?" Adam asked.

"I'd like your opinion first."

"I've never met him but it is obvious you have a high opinion of him," Adam said. "Judging by his application you might well be right but I will reserve judgement until I see him."

"Shall I invite him for an interview?" Barry asked.

"That is the next stage but I don't think you should do the interviewing in this case. You know him too well. It would be best if I see him."

"I think you are right. Will you let me know a convenient time to ask him to come?"

"I'll let you know later today," said Adam. "By the way, don't throw away the other six possibles. We may be able to offer them a different position."

Barry went back to his office feeling happier. He thought about his conversation with Adam and the sort of questions he had been asked. He shuddered as he decided that it would be quite an ordeal to be interviewed by Adam and he felt quite grateful he was here before he arrived.

Adam stood up and went into Sally's office.

"We must try to find a small desk for Julie," he said. "Then she will feel part of the team." He looked at Sally's desk. She had obviously been looking through the files.

"They don't tell us much," she said. "In fact, they are pretty useless."

"We are definitely going to have to make new files," he said. "Can you make sure that we have some in the storeroom and we will keep them ready in my office. I'm just going for a walk. I won't be long but if the architects come before I am back will you show them upstairs?"

He walked through the main office and out into the street. It was quite chilly and it reminded him that it wouldn't be long until Christmas and before that, his birthday. He wondered what present Leah had for him and smiled to himself. He sat in his favourite bistro and thought about what Alice might say that evening.

When he returned to the office he spoke to the receptionist.

"Has a desk been delivered?" he asked.

"No," she replied, "but two gentlemen arrived and Sally took them upstairs."

"Thank you," Adam said. "Will you let me know when the desk is delivered? I shall be upstairs."

He left the main office and went up to the first floor. He introduced himself to the architects and Sally went back down to her office. The architects had taken note of the dimensions of the space and had drawn out a rough plan. They had a full discussion about the project and they made one or two adjustments to Adam's original plan. They were about to go down for coffee when Barry came up the stairs.

"There is a large desk downstairs," he puffed. "Where do you want them to put it?"

"Ask them to bring it up and put it in the corner over there," Adam said.

The removal men struggled up the stairs with the heavy desk. Adam turned to Barry.

"You'd better offer them a cup of coffee after all that exertion," he said.

Barry took the men off to the staffroom and gave them some refreshments. Adam took the architects down to his office and asked Sally to bring the coffee in. They sat in the office and one of the men said:

"You have a superb space to work with and I can't see that there will be any problems. We will let Mr West have the plans by Friday morning. All the work will be indoors so there should be no delays because of the weather. When the plans are passed, we will send you copies and then you can contact local contractors. Make sure you get a reliable firm. This is a flagship development and we would want it to be completed to a high standard."

Adam thanked them and escorted them to the main entrance. He returned to his office and asked Sally to call Barry.

"I want you to come in as well," he said, "and bring your diary."

When they were all together, Adam told them what the architects had said.

"I can't believe it," Barry said. "We are going to get everything we hoped for."

"What does he mean by a flagship development?" Sally asked.

Adam thought for a minute.

"He means that it will be the only development of its kind in the U.K. We shall be the leading branch in our industry."

"I think your idea for a lecture room was a genius addition," Barry said admiringly. "That is absolutely unique."

"It seems that Mr West is fully in favour of it. He is not wasting any time getting it through the necessary channels," said Adam.

"He is certainly taking a personal interest in it," Barry said.

"We should have the go-ahead when he comes down on Friday," said Adam.

He looked at Sally and asked her if he had any appointments for the rest of the week. When she said that it was all clear, he turned to Barry.

"You'd better contact your friend Bill and see how soon he can come to visit us. Let me know as soon as possible?"

Barry left the room and hurried back to his office. Adam looked at Sally and smiled.

"Dominic is a fast worker," he said. "Don't let him hustle you."

"I know," Sally said wearily. "He can quite take your breath away. He is a complex character. Sometimes he is so sensible and business-like but at other times he can be naïve and annoying."

"He comes from a background where he was pampered as a child. He is used to having his own way and he relies on others to do his bidding but he means well and really wants to please you. It is just that having to think about someone other than himself is so new to him and you will have to be patient."

"I know," she said. "I shall do my best."

There was a knock on the door and Barry came in.

"I've spoken to Bill," he said. "And he can come on Thursday if that is convenient for you?"

"I'll see him at eleven o'clock on Thursday morning," Adam said. "Put that in the diary please, Sally."

"I'll phone him straight back to tell him," Barry said as he rushed away.

"I shall be leaving early today, Sally," said Adam. "I've promised to go and see Alice this evening. I hope we shall be able to get on with those files tomorrow. I should like to have finished looking through them by the end of the week."

He collected his briefcase and said goodbye to Sally. She watched him go out through the door and wondered how he managed everything, nothing seemed to faze him. She took a couple more files off the shelf before returning to her office.

Instead of going home, Adam drove straight to Leah's house. He let himself in with his key and looked for Leah. She was not in the lounge and neither was Alice. He called her name and she answered him from the top of the stairs.

"I'm busy," she said. "Make yourself a cup of tea."

Adam took his tea and went to sit on the settee. A few minutes later, Alice came into the room.

"Hello Dad," she said and kissed him. "You look tired."

"It's been a busy day," he said. "What have you been doing?"

"I've sorted out more black bags," she replied. "We are going to the charity shop tomorrow. A lot of my clothes are too big for me," she said sadly. "I must have lost weight."

"Be careful what you give away," he said. "You might fit into them as you get better."

They heard the doorbell ring and Leah came down the stairs with her student. She had a few words with his mother and then they both left. Leah went into the lounge and flopped down on her chair.

"I need a good strong cup of tea," she said. "That boy was hard work."

"I'll make it for you," said Alice and went into the kitchen.

"How is she?" Adam asked Leah.

"She has been very quiet today," she answered. "I think she has something on her mind."

Alice came back with the tea and gave it to her mother. Then she sat down by Adam.

"I've been thinking a lot about Jessica," she said, eventually. "I really would like to see her but I know William won't let her."

"I think it might be a good idea to invite Jonathan and Jessica to come to see you. William can hardly refuse them both," Adam said. "What about William? Do you want to see him?"

"I don't think I ever want to see him again," Alice said firmly.

Adam looked at Leah then at Alice.

"I don't understand," he said. "Are you saying that you don't want to go back to your house?"

Alice looked straight at Adam and said very clearly:

"I'm saying that I want to divorce William."

Leah and Adam were stunned by the tone of Alice's voice. It was sometime before Adam said:

"Are you sure about this? What has happened for you to make this decision?"

"Yes, I'm sure," Alice said. "I realised now that all his threats were meant to frighten me. He has told me nothing but lies. It was the way in which you explained his behaviour that helped me to understand what he had been doing to me."

"Have you thought about the children?" Leah asked.

"When I have my own house, I would like Jonathan and Jessica to live with me but I'm pretty sure Jonathan will want to stay with his father," Alice said. She turned to Adam and caught hold of his hand. "Will you help me?" she begged. "Will you both help me?"

"Of course, we will," Leah said. "We will do everything we can to help you."

Adam put his arms around Alice.

"It's not going to be easy," he said, "but yes we will do it." And he hugged her.

"What do you think William will say when he is told?" Alice asked anxiously.

"I would imagine that once he has recovered from the shock, he will try to find ways to make it work to his advantage," Adam said.

"How can he do that?" Alice asked.

"There are several ways he could try," he said. "He could try to hide some of his assets or he could refuse to allow you your rightful share of his pension. But whatever he tries to do, he won't succeed because you will have a top lawyer on your side."

"A top lawyer will be expensive, won't he?" Alice said with a worried look.

"He might be expensive but he will be worth it," said Adam. "A lawyer with a London address will make William think twice before trying any funny business."

"What would be the grounds for divorce?" Leah asked Adam.

"It would certainly be adultery but if he shows any signs of contesting it then we could add unacceptable behaviour through mental and emotional abuse," Adam said.

Alice shuddered.

"I don't want to have to talk about that again," she said, fearfully.

"I don't think it will come to that," Adam said soothingly. "I don't think William would want everyone to know what had been going on. I shall be seeing Dominic on Friday and I will ask him for his lawyer's name."

"Thank you, Dad," Alice said. "I couldn't do it without you and Mum."

"You have made a very brave decision," Adam said as he held her hand. "Now you must concentrate on getting well again so that you have the strength to see it through."

"I'm tired now," Alice said. "I'm not used to all this thinking. Are you staying here tonight?"

"That depends if the bed is clear of black bags!"

"I'll make sure it is," Alice said as she went out.

Leah stood up and moved to the settee beside him. He put his arm around her and they sat in silence. At last, Adam said:

"It was her own decision, wasn't it? She has never discussed it with me."

"She hasn't said a word to me," said Leah. "But I could tell that she had something on her mind."

"We must not say a word to anyone about it, not even Peter," Adam said. "I don't want William to have any idea until we have it all in place and he gets a letter from the lawyers. It might mean that Alice will have to take a trip to London to meet him."

"She is getting stronger every day," Leah said. "I think she will be able to manage that."

"It's been a busy day. I think I'll stay tonight and get up early in the morning. Is that alright?"

"Yes, of course, it is," she answered. "I much prefer my double duvet."

Adam leaned over and kissed her.

"I'm hungry," he said. "I haven't eaten today."

"We had cottage pie for our dinner," Leah said. "There is some left over in the fridge. I'll heat it up for you."

She went into the kitchen and Adam followed her.

"It will soon be my birthday," he said. "Have you bought my present yet?"

"Not all presents cost money," Leah smiled sweetly.

"Now you are up to your old tricks," he said pretending to be cross. "You are teasing me."

Leah just smiled and kissed him on the forehead.

"Eat your supper," she said. "I'll go and see if we shall be able to go to bed tonight."

She went upstairs and into the bedroom. There were still plenty of black bags around but the bed was clear. She peeped into Alice's room and saw that she was fast asleep, then she went back downstairs. Adam had finished his supper and was washing up his plate.

"Do you want a drink?" she asked

"No thanks," he said. "I just want bed."

"You go on up," she said. "I'll put the lights out and lock the doors."

Adam went upstairs and had a quick wash. He was soon in bed and half asleep when Leah joined him.

"Did you lock the back door?" he asked sleepily.

"No," Leah said. "I left it wide open."

"Ask a stupid question," Adam muttered as he kissed her goodnight.

As he lay there, he thought about his life and the events which had brought him to this moment. He had rediscovered his life and it was as if he had come full circle but not quite. He thought about Sally and her whirlwind romance with Dominic West; about Alice and her impending divorce and how he had been reunited with her and Peter, his son. His career had taken off and he looked forward to the work and being able to care for his family. Most of all, he thought, as he looked at her beside him in the moonlight, he had the love of Leah, his wife, the most important rediscovery of all. The future could not look brighter. He just needed to keep going and mend the final bridges which would bring him back into her life completely. That, he knew, was a matter of gaining her trust.

"I love you, Leah," he whispered in the darkness.

Outside the window, he saw the trees silhouetted against the sky. The season was turning and the branches looked darker. Autumn leaves, he thought and turned over to go to sleep.

Available worldwide from Amazon and all good bookstores

www.mtp.agency

www.facebook.com/mtp.agency

@mtp_agency